# A Guide to Measuring and Managing IT Benefits

Dan Remenyi PhD
Arthur Money PhD
Alan Twite BA

NCC Blackwell
MANCHESTER · OXFORD

British Library Cataloguing in Publication Data

Remenyi, D. (Dan), *1944 –*
Money, A. (Arthur), *1941 –*
Twite, A. (Alan),  *1949 –*
    A guide to measuring and managing IT benefits.
I.    Title   II. Money, Arthur    III. Twite, Alan
     658.4'038'0285

     ISBN  1-85554-138-6

First published in 1991 by:

NCC Blackwell Limited, 108 Cowley Road, Oxford OX4 1JF, England.

Editorial Office, The National Computing Centre Limited, Oxford Road, Manchester M1 7ED, England.

Typeset in 10pt Palatino by TechTrans Ltd, Kidmore End, Reading, RG4 9AY; and printed and bound in Great Britain by
Biddles Ltd, Guildford and King's Lynn

ISBN 1-85554-138-6

# Preface

So far no comprehensive economics of information has been developed.

By 'economics of information' is meant a systematic series of concepts and theories which explain the role which information plays in assisting the firm in its conception, production and delivery of goods and services in order to create wealth in society. Although much work has been done in the field of cost benefit analysis of information technology as well as user satisfaction with specific systems, little attempt has been made to produce a comprehensive approach to understanding the economics of how information is used to either boost the efficiency or the effectiveness of the firm. Also, the economics of the way information may be focused so that it becomes the basis of a new business strategy, or even how information can itself be used to establish a new enterprise, has not been well addressed.

A definition of information economics is not a trivial matter. A traditional definition of economics states that economics is the science of how wealth is created and managed and how this is achieved through exchange. A non-traditional definition of information would state that it is the presentation of facts and figures in such a way that decisions may be easily and quickly made. Therefore, it may be said that the economics of information is concerned with how facts and figures may be used to create, manage and exchange wealth. This is a very wide subject area which overlaps with many other aspects of business management.

As will be seen in the first chapter, IT has been used to help manage wealth creation for quite some time. This has been done through the processes referred to as automate and informate. However, the use of IT to create wealth is a relatively new process sometimes referred to as Transformate, which has only been understood for a decade or so.

There are probably several reasons why the economics of information has not been properly developed. One of the most important reasons is that the subject of information economics is a very difficult one and most practitioners respond to the challenges it offers by either attempting to ignore it, ie just get on with the day to day job, or by understating its importance. Unfortunately for IT practitioners and professionals, top management has begun to insist that much more attention be paid to the economic aspects of information

3

systems than ever before and this has lead to an increasing demand for a comprehensive and reliable IT metric.

This book provides a basic framework for understanding the main issues concerning the economics of information as well as some suggestions as to how the firm's IT efforts may be appraised. The book discusses a number of different evaluation concepts as well as reviews several approaches to cost benefit measurement. It takes a management approach to both investment proposals and to post implementation audits and describes how separate departments may be set up to specifically measure and manage IT benefits. In the final chapters an approach towards a number of IT Assessment Metrics (ITAM) is proposed which allows firms to measure their progress towards obtaining maximum value from their information technology efforts.

In all, this book provides a significant step towards an economic of information, but cannot be regarded as a definitive work of this enormous subject. It is a potpourri of ideas and approaches which most IT professionals and many business executives will find both stimulating and useful. Perhaps this book might be considered a guide to measuring and managing IT benefits.

Dan Remenyi PhD
Information Management
Henley – The Management College

P.S.    This book has been written by three authors. Although we have consulted together regularly, each has primarily written his own section. This resulted in some duplication. As editor I have eliminated nearly all of this, but on a few occasions I have allowed a few points to be repeated. Some things are worth saying twice!

# Contents

A diskette containing Lotus 1-2-3 templates and macros for the capital investment appraisal models discussed in this book is available. This includes a generalised macro which will allow risk analysis to be performed on a large number of Lotus 1-2-3 models.

To obtain this diskette send a crossed cheque made payable to TechTrans Limited for £49.95 (this includes VAT @ 17.5% and postage and packaging) to TechTrans Limited, Curtis Farm, Kidmore End, Near Reading, RG4 9AY United Kingdom. Please state whether a 3½" or 5¼" diskette is required. Please allow 28 days for delivery.

# 1 Why is IT Benefit Measurement & Management a Major Business Issue?

## 1.1 CURRENT TRENDS IN IT THINKING

There are a number of reasons why IT benefit management has become an important business issue today. But by far the most obvious reason is the rocketing level of IT expenditure experienced by many business organisations as well as government agencies.

For about 40 years, business, industry and government have been acquiring more and more computing power. This expenditure used to run into tens or even hundreds of thousands of pounds. However, by the beginning of the 90s many firms are spending millions or even tens of millions of pounds on their IT. In addition, they are employing vast numbers of staff, including data input personnel, programmers, analysts, systems co-ordinators, computer operators, computer managers, information systems directors, etc.

The phenomenal growth in this industry is totally unprecedented by any other human endeavour and is expected to continue for the foreseeable future. However, although computerisation has generally been welcomed by most business participants and observers there has always been a certain amount of scepticism about its real beneficial effects. The question which is sometimes asked is:

*Does this phenomenon represent the longest, sustained flow of beneficial investment in similar technology in the history of modern business organisation or is it just the greatest fad the world has ever seen?*

There is in fact growing concern especially among top executives about the effectiveness of what has been regarded as an extremely high level of investment and expenditure. Many CEOs are becoming more and more uncomfortable about the rate of IS spending and increasingly frustrated by their inability to find appropriate measures with which to evaluate its performance, let alone have a rigorous methodology for the management of benefits that IT generates. On the other hand, many IS professionals feel that it is getting progressively more difficult to assess IT value (Peters, 1988) and that the search for a measurement and management methodology is a fool's errand, and that an IT effectiveness metric is the modern day equivalent of the Holy Grail.

## 1.2    THE DEVELOPMENT OF ATTITUDES TOWARDS COMPUTER-ISATION AND THE BENEFITS SO DERIVED

Attitudes towards computers and computer benefits have evolved steadily over the past 40 years and may be described in three phases which coincide with the three distinct computer initiatives which are referred to as Automate, Informate and Transformate. The approximate dates of these developments together with the main impact they have on the organisation are illustrated in Figure 1.1.

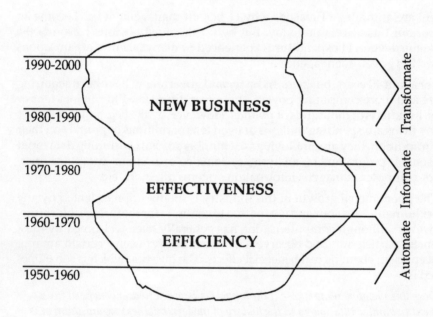

**Figure 1.1    Development of IS applications since 1950, illustrating Automate, Informate and Transformate**

### 1.2.1    Automate

During the automate phase the emphasis was strongly placed on reducing the labour required for the manual aspects of clerical work. The main perceived result of this initiative was the reduction of routine and tedious work with the primary benefit being greater speed of paper handling and greater accuracy resulting in better customer service, and possibly in some cases reduced costs. These systems are generally referred to as transaction processing systems (TPS).

These purported benefits were a controversial issue. In fact in these early days of the technology it was frequently said that computers were mostly acquired so that firms could demonstrate their modern approach to business. Increased profit or cash flow or improved ROI or competitive positioning were generally not considered main computer issues. It was often argued that computers did not actually save money but their introduction rather resulted in changes in the way firms incurred costs, ie clerks were not needed but programmers and analysts, a new breed of employee, were. The benefits were frequently described as being more to do with increased and improved capacity, accompanied by the issues described above of less errors, greater reliability, prestige, etc.

Nonetheless, despite the frequent lack of any real or measurable payoff, there were surprisingly positive attitudes towards computing during the automate phase with most businessmen and business observers believing that computers had a beneficial effect.

### 1.2.2 Informate

During the second phase, computers were used to deliver extensive management reports which were intended to facilitate the more effective management and control of the firm. The first attempt at this produced the phenomenon of Management Information Systems (MIS) which was closely followed by Integrated Management Information Systems (IMIS) and eventually Totally Integrated Management Information Systems (TIMIS). The industry's efforts in improving management effectiveness may be described as poor, and although some considerable success was achieved it was largely in the area of routine management reports which focused on efficiency. These reports represented regular and routine descriptions of how various aspects of the business were performing. They provided sufficient information for managers to be able to make important contributions to improving the organisation's efficiency. However, a material impact on the firm's effectiveness was not necessarily delivered. The supply of these systems together with the regular MIS reports has been referred to as the organisation's efforts to informate. This hybrid word informate was first coined by Shoshana Zuboff (1988) to describe information as a by-product of automate processes. Decision Support Systems (DSS) and Executive Information Systems (EIS) followed hot on the heels of MIS, but again with not much real measurable benefit in the business effectiveness area.

This second phase in computer development was not entirely without achievement and systems were delivered in many organisations which some-times dramatically improved the efficiency with which various functions were performed within the firm. Therefore the achievable benefits in this phase of computerisation may be attributed to savings obtained through applications such as better stock control and production management, im-proved sales forecasting and better credit management, etc. It is fair to say that in this phase vendors generally exaggerated the payoff of computerisa-tion as it related to improving business effectiveness, but organisations' efficiency continued to improve.

### 1.2.3   Transformate

Since the late 70s there has been a growing awareness that in some cases it is possible to radically change the way the organisation does business or even the actual nature of a firm itself through the way IT is deployed. There are now many examples of this, the more important cases being American Airlines, American Hospital Supplies, Meryl Lynch, Thompson Holidays, Benetton, and Xerox (Remenyi, 1990). These information systems are some-times referred to as Strategic Information Systems (SIS) or Competitive Infor-mation Systems (CIS) or Mission Critical Systems (MCS), and are intended to transformate the functioning of the actual business. Thus the word transfor-mate has been applied to describe what may be achieved by their use. These applications are frequently based on wide area networks (WANs) and rely on the strategic nature of data communications to develop electronic trading opportunities.

New frameworks of analysis have been introduced to help practitioners understand and manage these systems, the most important examples of which are the Porter Models (1985), the Wiseman Strategic Options Generator (1985) and the McFarlan Strategic Grid (1984). These are described in Figures 1.2 to 1.10.

### 1.3   A CONCEPTUAL FRAMEWORK FOR TRANSFORMATE SYSTEMS

There are a number of different frameworks which help explain how IT may be used for the purposes of transforming the business.

### 1.3.1   Porter's five forces model

The model portrayed in Figure 1.2 illustrates Michael Porter's five forces view of what determines an industry's attractiveness. Porter maintains that a firm's performance is considerably confined by the strength of the buyers and suppliers, the number of potential new entrants and substitutes available, and the rivalry among existing firms in the industry.

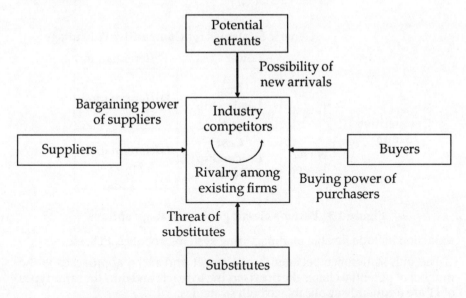

Figure 1.2   Competitive forces in industry structures

These five industry drivers or forces determine the relationship of the firm to its industry which in turn is a major factor in establishing the organisation's opportunity to make profits and sustain reasonable growth levels. The five forces model explains why some industries are highly profitable and others are not. Porter points out that IT may be used to change the balance of power in the industry by techniques such as locking in clients and creating barriers to new entries, etc. If used correctly in this respect IT can either transform the business or alternatively can lead to the creation of new products or even new ventures or enterprises.

### 1.3.2   Generic strategies

The second Porter model in Figure 1.3 describes the two generic strategies which a firm may adopt in its efforts to find and keep its clients.

In Porter's view a firm may either enhance its image in the market and as a result obtain a premium price, or offer a low cost no frills product or service. These two generic strategies can help firms become superior performers in their industry. IT may be used to support either of these strategies by using access to data to enhance the product or service, or by using IT to contribute to a direct reduction in the firm's cost profile. Examples of using IT to differentiate the firm include remote purchasing systems, client support systems and field maintenance systems. Examples of the use of IT for cost

**Generic Strategies for Competitive Advantage**

|  |  | Lower Cost | Differentiation |
|---|---|---|---|
|  | Broad Target | **Cost Leadership** | **Differentiation** |
| **Competitive Scope** |  |  |  |
|  | Niche Target | **Cost Leadership Focus** | **Differentiation Focus** |

**Figure 1.3   Porter's classic generic strategy options**

reduction include flexible manufacturing systems, robotics, EDI, etc.

The only difference between broad target and niche approaches is the number of potential clients the firm is trying to reach, and thus the same types of IT are frequently applicable to both strategies.

### 1.3.3   The value chain

The Porter Value Chain model in Figure 1.4 provides a detailed view of the major organisational components comprising a typical business firm. Porter argues that a strategy cannot be derived by considering the firm as a whole. He suggests that a detailed analysis must be undertaken which will provide

**The Firm's Chain of Value Activities**

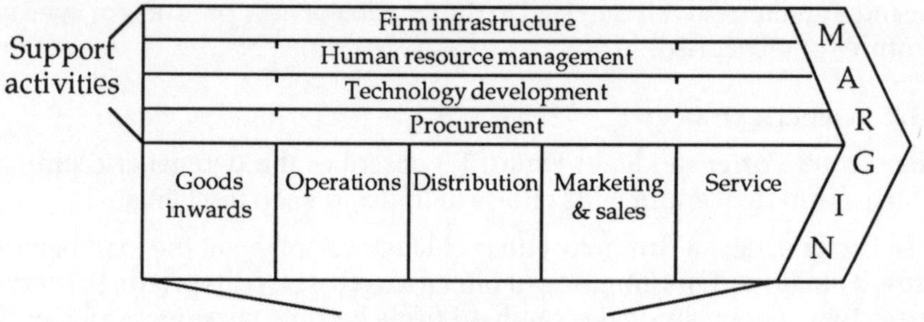

| Support activities | Firm infrastructure | | | | | M A R G I N |
| | Human resource management | | | | | |
| | Technology development | | | | | |
| | Procurement | | | | | |
| | Goods inwards | Operations | Distribution | Marketing & sales | Service | |

Primary activities

**Figure 1.3   Porter's value chain**

sufficient understanding of the business to be able to construct a suitable strategy. The value chain is Porter's tool for carrying out the analysis.

The value chain is described as the interrelationship of the *value activities* for the firm. Value activities divide the firm's operations into technologically and economically distinct activities which it must perform in order to do business. Therefore, by the nature of its business, its strategy and the industry in which it functions, firms will have distinctly different value activities and therefore distinctly different value chains.

### 1.3.3.1   *Value activities*

Porter identifies nine categories of value activity in a typical manufacturing firm. These are:

- Goods inwards
- Operations
- Distribution
- Marketing and sales
- Service
- Procurement
- Technological development
- Human resource management
- Firm infrastructure

This value chain concept simply segments a firm into strategically relevant activities in order that the cost and the potential for differentiation may be examined.

As all firms may be seen to have value chains it is possible to also consider suppliers' and customers' value chains. Looked at as a whole, it is therefore also possible to consider the industry value chain. All the value activities of the members of the industry value chain represent a potential for competitive advantage and superior performance through both cost leadership and differentiation.

Figure 1.5 shows some of the actual factors which may affect a firm's performance in each of the value chain activities. This diagram clearly shows the IT possibilities within a typical firm's value chain. It is important to note that the best opportunities are usually found in the links between the different activities in the chain. Thus IT is especially important in ensuring the smooth functioning of the interface between goods inwards and operations, operations and distribution, etc.

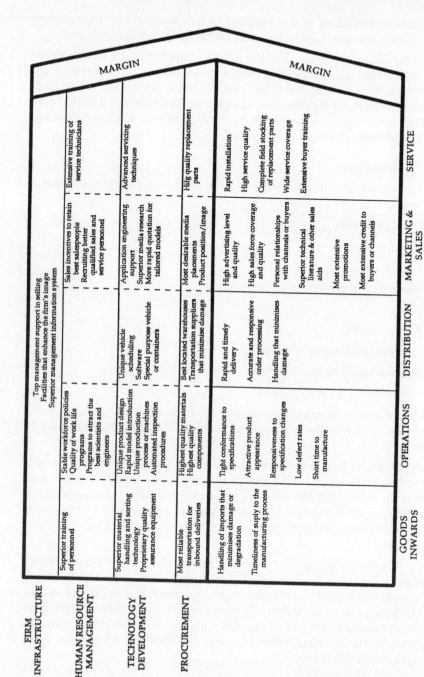

Figure 1.5    The ubiquitous nature of information technology in the value chain

### 1.3.4   The industry value chain

An important consequence of the value chain analysis is the notion that firms may link different elements of their own value chains to the value chains of other organisations in the industry. Figure 1.6 shows how a firm may link its operations to a buyer's distribution system, and its distribution (outbound logistics) to a client's goods inwards (inbound logistics). Firms may also make useful connections on the support activities level as well as between primary

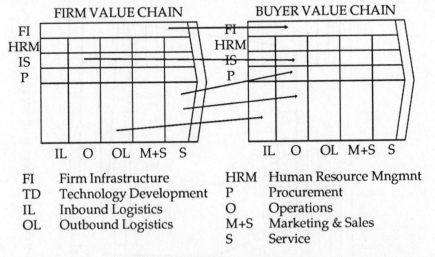

| FI | Firm Infrastructure | HRM | Human Resource Mngmnt |
|----|---------------------|-----|------------------------|
| TD | Technology Development | P | Procurement |
| IL | Inbound Logistics | O | Operations |
| OL | Outbound Logistics | M+S | Marketing & Sales |
|    |                     | S   | Service |

Figure 1.6    The industry value chain showing links between different organisations

activities and support activities. Such links or joins may really only be effective through the use of IT, and show how a firm may take advantage of its industry value chain, as illustrated in Figure 1.7. It is also possible for firms in different value chains to co-operate. This is usually referred to as establishing strategic alliances. In Figure 1.7 two industry value chains are shown, indicating how a strategic alliance may be set up. Firms which have successfully used IT in the above way have in numerous instances transformed their business, or given themselves very significant advantages in the marketplace.

### 1.4   THE STRATEGIC OPTIONS GENERATOR

Clearly Porter has made a major contribution in assisting firms in their search to apply IT to transforming their business. However, finding applications which will transform a business is not an easy task. Charles Wiseman has developed a methodology for identifying such systems which he refers to as

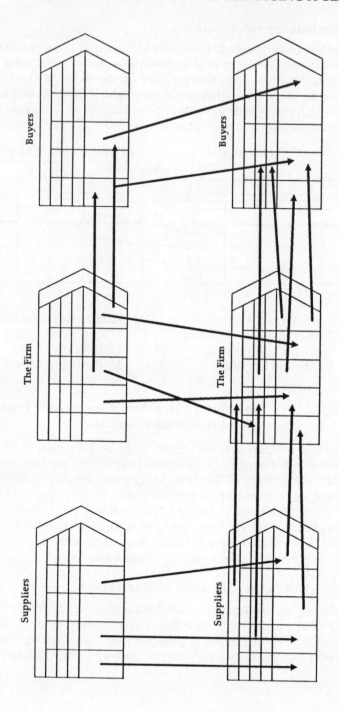

**Figure 1.7   Industry value chain showing strategic alliances with suppliers, buyers, competitors, etc.**

a Strategic Options Generator (SOG), and which is shown in Figure 1.8. The SOG is effectively a checklist which a business analyst may use to home in on areas of high opportunity. Wiseman claims that those who have used the SOG have never failed to find potential SIS. Wiseman believes that there are four dimensions to a SIS. The first of these is referred to as a *strategic target* and it is suggested that a SIS can only have one such target. This may be the firm's suppliers, customers or competitors. These targets are reached through a *strategic thrust*, of which there are five: differentiation, cost, innovations, growth and alliance. In addition to the target and thrust, a SIS operates in terms of a *mode*, which may be either offensive or defensive. Finally a SIS needs direction, and Wiseman argues that there are two directions, which may be referred to as use or provide. Use refers to the SIS itself being a strategic weapon used by the firm. Provide refers to the SIS being a facility which the firm provides to its clients to gain a competitive advantage.

Figure 1.8   Wiseman's Strategic Options Generator (SOG)

## 1.5   McFARLAN'S STRATEGIC MATRIX

The contribution of Warren McFarlan's strategic matrix, shown in Figure 1.9, is to put into perspective the three types of system referred to in the Automate, Informate and Transformate taxonomy. McFarlan's approach effectively re-defines these systems as Support, Factory and Strategic systems. He also adds a new category which he names Turnaround systems. The strategic matrix is based on the Boston Consulting Group's *Strategic Investment Analysis* approach in which investments are categorised into Stars, Cows, Wild Cats and Dogs. In his analysis McFarlan equates strategic systems to star investment, factory systems to cash cow investments, turnaround systems to wild cat investments and support systems to dog investments. McFarlan highlights the fact that all these different types of systems exist in any one given firm at the same time, that they require different management approaches, and that they deliver different benefits. It is also possible to match each of these system types with a different benefit measuring approach. This will be discussed in detail later in this chapter.

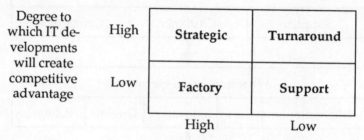

Degree to which the firm is functionally
dependent upon IS/IT today

Figure 1.9     McFarlan's strategic matrix

Although the McFarlan taxonomy is very helpful in understanding the use of IT within the firm, its comparison of support systems to dog investments tends to understate the vital importance of these systems to every organisation. The strategic matrix may be used as an effective planning tool (Remenyi, 1991).

## 1.6   ALTERNATE SYSTEMS CATEGORISATION

Another useful taxonomy with which to assess systems benefits is that of the four categories of Strategic Information Systems, Potential Strategic Information Systems, Critical Information Systems and Vital Information Systems, as shown in Figure 1.10.

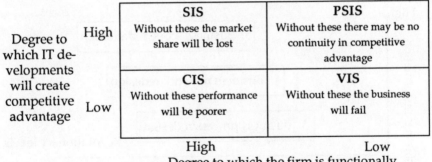

|  | SIS | PSIS |
|---|---|---|
| **Degree to** **High** | Without these the market share will be lost | Without these there may be no continuity in competitive advantage |
| **which IT de-** **velopments** | **CIS** | **VIS** |
| **will create** **competitive** **Low** **advantage** | Without these performance will be poorer | Without these the business will fail |

High                                              Low
Degree to which the firm is functionally
dependent upon IS/IT today

**Figure 1.10    Categorisation of information systems**

The definition of the Strategic Information System (SIS) and the Potential Strategic Information System (PSIS) are the same as those offered by McFarlan for SIS and Turnaround Systems, but the definition of the Critical Information System (CIS) becomes a system which is critical to the firms ability to achieve its required level of profitability. Without the CIS the desired profitability will not be realised. This concept and classification is more or less equivalent to McFarlan's Factory System but perhaps the meaning is slightly clearer. The Vital Information System (VIS) is defined as an information system which is essential to the continued existence of the firm but which, per se, does not contribute to any large extent to the effectiveness or efficiency of the management of the organisation. Examples of VIS are the payroll, bookkeeping, asset registers and other systems required by regulatory authorities. These are equivalent to McFarlan's Support Systems but the term VIS places them in a somewhat clearer perspective. These systems are not really equivalent to dog investments as the firm cannot actually do without basic record keeping facilities.

## 1.7    MIT90S

According to Morse (1991) another classification has been developed by researchers lead by Professor Michael Scott-Morton at MIT during the Management in the 90s project. Here information systems are seen as operating at either an evolutionary or revolutionary level. These are shown in Figure 1.11.

The evolutionary level is the equivalent of the automate and informate systems described previously, while the revolutionary level equates to the transformate systems. As may be seen in Figure 1.11 the MIT90s study identified two sub-groups in the evolutionary level and three in the revolutionary level. The three revolutionary level groups provide some useful

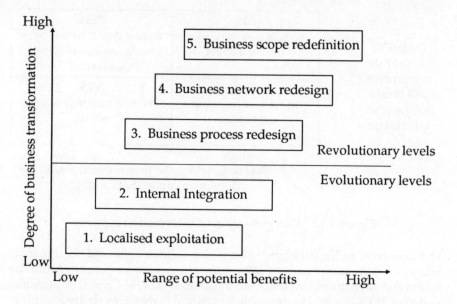

Figure 1.11    The MIT90s five layer model

ideas as to how a firm might apply transformate systems. Thus *Business process redesign* refers to employing IT to radically change the way the firm functions internally. The *Business network redesign* phase requires the firm to be connected to its buyers and sellers through its information systems. The *Business scope redefinition* requires an even broader view of the firm and its environment to be taken.

Theoretically, the potential benefits delivered by the strategic information systems can be enormous. However, they can also backfire and deliver no benefit or actually put the firm in a disadvantageous position. Recent research suggests that vendors, consultants and academics generally tend to exaggerate the payoff or the ability of computerisation to transformate.

## 1.8   A PORTFOLIO OF IT WITHIN THE FIRM

It is important to state that although the three phases of automate, informate and transformate may be seen as the historical development of IS, all three are currently relevant, and today's systems in any contemporary firm which is effectively exploiting its IS potential will be using all three types of approaches to IT. This co-existence of the three types of IT within the same firm is illustrated in Figure 1.12, and is critical to any systematic approach to the measurement of IT performance within the firm.

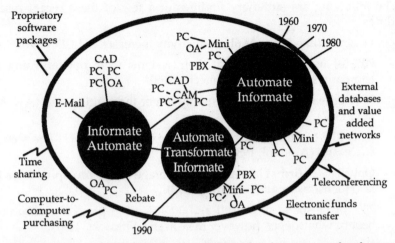

**Figure 1.12    Typical systems used in a business organisation**

It is most important to note that a single system may simultaneously have automate, informate and even transformate implications; for example, a CAD/CAM system clearly makes a major contribution to automating the design and engineering drawing process. However, CAD/CAM systems also supply copious information to management to assist in manufacturing decision making. At the same time, through its ability to reduce product development life cycle, CAD/CAM can make a significant contribution to transforming a business in the marketplace. End user computing and EPOS are two other examples where there is extensive overlapping of systems functionality.

The main conclusion which may be derived from the historical description of IS development is that the three different types of systems require three different types of approaches to benefit measurement and management. There will be a different approach to objective setting for each type of IT. These will be different staffing requirements as well as different investment profiles. Extending this concept to the area of IT performance measurement means that there will be a need for at least three different metrics, if one metric is adequate to measure each of the dimensions of automate, informate and transformate.

## 1.9    CHANGING ATTITUDES IN THE 90s

In some ways there is now greater cynicism about IT benefits than ever before. There is also today a much greater propensity to conduct research into how business actually performs as well as how business people feel about important issues. In the last few years several dozen major research assignments into how firms view their investment in IT have been conducted.

The following are summary findings of a few of these recent research findings:

- IT is not linked to overall productivity increases (OECD,1988).

- 70% of users declared that their systems were not returning their company's investment (Romtech, 1989).

- IT overhead costs are consistently larger than anticipated (A.T. Kearney, 1987).

- Only 31% of companies report that the introduction of IT has been very successful (Amdahl, 1988).

- Only 24% of firms claim an above average return on capital from their IT (Hochstrasser and Griffiths, 1990).

- 20% of IT spend is wasted and 30-40% of IS projects realise no net benefit whatsoever, however measured (Willcocks, 1991).

Another research report found that firms did not have a systematic approach to evaluating their IT investments. It is estimated that as many as 90% of organisations perform no systematic IT investment evaluation. In fact it is probably the most significant aspect of IT benefit management that few firms really know what IT investments actually cost and even fewer firms have any idea how to measure the effect of these investments. Recent research has concluded that there is a lack of conviction in business that IT investment costs and benefits can actually be estimated with adequate accuracy. Further, there is frequently an additional complication in the fact that after investment funds have been agreed, ongoing costs are generally not well analysed before commitment, which leads to situations of inadequate control. The spectacular growth in end user computing has further aggravated the situation. The problem of not knowing the exact costs of systems increases daily as more and more firms commit higher and higher proportions of their IS resources to end user or desk centred computing for which there is, generally speaking, very poor record keeping. According to Willcocks (1991) 25-40% of IT expenditure is incurred outside of the ISD budget. Some observers claim the end user costs are deliberately fudged in an attempt to understate the full cost of the IS function to the firm. Figure 1.13 shows some of the arguments for and against recording the costs of end user computing.

Those firms which have measured the return earned on their IT have found confusing results. According to Paul Strassman (1990) there is in fact no correlation between the amount invested in IT or the amount spent on IT and the return earned on the investment. Strassman claims that the amount spent on IT as a percentage of revenue, which has been used for some time as a measure of the firm's commitment to IT, is a misused indicator. For some time

| Pros | Cons |
|------|------|
| Better insight into work patterns | Needs time recording procedures |
| Closer approximations of cost/effort required to implement systems | May frighten off investment |
| | May prevent the learning experience |
| May discourage fatuous systems | End user's time is already paid for |

**Figure 1.13    Should end-user's time be recorded ?**

a number of organisations believed that it was necessary to spend a target percentage of their revenue on IT in order to obtain a desired level of benefit. Figures 1.14 and 1.15 are scatter diagrams showing shareholder returns plotted against IT budget (ITB) as a percentage of revenue, and return on assets plotted also against ITB as a percentage of revenue.

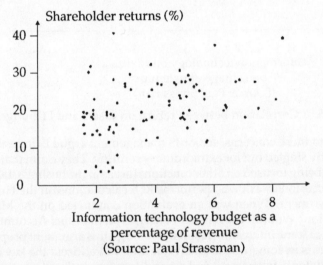

**Figure 1.14    Correlation between shareholder return and IT budget**

The effect shown by these scatter diagrams is that of a shotgun with no discernible pattern or correlation. An interpretation of Figure 1.14 is that for firms in this sample no more benefit is derived by firms spending 8% than by those spending 2%. This of course leads to the question "Why spend more than the minimum finance?" Figure 1.15 shows similar information but using a slightly different ratio. Again there is no correlation between expenditure on IT and business performance. Therefore from this research it appears that there is no advantage to spending a greater percentage of the firm's revenue or income on its IT. This puts the whole question of the value of business computing, especially the traditional ideas of how firms should monitor their IT expenditure, in grave doubt, and leads many to suspect that much of the claimed success for firms spending large percentages of their income on IT is simply industry hype.

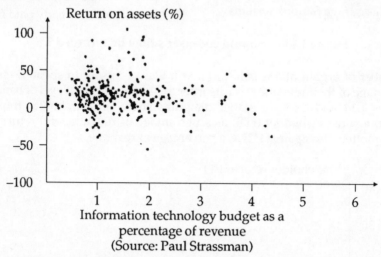

(Source: Paul Strassman)

**Figure 1.15    Correlation between return on assets and IT budget**

In response to these concerns, senior IS management argue IS investment has been unfairly singled out for extraordinary scrutiny. They claim that such attention is not being focused on other functional areas in the business. In their defence, IS professionals ask who performs ROI calculations on the Human Relations Department? When was an evaluation conducted on the Market Research Division? Wouldn't cost benefit analysis on the Chief Accountant's function produce some interesting results? Although this argument proposed by IS executives is in some way attractive, it does not address the key issue which differentiates IS investment and expenditure from other departmental investment and expenditure, which, inter alia, is the risk profile. Risk is discussed in some detail in Chapter 5.

## 1.10    THE MANAGEMENT OF THE ISD

One of the keys to the IT benefit evaluation and management process is the way the firm fulfils the information management function which is quite a unique one and which is frequently not well managed. This is because in many firms the measuring and managing of IT benefits is regarded as being the domain of the ISD.

Information management is a relatively ambiguous term. It is not entirely clear whether it refers to the management of the information systems department or to the management of information flows which is only part of the responsibility of the whole information systems department. Often the term information management refers to both.

Information management is sometimes perceived as highly technical and therefore the domain of "techies". This view has been encouraged, at least some of the time, by IT professionals. Without a clear definition and with the technical image it sometimes projects it is perhaps not surprising that Information Management is a relatively neglected area in business. At least the management of the information systems department is frequently neglected. Quite a lot of research work has been done in a number of technical areas which relate to the application of information systems in the business. Examples of this are MIS, EIS EUC and SIS. However, how the ISD itself should be managed has not received anywhere near enough attention. It is simply assumed that the information management team engages in the usual processes of planning, organising, motivating and controlling.

There is often a general assumption made that the way the ISD is managed is simply a microcosm of the business as a whole. Therefore the ISD is usually portrayed in terms of the classical Anthony paradigm with the classical sub-divisions of Top, Middle and Supervisory management. However, as was pointed out in recent publications (Owen, 1986 and Madrick, 1987), this model does not necessarily reflect what is happening in the ISD. In the first place, there has been considerable pressure put on the ISD to escalate its importance or relevance in the firm. This has meant that the ISD has expanded the area of its influence at the higher levels of management and has thus, in some firms, become involved in strategic planning, financial analysis, sales forecasting etc. On the other hand, the ISD has often had to take on additional responsibilities such as the provision of information centres or end user computing and this has skewed the lower part of the triangle. Figures 1.16 and 1.17 are graphical representations of the actual structure of some ISDs.

It is argued by some that the result of stretching the top portion of the triangle and extending the base has been to distract the management of the ISD away from some of the more routine issues with which it should be involved. The result of this is that the ISD's performance has been reduced.

One of the regular functions of the ISD should be to measure or evaluate its own performance. Most departments within a firm conduct on a weekly or monthly basis, assessments of their activities. This is typically undertaken by creating cost centres or profit centres or even investment centres and by producing appropriate management accounts to reflect each function's act-

**Figure 1.16   The Anthony paradigm in the ISD**

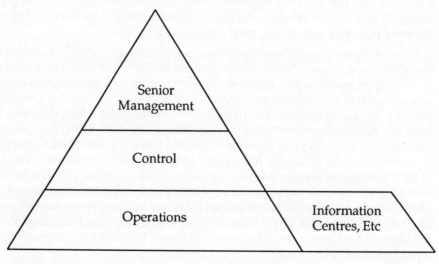

**Figure 1.17    ISD structure incorporating additional responsibilities**

ivities. Although this is sometimes done for the ISD it is usually only conducted in a very limited way probably addressing nothing more than a simple budget. This is just not adequate as the activities of the ISD are among the most complex in the firm and have the potential to be the most far reaching. Frequently it is said that the ISD is at the centre of the business, and that they are the only people who know exactly what is happening throughout the whole spectrum of the firm. Clearly this is true in some sense, at least as far as the information flows are concerned. This attitude of the ISD being at the centre of the business can cloud many other important issues as well as lead to unsatisfactory relationships between the ISD and other departments. However, if it is true that the ISD plays a central role in the firm then it may be argued that it should be involved in managing the success of the systems which it implements. Of course in some firms the ISD is quite reactive, not looking for systems opportunities nor finding ways to assist users in optimising the use of their systems, while in other organisations it is quite proactive. A proactive ISD will not only look for IT opportunities but may also help manage them. Furthermore it is not perfectly clear whether a proactive ISD will actually produce better results.

A key issue is that of responsibility. The introduction of a new system always results in a change as to how certain processes are handled in the organisation. A critical question is "Who is responsible for the change effort?" In most cases the ISD is responsible for the systems development process, and is thus the change agent. The ISD is nearly always independent or external to the user department. The fact that the ISD hands systems over to user departments frequently leads to a lack of commitment from both the ISD and the users themselves. From a change theory perspective it is obvious that the change agent can never truly assume responsibility for another's change because only that individual is capable of changing his/her behaviour. The change agent can only facilitate or inhibit individual change through the handling of the change program (Bostrom & Heinen, 1977 (a) and (b)). Perhaps one of the main reasons why the ISD performance, especially with regard to the systems it delivers, is not rigorously examined is that IS benefits are often believed to be so difficult to measure.

The management of IT benefits is an issue that must be addressed in a multi-functional and multi-disciplinary way, and therefore it is important to look at how users and other groups perceive the situation. The question of how financial management, IS staff as well as the general management perceive the utility of the ISD is of critical importance. The issues of perception and context are discussed in a later section.

In general most observers agree that the management of the ISD is a very difficult business. The ISD is expected to exhibit technical excellence, it is expected to be highly flexible, it must be highly responsive. The ISD must have strategic vision as well as being able to master the finest detail of very complex technology. The management of the ISD must understand business issues as well as be able to express highly technical matters in simple terms.

The issue of benefit management begs several other questions.

–   Not all IS applications will generate benefits. In fact some applications may generate dis-benefits (or negative benefits). It could even be ar- gued that benefits are only a matter of definition in that costs and assets may be the same physical items but treated quite differently, and whether these items are expended in the profit and loss account or capitalised in the balance sheet is frequently determined by the opinion of the financial director.

– Even if there are no discernible benefits the question of what the firm would do without the system has to be faced. It has been estimated that after three months the average system has been totally internalised within the firm and that the firm could not function without it. Systems are never removed from firms even when they are showing no apparent benefit. Therefore the question may well become, what cost can the firm bear in order to have the system?

## 1.11  WHY FOCUS ON IT BENEFITS?

When a firm undertakes a major reorganisation it is unusual for it to conduct a cost benefit analysis. The costs of this sort of work are usually absorbed into the ongoing expenses without being separately highlighted. On the benefit side it is usually assumed, without detailed enumeration, that the reorganisation will produce more than adequate benefits to justify whatever costs were incurred.

Computers are frequently nothing more than a tool for reorganisation or change. They provide the infrastructure which allows management to reconsider the way different parts of the organisation function and relate to one another. It is therefore sometimes assumed that like a general reorganisation, it is not necessary to measure the benefits, nor try to manage them. The assumption is that the benefits actually take care of themselves. However, this is in reality, clearly untrue, as benefits do not generally materialise without considerable attention from management. Furthermore, computerisation is quite different to other forms of reorganisation, frequently requiring considerable cash investment as well as the adoption of new technology which brings a new risk level to the reorganisation's activities, as well as to the general business of the firm.

The risk issue is perhaps one of the most important reasons why it is necessary to carefully focus on IT benefits. There are a number of dimensions to IT risk which include: structure of project, size of project, firm's failure record, novelty of technology and novelty of project. All of these issues directly impact on the project's likelihood of success. Risk, which is a fundamental aspect of IT, and which is often ignored, is discussed at length in several subsequent sections.

## 1.12  WHAT IS MEANT BY MANAGING IT BENEFITS?

In pursuing the measurement and management of IT benefits several systems realities must be kept in mind. IT benefits are the product of a successful implementation of information systems. When new IT is to be introduced into the firm, feasibility studies, costs benefit analysis, detailed specifications, etc, are carefully prepared. Once the system is produced training, commissioning and implementation are the main focus issues.

Sometimes accountants carefully scrutinise the cost of the investment as well as the ongoing expenses and make sure that they are continually monitored so that they can be kept under control. Improvements in performance are also sometimes looked for. However, hardly ever is the same emphasis given to making sure that the benefits are delivered that is placed on ensuring that costs are held within the budgeted limits. There seems to be an implied assumption that benefits are passively produced, although costs are actively controlled. This attitude is particularly strange as there is ample evidence that benefits do not simply generate of their own accord. One of the reasons proposed for the lack of benefits management is that benefits are not actively pursued because control of the project is invariably handed over to users too busy or not sufficiently involved with the project to ensure that the benefits are actually delivered. This attitude has been described by Parker et al (1989) as arising from an urgency to get on with the job, combined with a distinct lack of appropriate disciplines.

## 1.13 ASSESSMENT OF IT BENEFITS

The benefits to be derived from an IT investment should be assessed a number of times during the project's life-cycle. Figure 1.18 indicates the stages at which assessments should occur.

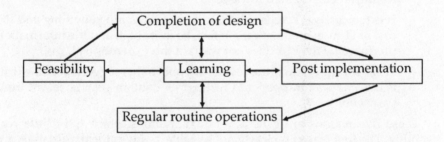

Figure 1.18    Appropriate stages at which to conduct IT investment assessment

It is most important to note that the main purpose of IT investment assessment is to ensure that the firm learns about the costs and the benefits associated with this activity. As all the costs and benefits cannot be fully understood before the project begins, it is necessary to perform this procedure a number of times. On each occasion, the organisation should learn from the experience and some of the learning should be passed on to the next stage.

One of the most critical stages at which this assessment should be performed is post implementation, and following on from this, at regular intervals. This is essential in order that the firm may incorporate the lessons learnt into the next feasibility study undertaken.

## 1.14   POST IMPLEMENTATION AUDITS

Furthermore, although post implementation audits (PIA) are regularly included in systems development standards, they are frequently not conducted or are very poorly attended to. In research conducted by Butler Cox four reasons were attributed for the lack of attention given to post implementation audits. These four, plus one other excuse which is regularly heard, are listed below:

- **It is not necessary.** If the investment appraisal was conducted correctly then the results should be automatically delivered and therefore any attempt at a PIA is superfluous.

- **It is too difficult.** IT produces complex results which cannot be easily discerned or disentangled from other business activities or general noise in the environment in which the firm functions.

- **It is against our culture and philosophy.** Acting as an auditor or a policeman is not appropriate in the firm and will produce negative feeling among the staff towards IT.

- **It is too costly.** There is a definite cost to measuring anything and the cost of IT measurement can, in fact, be quite high and the information produced by the PIA does not warrant this expense.

- **What would we do if the results are poor?** This suggests that the firm is in some way trapped and furthermore nothing can be learnt from past actions.

These five reasons are generally rationalisations which have little real validity. The first reason is clearly not sensible, as investment appraisals are regularly conducted with very scanty information and therefore frequently do not accurately represent what will actually happen. The second reason has a greater truth content but nonetheless, for most organisations it is possible to perform some degree of post implementation audit without too much strain. The third reason is pure excuse. Post implementation audits may be conducted in an atmosphere which does not suggest that the head office accountants are prying or spying on the users. The fourth reason has some degree of truth. The performance of highly detailed data gathering and calculations may incur considerable expense. However, in many situations rough estimates which may be compiled with little expense are perfectly adequate. Finally, the fifth reason is perhaps the most honest but misses one of the most important points of IT benefit measurement. IT investments, as with most other investments, are evaluated in order that the organisation can learn from its experience. If the results of the investment are rated poorly then the organisation may learn from this experience and not repeat that type of investment again. If no assessment is done then the firm might continue to re-invest in this area of poor returns.

The reason why post implementation audits are not performed is probably much more simple; because the organisation does not demand them. Accounting is performed primarily because a statement of account is required by law. Management accounting and business performance measurement is a by-product of the statutory accounts, and in any case management accounting and business performance measurement is required because many managers are directly rewarded on the basis of the responsibility they accept and how well their duties are executed. Few managers are directly rewarded on the results of IT. As mentioned earlier, there is a general problem relating to the fact that the ISD frequently produces the change agent while someone else has to carry out the system initiated by the change agent.

Until firms re-orientate their thinking with regard to responsibility, the issue of IT benefit measurement and management is likely to continue to be fudged. Fortunately many business firms and government organisations are doing precisely this today.

## 1.15  SUMMARY

IT benefit measurement and management is a central business management issue. It is a distinct discipline which falls within the responsibility of user management but which requires the direct support of information systems staff. It also requires the direct attention of the top management in the information systems department as well as commitment from the various user departments involved. It is a complex issue and must therefore be handled carefully if meaningful results are to be obtained.

As a first step IT benefit measurement and management requires IT systems to be categorised as Automate, Informate and Transformate. Many information systems have multiple functions such as both automate and informate aspects, or informate and transformate aspects. As a different measuring approach is relevant for each of these IT categories the next step is to choose the appropriate set of metrics. Where an information system has more than one function it is necessary to isolate the different functions, and to apply different metrics to each of these functions. Finally, data must be collected and calculations performed.

# 2  Some Aspects of the IT Investment Decision Process

## 2.1  ARE IT INVESTMENT DECISIONS DIFFERENT?

Many firms have rules for information technology (IT) investment decisions which differ from those adopted for core business investment decisions. Signing limits are frequently different, or the decisions may be restricted to staff in the IT function or department. Some firms have an IT version, or sub committee, of the capital approvals committee. An important question which must be addressed is how far can these, or other, differences be justified or explained by the characteristics of IT? In other words, are IT investment decisions fundamentally different to other investment decisions?

This chapter considers some characteristics of decisions about IT invest-ment, comparing them with other business investment decisions. The analysis points to problems of understanding and credibility rather than to any fun-damental difference between IT and other aspects of business, and the chapter concludes with some suggestions for overcoming these problems.

Some firms have in the past, taken a strategic decision to encourage more use of modern computer technology. In such circumstances, the rigour of a case by case appraisal process might be relaxed, or the required rate of return for any particular project could be lower than for other, non IT, projects.

### 2.1.1  The strategic potential of IT investment

One such example of this type of strategic thinking occurred in the late 70s when British Telecom (then Post Office Telecommunications) decided that it needed to quickly raise the computer literacy of its staff. The firm relaxed its normal financial rules and "seeded" the organisation with a large number of small business computers. The reasoning was that such an investment would raise the computer consciousness of the staff, suggest numbers of new appli-cations and uses and thus bring about long term improvements.

Pretty much as hoped, staff throughout the organisation worked on differ-ent problem areas. In many cases a number of personal computer or small business computer-based solutions were developed independently. The firm picked the most promising for further, generally professional, development.

37

Such an approach has a number of advantages. It harnesses the creative abilities of large numbers of staff and ensures that staff working in particular problem areas are able, in some small way, to direct IT development. A further spin-off was that the use of PC based tools such as word processing, spread-sheets and databases is now widespread throughout British Telecom and that there is a substantial group of staff and managers who have a familiarity with the concepts and practices of PC based IT.

Whilst such an approach may have had its successes it can probably only be attempted on such a scale once in any firm's life. As far as is known, no attempt was ever made by British Telecom to cost the experiment. It relied on the visionary approach of one man, Sir George Jefferson, the then new Chairman. It may be considered doubtful whether any but a nationalised industry generating a large amount of cash could consider such a step. In short, this sort of situation is fairly unusual and certainly not a basis for normal business decisions or practice.

In normal circumstances a firm only invests if it considers that the return on the capital utilised is sufficient to meet the long term objectives or needs of the business. In other words the benefit gained is worth the expense. The capital utilised in this way costs the same whatever its intended application, and there are likely to be a number of ways the capital can be spent to gain a similar goal. It should therefore be expected that the same appraisal rules and criteria apply to decisions about IT as they do to any other investment. Except in unusual circumstances, similar to those described above, IT should never be regarded as something good, or bad, in its own right so that it need only achieve some lower rate of return. IT has to take its place in the queue for all too scarce cash resources, and the rules for justifying the expenditure must be the same as for any other project.

A more sophisticated argument is that, because the risks inherent in deci-sions about IT are higher, the expected return on investment (ROI) must be higher before an investment can be justified. As described below, decisions about IT do carry substantial risks in that they tend to involve large sums of money and have a high potential to damage the firm. This chapter will argue that this combination is not unique to IT, for example, a new product launch is equally risky. But, fundamentally, decision makers are frequently less comfortable about IT because of their ignorance of all the issues and because they lack faith in the estimates presented to them.

## 2.2   MUST-DO IT INVESTMENTS

There will be occasions when a firm undertakes an investment which gives no return at all, or perhaps gives an intangible return which is difficult to measure. Complying with some legal requirements is an example of the first, PR or training might be examples of the second. These cases are discussed in greater detail below.

But there is another side to the issue of investment; do the characteristics of information technology mean that there are, or should be, differences in the way that decisions about IT are arrived at? That is, are there good reasons why there should be different processes for making decisions about IT expenditure?

Some of the characteristics of investment decisions are discussed below, comparing IT with core business and assumes a firm whose core business is not IT. Three examples are considered, core business, prestige project and IT project. Obviously there will be certain generalisations but some underlying characteristics of each example will become apparent.

One class of decision, or of investment justification, will not be discussed in any detail; that is the "must do" changes. They typically result from legislative changes. For example, firms had no choice but to change their systems to provide VAT information to Customs & Excise, or to implement the provisions of the statutory sick pay regulations, when these were first introduced. Because the firm has no choice but to comply there is little point in indulging in a formal justification or worrying about decision criteria. But, even in these cases, there is considerable merit in investigating, and costing, alternatives. If there are realistic alternatives, as there certainly are in the examples above, then the "must do" solution is the cheapest. The more expensive solutions are all optional. The additional expenditure, over and above that required for the cheapest solution, must be justified as though it were an optional project.

## 2.3   A CORE BUSINESS INVESTMENT DECISION

Decisions about investment in core business are, by definition, what the firm's managers know most about. The decision to re-equip the production line is easy to cost, so many machines at so much each, plus installation, a lick of paint and re-training. A certain simplification of the details may perhaps be forgiven. The number of options will probably not be large, the new machines have to fit the existing space, work with the remaining machines and be capable of producing the product.

The benefits will be inherent in the reason for considering the decision. It might be that the old machines are getting too expensive to maintain, having too much down time, or are turning out products of insufficient quality. Or it might be that the firm is changing its product line and this change is necessary to accommodate the new products. The benefits are thus fairly easy to identify and generally fairly easy to cost.

Similarly, the implications of not proceeding with the project, or not changing the machines, are fairly easy to identify; continuing high maintenance costs, high reject ratio, or the inability to produce the new product. However, this "do nothing" option is often not fully costed, especially when the alternative is not to undertake some new work. The people putting together the financial case are likely to be departmental managers and have limited accounting, financial or investment appraisal expertise. They will probably be emotionally committed to the project and may be under an implied directive from above. This leads to the observation that many such investment cases are a result of an earlier decision, and do not, in fact, represent a true choice but are a means of exercising management control of capital expenditure that must be undertaken because of that earlier decision. The decision to launch a new product is a case in point.

There will also be intangible benefits; the production line workers may prefer newer machines, feel they are participating in technological progress, feel pride in using leading edge technology. And they may feel happier that the firm has enough faith in them and itself to invest in their future. So their morale, and maybe their productivity, will rise. On the other hand some workers may not like the change; the new machines are likely to be from a different manufacturer, perhaps foreign, and they may feel that "all change is for the worst". Some upheaval and re-training is probably inevitable. These attitudes would be a distinct disincentive.

The intangible benefits and disadvantages would not normally be costed. Indeed, in some firms to even mention them in an investment appraisal case would be to risk the accusation of going soft.

However, the difference between the positive and negative attitude is quite likely to result from the way that the change is proposed by management. In other words, in any project, managing the way that the subsequent changes to working practice are communicated will be an important part of the implementation process. The difference between doing this well and doing it badly or not at all may well make the difference between a successful implementation and a disaster. Ignoring the value of a change in the workers' attitude in the investment appraisal may be acceptable; but if that leads to the issue being ignored altogether it may sink the project.

The case for investment will be prepared by managers in the department concerned, then pushed up the management chain, each level committing its own personal credibility to the case, until it eventually arrives at the Board of directors, or capital approvals committee. It is likely to be considered very much on the merits of the case as presented, and on the financial situation of the firm. The people making the decision will be well versed in the issues surrounding the decision, or at least believe that they are (or want other members of the committee to believe that they are).

The above case can be summarised in the following way:

- There are relatively few options,
- The decision makers are "at home" with the relevant issues,
- It is comparatively simple to cost and the benefits are relatively obvious,
- The cost of not undertaking the expenditure is obvious, though probably not costed,
- Any intangible benefits will probably be only slightingly referred to and will not be costed.

## 2.4 INVESTMENT IN A PRESTIGE PROJECT

For most firms investment in prestige projects are not regular events. However, the prestige project case has strong parallels with much expenditure that does not have an easily quantifiable return, such as advertising or PR for example. These decisions will generally not require much specialist knowledge. Even though experts will probably be invited to give advice, most managers involved will feel fully qualified to give an opinion, or hold an opinion at variance with the experts.

Consider a fairly new, rapidly expanding firm, which has its head office in a small building in a back street of a provincial city. It has outgrown this office and is looking for larger accommodation. Having illusions, or perhaps delusions, of grandeur it is looking for a building that will become the corporate headquarters of a large conglomerate. It will have a number of alternatives available, from old office blocks just like the present one but bigger, to glass and chrome monstrosities in the science park. Or it could just take over the equally small building next door and join them together. This last alternative is likely to be the cheapest option.

The financial case, or justification, for these alternatives is somewhat more difficult to put together. There will be many possible options, albeit many of the elements will be common and a few large costs will tend to swamp the smaller variables. Not all of the costs will be fully predictable, especially if the proposed new office is some distance from the existing one.

In these circumstances the project will almost certainly show a large negative figure at the end. The costs of moving office are very large. What are the measurable money benefits? Practically none.

The most obvious implication of not moving is that the firm cannot expand; but this may be stated in a loaded manner, "firms either expand or die".

In this case there are lots of intangible benefits to be considered:

-   A smart office will impress customers and creditors, so will be a benefit in itself.

-   A smarter location will improve staff morale, and thus improve productivity and staff retention.

-   A purpose built office will improve efficiency.

There is probably some truth in these arguments. But how does the project manager go about costing them, measuring them or controlling them? In the event there will almost certainly be no real attempt made to cost them. Whether they are considered to justify the expenditure will be a rationalisation after the decision is made.

The case will probably have been overseen from the start by Board members. They will have a fair bit of personal credibility tied up in the issue, indeed the genesis of the project may owe more to their view of the firm than any real need to expand. The decision will probably eventually hinge on the personal views of one or two influential people, essentially "the Boss".

Lest the above be considered an excessively cynical view of the decision making process in firms, it is only necessary to look to the centre of London. The headquarters buildings of many large firms are built at vast expense on ruinously expensive plots, and rely on staff spending large parts of their days in useless and tiring commuting. Whilst the expense of the buildings and of attracting high calibre staff to central London is readily admitted, the location is generally justified on the grounds that a firm of this importance is "expected" to have a presence in the Capital. This is so even amongst firms whose main product is communications – whether physical or electronic – failing to take the advice they liberally offer to others.

The spending of large amounts of money on a project which shows a negative NPV, or whose benefits are not assured, is not unusual. Prestige projects aside, mention has already been made of training and PR. Neither of these types of investment can be unambiguously evaluated in strict financial terms. The launch of a new product is surrounded by uncertain estimates of likely benefits. However, most firms will have launched new products before and will thus have a track record on which to form a judgment of the realism of the sales estimates. The new product will also probably be related to existing core business; indeed, firms which launch into totally new fields have a much lower chance of success.

In the case of a negative NPV for an optional project it must be assumed, if the firm is behaving rationally, that the un-costed intangible benefits are considered to generate an adequate return. In these cases the firm has put an implied or imputed cash value to those intangible benefits.

This case may be summarised in the following way:

- There are a large number of options.
- The decision makers are probably driving the project.
- It is not straightforward to cost and there are few obvious financial benefits.
- The cost of not undertaking the project is not obvious.
- The intangible benefits will probably carry the case. The weight given to these benefits will be decided arbitrarily.

A simple observation that flows from some of the comments above which should come as no surprise, but which is frequently overlooked, is that firms are made up of people. These people do not in general behave as automata, following strictly logical and predictable paths. Emotion, personal preferences and even sheer cussedness play an important part in decision making in many firms. A consideration of the likely personal views of the individuals is thus important in understanding much company behaviour. The imprecision which dogs much social policy, because people do not always behave exactly as predicted, affects large scale changes in firms as well.

## 2.5  AN IT INVESTMENT

Decisions about IT generally involve large sums of money. Quite what constitutes "a large sum" differs from firm to firm of course, but a bigger firm tends to need bigger, more expensive, computing. So to some extent that is self compensating. Because the decision does involve a lot of money it is generally pushed some way up the company tree. It is a sad fact that most of the men or women in this exalted position are unlikely to have any real knowledge or understanding of IT (some striking exceptions to this generalisation are referred to below).

The characteristics of the decision may include elements of both of the previous examples. The computer or system is likely to be intended to assist the core business, either directly by automating some aspect of the operation, or by improving some back office function. Thus the ostensible purpose of the project may be understood although the details will probably not be. This understanding will not necessarily work in favour of the project, however, as the proposal may well involve changing some long established working methods.

Modern computer technology is so all-pervading that examples of its application throughout all parts of a firm can be expected. However, any decision about the use of IT requires an understanding both of the technology and of the application area. This makes the problems of insufficient understanding all the more severe, especially in a diverse firm. A senior manager is unlikely to have a good understanding of the basic processes and operations in every part of a reasonably large company. Indeed, he or she may have joined the firm directly at a senior level and thus have no first hand knowledge of any of the working departments.

In the days when most IT was used to automate basic processes the benefits were relatively easy to specify and measure; three invoice clerks replaced by a small business computer, for example. However, as more of industry's basic processes are already automated a growing proportion of new IT investment is intended either to marginally improve an existing application or to assist management rather than the shop floor. Whilst the first of these two has strong parallels with the replacement of obsolete equipment of any kind, the second class, helping management, is intended to deliver benefits which will be very difficult to pin down with the same precision.

Projects of this kind are often described as intended to informate a business, to distinguish them from those designed to automate. Not only are their benefits more difficult to measure they are also more difficult to describe in advance. However, these benefits will probably be potentially much larger than those delivered by automation projects. Managers used to strictly money based capital approvals may feel that the benefits claimed for such systems appear wishy washy or intangible. However, whilst it may well be difficult to put strict money values to them, these potential benefits are very real, may be very important to the firm's profitability, and certainly need to be carefully managed.

The third wave of systems is often described as those which transformate (or transform) a firm. These systems have meant the difference between gentle decline and highly profitable survival for some of the firms which have mastered them. There is little methodology available to put money values to such benefits, and probably little merit in the attempt. In some senses they are close to the prestige project described earlier; likely to stand or fall on the vision of a few senior executives (who are likely to be an exception to the generalisation suggested earlier). Whilst the successes, and a few failures, are well known there is no evidence about the firms, that must surely exist, which decided not to go ahead with a system that had the potential to transform their business because they could not see the point, or did not dare risk the investment.

Thus there is a spread of potential benefits, ranging from reasonably straightforward cost based, to those based on little more than the vision of a few senior executives. (This is not to imply that senior executives have less faith or vision; but it is only the view of the decision maker that is relevant in this regard.)

An element of prestige will probably also be involved. As IT is still relatively recent, and considered by many to be a good thing in its own right, many firms will be interested simply in leap-frogging competitors without necessarily fully understanding or considering all the ramifications.

The number of options to be considered will depend on the type of project. The first implementation implies a free choice amongst a number of suppliers, as well as the option of continuing the current manual process. Subsequent additions or enhancements will be more constrained, but eventually the firm will reach the point when they could make a break with their existing suppliers and the choice again widens out. In general the number of options is large.

### 2.5.1 Difficulty in costing

The project will be difficult to cost accurately. The difficulties of costing software projects are well documented; similar, though less well researched difficulties, exist with large implementations. A naive purchaser will also find that apparently firm and final quotations from hardware suppliers can be surprisingly flexible; a few more pounds will always buy that suddenly vital extra feature. In addition, there will be a low confidence that the cost estimates will prove accurate.

If there are doubts about the costs, the estimates of benefits will be even more problematic. These estimates will probably have been made by the analyst who devised the system. Because significant benefits are possible from good, well implemented, systems, and because the analyst will put the best gloss on his own proposals, the estimates may appear unbelievably large. Reactions from the line managers will vary from simple disbelief to alarm about loss of staff and perceived loss of status. More senior managers, including those involved in the investment decision, are likely to view the estimates with considerable scepticism. This is unfortunately well founded as in many, perhaps most, firms there has been little history of post investment audits sufficiently detailed or thorough to authoritatively establish what benefits were gained from new systems. And if the benefits were not measured they were probably not managed, nor was any real attempt made to ensure the forecast benefits were achieved, let alone maximised. In such circumstances personal opinion or prejudice has free rein.

The cost of not proceeding may be difficult to ascertain and not well understood by the decision makers. This will especially be true if the project involves an upgrade to an existing system. Anecdotal stories abound that IT projects or departments are a black hole for money, always wanting to buy the latest gizmo. No matter how much growth there has been recently there may be a suspicion that the project is really nothing more than an admission that the original implementation was under-specified. Where there is ignorance, suspicion is not far behind.

### 2.5.2   Intangible benefits

Significant intangible benefits will be possible and some will be quoted in the project justification:

- Customer perception will improve if front office staff are seen to be using modern technology, or demonstrate the benefits of that technology by having instant access to the firm's information about the customer.

- A mention in trade journals or general press because of a large new system is good publicity.

- Giving management access to better, more immediate, information will improve decision making.

Equally, large disadvantages are likely if the system or implementation is not all that it should be. Also, intangible benefits are unlikely to be well understood and will often not be costed. The putting of financial values to such intangible benefits is not easy, and is discussed elsewhere in this book.

A summary of the above shows the following characteristics of IT decisions:

- There are a large number of options.

- The decision makers will probably not understand the details of the project, though they may have an understanding of the process to be automated.

- Not straightforward to cost, low confidence in the estimates.

- Relatively difficult to estimate benefits. Low confidence in those estimates based on past experience.

- Cost of not undertaking the project not understood or accepted.

- Intangible benefits will not be quantified, though they may be an important part of the justification.

### 2.5.3 Making the decision

There is a range of types of decision regarding investment in IT. At one extreme the decision is little more than a question of when it suits the firm to replace an obsolete part of the production machinery. At the other extreme, a firm may be considering spending significant amounts of money with little in the way of hard financial justification. Such decisions are taken in other instances by many firms with equally little hard evidence. A mistaken advertising campaign can be stopped. Poor training will probably not cost more than the wasted courses. A bad choice of new office is unlikely to significantly affect costs or productivity.

However, a bad decision about a large new computer system will affect the firm at least until a replacement can be installed, which may be a long time, and which the firm may not be able to afford. In this time there may be significant deleterious effects on costs, productivity and customer service. These effects may be enough to destroy the firm. A mistaken decision not to go ahead with a system may also destroy a firm. Simply refusing to consider big IT projects is definitely not a way of playing it safe. Thus decisions about major computer systems carry a high risk, as well as a high price tag. Probably only decisions about major product launches have as much potential for good or bad in most firms.

In conclusion, it appears that decisions about IT investment have similarities with many other sorts of decisions taken by firms. Although they are not unique there are certain differences, which result partly from the characteristics of IT and partly from the way it is perceived by management. The main points are:

- IT is high risk, high cost, but capable of delivering substantial benefits so cannot be ignored.

- Expenditure on IT will probably constitute a significant proportion of a firm's capital expenditure.

- The rapid pace of change of the technology, and its wide use, make it difficult for managers to be sufficiently conversant with all aspects of the decision.

- In most firms there is no trusted track record in reliable estimates, or subsequent measurements, of costs and benefits.

The overriding impression is of senior managers who, ignorant and distrustful of IT, attempt to make a decision based on inadequate and unreliable information, but at the same time are subjected to a steady diet of propaganda telling them of the enormous benefits competitors have realised from modern computer systems.

Should the decisions, then, be left to the computer professionals, who at least understand the technical issues?

## 2.6   A WAY FORWARD

The following are some suggestions as to how the IT investment decision process may be improved.

### 2.6.1   Getting together

Decisions about IT investments cannot and should not be left solely to IT professionals any more than decisions about product launches should be left to the factory managers. Of course, detailed technical points about the way the machines and systems run are best left to experts but any decisions about large sums of money, or affecting the firm's core processes, must involve the general management of the firm.

The problems of managers' ignorance and inadequate information need to be tackled. Much research into this question shows that the greatest benefits are achieved by firms which have an agreed, thought through, IT strategy. A result which seems obvious.

It also seems obvious that once such a strategy has been developed it must be adhered to. So the firm needs a mechanism for developing a strategy and a mechanism for ensuring that all proposed investments are within that strategy. Both the IT professionals and the general management of the firm need to work at this issue.

The IT professionals are clearly a valuable source of expertise within the firm. But too many prefer to stick to their chosen speciality rather than (as is common for many managers in large firms), being prepared to spend time gaining experience in other, core business, units. There are risks to the individual in gaining such exposure, and problems, largely related to pay and grading, for the firm. The benefit is primarily a manager with a more rounded outlook who is likely to be more committed to the firm.

Similarly, information technology is now too all pervasive in any modern firm for an operational manager to be able to justify almost total ignorance of it. He has to be familiar with the major issues and problems in order to fully understand the workings of his own department.

It is not within the scope of this discussion to describe how a firm can develop managers with an understanding of both core business and IT. However, on the assumption that the managers concerned are willing to learn and to try, a powerful way of focusing attention and teaching both operational and IT managers some of the key issues is to ask both to co-operatively develop an IT strategy, and to police it. This is a task which is too often left to the IT professionals alone and then rubber stamped by the Board.

The development of a strategy for the use of modern information technology within a firm must be based on a thorough understanding of a number of factors:

- The firm's overall business strategy.
- The firm's position in its marketplace, including an analysis of the facilities available to the competition and of the service expected by the customers. (Taking into account the concept that successful firms seek to pleasantly surprise their customers with new, more efficient, levels of service, not just grudgingly follow expectations.)
- The firm's financial situation. A well thought through strategy which would bankrupt the Bank of England is no help to anyone.
- The firm's current level of IT expertise. As everyone needs to learn to walk before they run, it may be appropriate to introduce a cheap, simple, system for a few years before proceeding to a state of the art system.
- An analysis of current IT trends and standards.

A strategy based on these points cannot be completed by either IT professionals or operational managers working in isolation. Development of such a strategy can only be undertaken by the two working together and having a great deal of understanding of each other's specialism. To have any real chance of success the strategy needs to have the visible commitment of senior management. Probably the simplest way of ensuring this is to involve such managers in the original process. And the strategy needs to be regularly reviewed; which implies a mechanism to keep a group of senior managers thinking about current trends in the IT world in general and in their own firm in particular.

Many firms seem to regard the, admittedly large, investment of senior management time and effort such advice implies as somehow wasted on a narrow specialism. Such criticism can perhaps best be answered by reference to the amount of money modern firms spend on IT, and on the vulnerability of most firms to bad decisions on the subject.

Once a strategy has been established, all investment decisions for information technology can be tested against it. Typically this would not be an onerous job as few cases will be submitted which breach published company policy. A pre-review by the IT group would be appropriate before cases reached the capital approvals committee.

It can be seen that the development of an IT strategy is only possible if senior managers and the IT professionals get together and learn from each other. Maybe it is not so surprising that firms which have developed such a strategy succeed.

### 2.6.2    Improving information flow

The other side of the problem described above is that the information about costs and benefits of computer systems is unreliable and inadequate.

There is no easy answer to this. It is an issue which requires patient and diligent application over a number of years. Much research has been done into the forecasting of system development costs and timescales. However, most firms completely neglect the measurement and control of benefits.

Contrary to the beliefs apparent in many large firms, merely estimating the benefits in the financial case does not guarantee that they will be achieved. Simply assuming their achievement, and cutting departmental headcounts accordingly, whilst having the satisfying smack of strong government, is no answer unless some attempt is made to measure real productivity. Otherwise, it is all too easy for a department to reduce its real level of service in line with the headcount reduction, instead of taking full advantage of the new system.

The measurement of benefits, a subject in its own right, starts well before the system is implemented. It must be monitored for months, or years, after implementation if the firm is to maximise the return on its investment and ensure that all departments using the system are gaining equal benefit. Such a programme will almost certainly require the establishment of a benefits monitoring group, staffed by operational as well as systems experts.

Only when a firm has a record of successful implementations, monitored and controlled to the satisfaction of all parties, will the doubt and mistrust described above begin to break down. It is likely to be neither a quick nor an easy process.

### 2.7    SUMMARY

Sometimes it is argued that IT investments are fundamentally different to all other business investments. It is said that IT investments are different becuase their effects are often far reaching beyond their immediate and obvious impact, and that their benefits are often intangible. However, on close examination, many non-IT investments also have knock effects, and have intangible benefits associated with them. Thus IT investments are not unique.

To be more effective in measuring and managing IT benefits it is necessary for firms to change their attitudes towards IT investments in several different ways. IT investments must not be seen as being materially different to other investments. Decisions about IT share many characteristics with core business decisions but often involve high risks and large sums of capital. Traditionally top management have tried to "ignore" IT decisions by delegating them to specialist management. In an era when most firms' core business and competitive advantage is critically affected by the successful use of IT, and when huge sums of money are involved, this practice is no longer acceptable.

Many firms do not give sufficient senior management attention to the use of IT, especially for strategic applications. Furthermore, many firms do not educate their IT managers in core business issues, and this sometimes causes them to be business illiterate. As a result senior managers do not sufficiently understand the issues inherent in IT capital appraisal, and IT staff feel insufficient commitment to achieving benefits in core business areas. In fact there is frequently a fuzziness as to the responsibility for achieving IT benefits.

Most firms have little history of monitoring or managing the achievement of benefits from previous use of IT. They consequently have little faith in estimates of benefits included in the appraisals. Both the ignorance and the lack of a trusted track record of benefits monitoring must be tackled in order to improve the chances of picking IT "winners".

# 3 Managing Operational Benefits and Dis-benefits

## 3.1 OPERATIONAL BENEFITS

A wide variety of benefits may be delivered by the appropriate use of information technology. This chapter considers some of those benefits, fitting them into a classification, and describes dis-benefits that may also be encountered. The subject of intangible benefits is also discussed and an approach to the measurement and interpretation of such benefits is described.

## 3.2 WHAT IS A BENEFIT?

At the outset it is useful to establish basic definitions. *The Shorter Oxford English Dictionary* defines the word benefit as follows:

A/ Substantive
   1: A thing well done; a good deed. (1811)
   2: A kind deed; a favour, gift. (archaic, ME)
   3: Advantage, profit, good. (The ordinary sense, 1512)

B/ Verb
   1: To do good to, to be of advantage or profit to;
      to improve, help forward. (1549)

For our purposes the definition that the dictionary refers to as the ordinary sense of the word will be adopted. Thus:

*An IT benefit is an advantage or good, something produced with the assistance of computers and communications for which a firm would be prepared to pay.*

*In functional terms the benefits derived from IT relates to the fact that the technology allows more tasks to be completed with greater accuracy and quality in less time and for lower cost.*

How much a firm would be prepared to pay will obviously depend on the circumstances and is one of the key issues discussed below. The advantage might be better productivity, faster cash flow, or better quality; or it might be less tangible, like ensuring customers have a better image of the firm, improved response time or improving staff morale. In all those cases, and in many more, the firm would be prepared to pay money to achieve the good.

53

From the above the definition of a dis-benefit is also clear. It is any negative effect that the firm would be prepared to pay money to avoid. Again this might be quite difficult to put into financial terms, poorer quality of customer service, reduced staff morale or bad publicity (if it is believed that such a thing is possible). Any rational firm would pay some money if it could be certain that as a result it would avoid a reduction in staff morale or a worsening of its image in the marketplace. Note that a dis-benefit is not the same as failure to deliver a benefit. this point is amplified below.

Any change in a firm, including implementation of a new computer system, is intended to achieve a benefit. However, it may also involve a dis-benefit. Good management seeks to maximise the benefits and minimise the dis-benefits. Before these efforts can be fully effective we need to understand the potential benefits that any system may deliver, and the potential dis-benefits that are threatened.

## 3.3　TYPES OF BENEFIT

The first step is to establish the classes of benefit that a system might be expected to achieve. Though these may seem somewhat obvious the classification does make the later discussion of measuring benefits easier.

### 3.3.1　Regulatory compliance

This type of benefit is achieved by a system whose purpose is to comply with some legal or company policy requirement. It may be achieved by a system which also delivers other benefits. An example might include the company accounts system which, inter alia, delivers VAT information to HM Customs & Excise, or a personnel system which produces statutory sick pay records.

In terms of benefits, regulatory compliance is of little interest. The requirement is either met or it is not met and, whilst it is possible, useful and necessary to investigate whether the requirement could be met at lower cost, the concept of maximising the benefit is not meaningful.

However, it would be somewhat unusual for a system to be introduced solely to meet some regulatory need. There cannot be many managers who would lose the opportunity offered by such a change to effect some other improvements thus entailing other types of benefit.

### 3.3.2　Financial

Financial benefits are those which can be identified and measured in strictly cash terms. These benefits include:

### 3.3.2.1   Improved productivity

Doing the same work with fewer staff, or de-skilling a job. Both reduce salary costs either by reducing staff numbers or overtime, or by reducing wage levels. If the reduction is dramatic it may be offset by relocation or, in the extreme, redundancy costs.

### 3.3.2.2   Reductions in the cost of failure

This might be achieved by reducing the re-work necessary because of failure to achieve quality standards. Another example would be reductions in apologies to customers and bills waived for making mistakes in handling their orders or correspondence. In most firm this is a large potential area of possible savings.

### 3.3.2.3   Improved cash flow and reduced bad debts

Evidence shows that the more quickly a bill is presented the more chance there is that it will be paid and the lower the eventual level of default. In addition a more comprehensive and accurate record of customer details will help in the recovery of bad debts. Giving billing enquiry staff immediate access to full bill details will settle a majority of queries on the first contact. The alternative may be a protracted correspondence with a diminishing chance of recovering the full amount.

### 3.3.2.4   Reduced computer costs

More modern machines should have lower overall maintenance costs. Although the maintenance contract may be no cheaper, the number of unscheduled breaks, and consequent wasted time, should be lower. Software maintenance costs do generally increase with the age of the system, as modifications are built onto modifications to cope with situations that were never foreseen in the original design.

### 3.3.2.5   Reduced overhead costs

Implementations will reduce several types of indirect costs whilst increasing others, for example conversion to microfiche reduces the costs of storage.

### 3.3.2.6   An example of financial benefits

In the early 80s a large mail order firm changed the way it handled queries and complaints from its agents.

The agents sent orders, collected from customers, to the central office. The order details were keyed onto an order processing system, then the original documents were stored in a purpose-built stationery room; they were destroyed after two years. The order processing system produced picking lists for the warehouse staff, who were required to confirm whether or not items had been sent. Daily despatches were made, the firm attempted to despatch all goods within twenty four hours of receipt of order. Partial despatches were made if parts of an order were out of stock. Despatch documentation was kept in the warehouse. A statement was sent to an agent about a week after any order. This statement consolidated all amounts outstanding, and itemised the goods in the latest order. Many agents sent in two or three orders a week, thus receiving a number of statements every week. Copies of all statements were stored, for two years, in several hundred filing cabinets in the accounts office.

Telephone queries from agents were handled in the accounts office. Most enquiries were about non receipt of goods, or the receipt of incorrect goods. These queries could generally only be resolved by reference to the original order, details on the order processing system and the despatch documentation in the warehouse. This usually entailed a number of phone calls and a visit to the stationery store to examine the original order. Thus the majority of queries took several days, and a number of return phone calls, to resolve. Confusion caused by missing, or out of sequence, statements accounted for about 20% of queries. These could usually be resolved within about ten minutes, with the agent still on the phone.

Although not many queries were received, as a percentage of total orders, the firm was aware that its agents had a very low opinion of the complaints process. The rate of defaults on orders which had been queried was about ten times higher than for all orders, and this rate increased sharply if the query took more than five days to resolve. Once an agent had defaulted they were unlikely to place more orders; probably transferring their custom to another firm.

Analysis of the complaints showed that about 60% were due to mistakes in order entry or despatch, 20% were the result of confusion on the part of the agent, and 20% were for other reasons.

In 1983 the firm installed a microfiche printer which was used to print details of all despatches and statements for every agent. At the same time it started to microfilm all orders received from agents, destroying the original order. Copies of the microfilmed orders, despatch details and statements were stored in the accounts office.

After a transition period the firm was able to close the stationery store and remove most of the cabinets in the accounts office. The accounts office was reorganised to take advantage of the extra space, moving the desks into small clusters with low screens between and giving all staff an external view.

The firm's staff now had the information to answer the majority of queries during the initial phone call. An analysis some six months after the change showed that about 70% of queries were resolved immediately. Because the microfiches were easier than paper documents to file and handle, call holding times were reduced. The default rate following disputes fell to three times the overall average, and the number of agents becoming inactive after a query reduced by about 80%.

The main financial benefits of this change were: the savings as a consequence of closing the stationery store; improved cash flow for those disputes which were resolved more quickly; reduced default rate; and a reduction in outgoing telephone call charges. There were offsetting increases in costs; extra energy costs for the microfiche printer and the viewers in the accounts office, and the costs of microfilming orders being the principal ones.

There were a number of other benefits. For example: a better service to the agents, and thus for their customers; improving the agents' image of the firm, and their confidence in its administration; improving the working environment in the accounts office, and improving the job satisfaction of the staff. These benefits are discussed below.

### 3.3.3 Quality of service

These are benefits that directly affect the customer. They can often be given a direct financial value because the firm will have much experience in achieving a certain level of service in their core business over the years. This category of benefits includes:

#### 3.3.3.1 *Improved response times*

Staff dealing with customer queries or orders, either face to face or over the telephone, who are given access to a faster system with more customer and product information will be able to handle those contacts more quickly. This reduced handling time, as well as being a benefit in itself, will result in shorter queues for all customers. Note that this is very similar to the improved productivity described earlier. In effect the firm has the choice of taking the benefit as improved productivity or as an improved quality of service. It is generally possible to put a financial value to the improvement because the firm is likely to have historical data about numbers of staff necessary to achieve certain queue lengths. Typical cases are telephone sales offices, or building society counters.

#### 3.3.3.2 *Improved interface with clients*

More accurate, more detailed, more friendly correspondence (including invoices, letters, phone calls) with customers can result from improved system design. British Airways use the name and address details taken for issuing a ticket to automatically produce a personalised letter thanking the customer for choosing BA and specifying the itinerary and travel times. More detailed invoices reduce queries and so tend to improve cash flow in much the same way as described earlier.

### 3.3.3.3    *Improved resource utilisation*

Better scheduling of field staff gives an obvious benefit to the customer who is waiting for a service call. It may also improve productivity but in this case the two are unlikely to be in conflict. Better stock control and control of delivery also improves the quality of service as perceived by the customer. Many of these benefits can be given a financial value because firms aim for a particular level of service and as a result of the new system, can now get that level with (measurably) less effort.

### 3.3.3.4    *An example of quality of service benefits*

A firm which maintains a large number of electrical appliances in domestic and industrial premises employs maintenance technicians who work from home. Every morning each technician used to be expected to phone the repair service centre to report that he was "at work" and collect the details of his first call. There were about 25 technicians for every incoming telephone line at the service centre and thus considerable congestion and time wasting occurred. In addition, technicians complained that they were not classed as at work, and therefore paid, until they had made contact. This led to considerable resentment.

In an attempt to improve matters the technicians had been given nominal time slots of two minutes each. This had not been very successful, partly because two minutes was often not long enough for the first contact of the day. In addition, even if the system worked well, the 25th slot was nearly an hour after the centre opened and thus the start times had to be staggered whereas most customers wanted an early call. The service centre opened at 7:30am and the first customer visit slot was 8:00am. Only about 20% of visits booked for the first slot were achieved on time. This failure caused increasing problems during the day and the service centre had effectively abandoned quoting specific times to customers. This was considered to be a significant worsening of the quality of service the firm offered its customers.

Another idea introduced was to give the technicians their first job on the night before. However, this resulted in similar congestion in the late afternoon; with the difference that the technicians were very much less inclined to persist in their attempts when this activity ate into their leisure time. In any event, most faults in domestic equipment were reported in the late afternoon and early evening, when the customers returned home from work but after the technicians had finished.

In 1988 the firm invested in a new system based on hand held computers issued to the technicians. These devices were left in a charging cradle overnight, where they were connected to a modem, and were programmed to call the service centre during the night. The calls were connected to the service centre computer which passed details of the technician's first call direct into the hand held computer's memory. The decision about which job to pass to each technician was still taken by the service centre staff.

In the morning the technician keyed in his PIN, which was logged as his start of work, and read the details of his first call. He was then able to travel to the site without contacting the service centre, the only requirement being a call during his first two hours to assure the service centre that he was at work. During the day he used an acoustic coupler to connect his computer to the service centre and feed details of the faults he had found and the spares he had used to the centre. In exchange he received details of his next call. Additionally, the computer automatically produced a timesheet at the end of the week, and was capable of analysing the week's work into travelling, ineffective and effective times, or of analysing faults and times by product.

This system was intended to deliver a number of types of benefit, not least increased productivity but a major benefit was the improvement in the punctuality and predictability of the technicians' calls.

As a result of the introduction of this system, the success rate in making the first visit on time improved to 80%, and this ratio was maintained during the day. This was partly because the technicians got the details of their calls more promptly and partly because, as the number of calls to the service centre reduced dramatically, the fault distribution staff had more time in which to plan which technician to send to which job. The practice of quoting a (rough) time to the customer was re-introduced.

The cost of achieving this benefit by conventional means, more technicians, more service centre staff, better communications, etc, could be estimated fairly easily by the service manager. This figure was used as part of the justification for the system. The value of the benefit in terms of increased customer satisfaction was measured by surveys of customer opinion before and after the change. The firm made no attempt to put a financial value to the increase in customers' satisfaction.

### 3.3.4  Customer perception of the firm

This class of benefit might be regarded as a subset of improved quality of service. However, it differs in that it is much more difficult to put a financial value to the benefit. Indeed these are a class of intangible benefits. The following are some examples:

### 3.3.4.1    Increased customer confidence

The feeling of increased confidence a customer experiences when he realises that the person dealing with his call knows his details. This may be very simple, responding to a customer by name immediately when he has only specified an account number; or knowing the details of a transaction or conversation which the customer conducted with another clerk. These examples of customer care, as much a product of good training as of the technology which makes them possible, give the customer a "warm glow", a feeling that the firm does understand and is likely to deliver. It is difficult to express this benefit in financial terms.

### 3.3.4.2    Increased staff confidence

In a similar vein, staff dealing with calls from the public or from customers show a perceptible increase in confidence when they are backed by a system which actively helps them to do a good job. This confidence tends to give the caller an increased confidence in the firm. By reducing the strain on the clerks it also frees them to be more relaxed and friendly with callers. Experience has shown that customers react positively to such an approach and tend to accept the answer to their query as more authoritative. Firms such as Adlink use similar technology to help their staff answer direct calls from the public in response to several dozen different advertising campaigns; something that would be technically possible with a manual system, but so much less effective that it would not be worth doing.

### 3.3.4.3    An example of the associated benefits

A chain of garages introduced a computer based system for booking vehicles in for service. A record of all regular customers, including details of their vehicles, was maintained by each garage in the firm. This ran on a stand alone computer, also used for payroll and accounting purposes, in each garage. Thus each branch maintained completely separate databases.

An important benefit of the system was that it gave the service receptionist details of the garage's dealings with the customer; including a history of the work done, and outstanding, on his car. Customers were relieved of the necessity of explaining, for the fourth time, about the persistent difficulties in starting the engine on Monday mornings. The firm also spent some time training the receptionists to identify a customer's particular likes and dislikes, then to record them on the system and react to them on the customer's next visit. Thus a note to the effect that the owner had complained that the car radio had been re-tuned could be used to ensure that the mechanic did not use the radio next time the car was serviced.

The individual computers in the garages were eventually linked together, mainly to provide consolidated accounting and personnel information and permit the centralisation of these functions. The firm was aware that many of its customers used more than one branch, one near home and one near the office was a typical pattern. It was also aware that many customers also used a second, competing, garage for similar reasons.

The connection of all the separate machines allowed the interchange of information about customers and their vehicles and the firm took advantage of this by launching a "service club". This was principally intended to persuade customers to remain loyal to the chain. Information about the members of the club, and their vehicle, was made available to all branches. The firm was able to treat a customer visiting any branch of the chain as though he was visiting the garage that had last worked on his car. His usual credit arrangements were available, the garage knew the history of the car, any outstanding work necessary and any personal likes or dislikes of the owner.

The benefit perceived by the firm was that owners would believe that this was a professional organisation and was thus more likely to also be very professional in the quality of its workshops. The garages charged fairly high rates compared to some of their competitors and part of the premium was felt to be justified by the impression of high quality and the convenience offered at the service reception point. The firm did not attempt to put a financial value to this benefit.

### 3.3.5   Internal management benefits

These are another class of intangible benefits. They include advantages such as better decision making, or improving manager's productivity. This class of benefit is extremely difficult to monitor and control.

#### 3.3.5.1   *Improved decision making*

In theory a decision can only be as good as the information available to the decision maker. The more, relevant, information available the better informed they will be. So a system which delivers information which is more up to date, more encompassing and, very importantly, which is processed into a useful format will help a decision maker to make better decisions. Unfortunately there is little practical way of measuring the effectiveness of decisions in industry. All decisions can only be considered in hindsight, by which time the conditions, and information available, will have changed. There is also the question of noise in the environment which prevents all the facts from being known or understood. There is little time, or inclination, in most firms to attempt to unravel the changed circumstances from the quality of the decision.

### 3.3.5.2   Improved management productivity

Similarly, improving a manager's productivity is difficult to measure. It is perfectly possible to measure some mechanistic aspect of his job, for example, how quickly he or she clears an in-tray. However, a manager's job is not principally to undertake such mechanical tasks, it is to motivate and help his staff. A better measure might be how much time the manager is able to spend "walking the job". But, by itself, this measure is open to some obvious weaknesses.

### 3.3.5.3   An example of internal management benefits

The garage chain mentioned in the last example produced monthly accounts consolidated from all the branches. At the end of each accounting period, each garage sent a disk containing a standard report generated by the accounting system. These were loaded onto the central office machine.

Once the machines were networked, the information became available in real time and permitted the centralisation of the book-keeping and procurement functions. A number of benefits flowed from this, for example reduced staff costs and the bulking together of orders and payments to obtain better discounts.

Another benefit was that it gave the firm's accountant immediate information on cash flow and enabled him to use the cash the firm had at its disposal to best effect. It also gave the firm's senior management immediate information on the amount of business each garage had booked, something that had been impractical when the time necessary to send the information to head office was of the same order, or longer than, the customer lead time for most jobs.

The firm had a range of special attractions, cheap petrol days, free check-up days, etc, which could be arranged at short notice and they used the information to co-ordinate these. They also balanced the load between garages in the chain when appropriate. Such action had been possible using a manual system, but had been so time-consuming and cumbersome to arrange that it had rarely been invoked.

The firm made no attempt to put a financial value to the management effort saved. Individual promotional events were costed and compared to the extra business but the firm did not try to calculate the effect of the more frequent use of such events made possible by the networking.

The benefits above are obviously not an exhaustive list. More importantly the different benefits are in no way mutually exclusive. Although a system may well be principally intended to deliver one particular benefit it would be most unusual if it did not also include elements of all the classes described above.

## 3.4   RECENT RESEARCH

Recent research conducted by the Kobler Unit at Imperial College in London categorised the main reasons for firms investing in IT. Figure 3.1 shows that IT investments may be described under the following headings:

- – IT helps gain a competitive advantage.
- – Business would be impossible without it.
- – Individual departments justify the investment.
- – Rigorous methods are used to calculate the benefits.
- – Aim to match investment levels in the market.

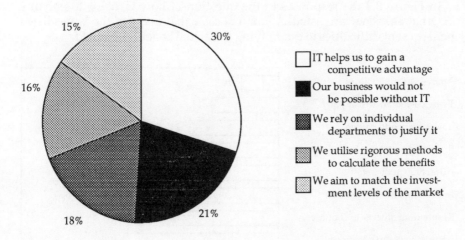

**Figure 3.1     The main reason for the IT investment**

Figure 3.2 shows that respondents considered that there were 10 major ways in which IT helps to improve internal efficiency. It is clearly noticeable that not many of the benefits listed here are quantifiable.

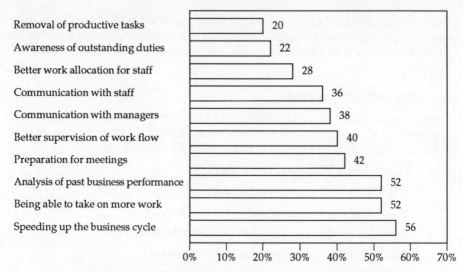

**Figure 3.2      How IT improves internal efficiency**

In Figure 3.3 the responses to the question of how IT helps to enhance external efficiency are listed. Again it is clear that many of the issues listed here present difficulties in quantifying the actual benefits obtained.

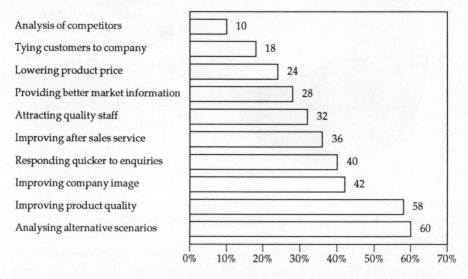

**Figure 3.3      How IT improves external efficiency**

## 3.5   DIS-BENEFITS

There is a school of thought that in a perfect implementation, admittedly a rare occurrence, there will be no dis-benefits; that is, no down side. However, evidence of any implementation that has achieved this remarkable feat is difficult to come by. Potential dis-benefits are of two sorts:

- Those which are caused by a badly executed implementation;
- Those which are inherent in the change, which no amount of planning or forethought could completely eliminate.

In the first case the problem might be a failure to achieve the level of benefits forecast, or it might involve some unforeseen negative factor of the implementation, poor communication leading to industrial action for example.

In the second case the task of the implementation team is to recognise the existence of dis-benefits, and to manage them. It follows that these inherent dis-benefits are not the same as a lack of benefits, they might more usefully be thought of as costs. This section will solely discuss the inherent dis-benefits, not the mistakes.

Inherent dis-benefits occur for a number of reasons. They can loosely be grouped into three categories; the people, the job and the computer. Only the third group are peculiar to computer systems, the first two are a feature of any change.

### 3.5.1   Dis-benefits related to people

People dis-benefits are largely caused by the way individuals react to change, they are not specifically anything to do with IT. However, because of a certain concern about IT, these reactions will probably be more marked when a computer system is being introduced than with most other forms of change.

These problems occur mostly because staff frequently mistrust management motives. People fear loss of their jobs, as the new system will presumably be more efficient than the old. They may very well fear potential discomfort or health problems, although these are less likely now, as more implementations involve changing an existing system, not the initial introduction of terminals.

Staff may very well see increasingly sophisticated computerisation as giving management more information, and more control, about the day to day work. Data entry systems which give key stroke counts are an obvious example. (A slightly different example occurs with electronic mail systems which time stamp all messages. These appear to encourage managers to send all messages either very early in the morning or very late at night.)

Most of these concerns have little to do with computer systems. The level of distrust will be determined as much by the prevailing industrial relations climate as by the amount and quality of the communication undertaken for this change. But, however good a firm, at least some staff will always suspect anything that the firm does, simply because that is how people are. The fears, whether real or imagined, may be played upon by an existing trade union, or one attempting to gain recognition and therefore looking for an issue.

A new, different, system will mean re-training. Apart from the cost and time away from the job, this re-training will upset the working of the group in other ways. Staff will not be as efficient until they have been working the new system for some time. Silly mistakes will occur no matter how much training is undertaken. This may be thought of as analogous to the tendency, after one has spent some weeks on holiday driving on the other side of the road, to suddenly drive off on the wrong side after a moment of inattention. Whilst trying to come to grips with the new system, staff will be under more pressure and may snap at each other or at customers. Dismissing these manifestations as trivial is all too easy for the implementation team who have probably been chosen for a somewhat broader outlook than the majority; to staff who enjoy the atmosphere in their department, they can be very de-motivating.

Some staff will not be re-trained because they are too close to retirement. Even though the retirement may not be brought forward as a result this is likely to affect morale in the entire work group. Informal pecking orders within work groups will frequently change. Such changes will probably favour the newer, younger, employees who learn more quickly. The older staff may lose prestige because their knowledge and experience is largely tied to the old system.

Because the people who are subject to such fears will be very different to, and probably much older than, the implementation team it often happens that this situation is badly handled. However, even when handled well, some suspicions and loss of morale inevitably occur.

### 3.5.2   Dis-benefits related to the job

Most jobs only work because of informal procedures that mangers know little about and the systems analyst did not discover. This is often a difficult concept for many managers to accept but can most commonly be seen in the way staff obtain materials to complete jobs. A change to a new system will almost certainly destroy these practices. It may take months or years for the informal procedures or networks to be re-established. During that time the work group's performance will be degraded for no very obvious reason.

Mechanised systems are less flexible than paper systems, they do not normally offer the facility of scribbling special instructions or explanations in the margin of a form. Especially in the early days, this will be seized upon by the Jeremiahs as further proof that the change will result in a worsening of customer service.

Even if the system can cope with unusual procedures, the initial training will probably have concentrated on the run of the mill, ensuring that staff are as efficient as possible for the majority of cases so the staff may not know how to persuade the system to accept unusual orders or amendments. There is little more calculated to enrage staff than standing in front of a customer staring at a meaningless error message on a VDU.

### 3.5.3 Dis-benefits related to computers

Dis-benefits in this category tend to be risks not certainties. They will only occur if things go wrong, either the system suffers some major catastrophe, or performs well below expectation.

Computer systems are by their nature more vulnerable to catastrophe than manual systems. The more you rely on the system the more helpless you are when it is not there. Recent research suggests that 80% of firms which have suffered a major IT catastrophe did not survive. Many of these firms did have some disaster recovery plan and back ups. But in the event they either proved inadequate or too expensive to implement. The cost of backups and preparing for disaster recovery is of course a well known dis-benefit in its own right.

When the IT function is not performing well, it can absorb an inordinate amount of senior management time; time they should be spending on their core business. If some part of the business is not working well you would expect managers to be devoting a fair bit of their time to the problem. If the cause is a manual system they will probably have a good understanding of how it works. Resolution of the problem will probably be within their own control. But if the problems are to do with a computer system, many managers will not have this degree of understanding, nor the ability to immediately implement a solution. Obviously this is a generalisation. There will be situations where the solution is simple; more terminals, better lighting, whatever. But when the real problem is that the system is not performing as expected, or the hardware is overloaded, the solution is more likely to lie with the IT professionals than with line managers. The line managers will either have to spend a lot of time learning about the issues, or will have to trust their experts.

Resolution of the problem is also likely to take time. None of these factors is likely to reduce executive blood pressure. In fact, what often happens is that some complex paper system is devised to overcome the computer's shortcomings. An appalling waste of resource, and a waste of opportunity.

It could be argued that the root cause of this weakness is the very low appreciation of IT amongst too many managers, and that this is an issue more correctly categorised as a people problem; ie that the level of ignorance displayed by many senior mangers is just as much a cause for concern as the fears demonstrated by the shop floor workers. No matter how much truth there is in this view, it has to be admitted that a computer system will always be more complex, and less susceptible to immediate management alteration, than a manual system.

## 3.6 SUMMARY

To be able to measure and manage IT benefits it is first necessary to have a framework with which to identify types of benefits which are likely to be generated. One way of categorising benefits is under the following headings:

1 Regulatory benefits

2 Financial benefits

3 Quality of service benefits

4 Customer perception benefits

5 Internal management benefits

Analysts should also be aware of and on the lookout for serendipitous benefits. Finally, the issue of dis-benefits should also be incorporated in any IT management exercise.

# 4 Issues and Techniques for System Evaluation

## 4.1 A CONCEPT OF VALUE

The objective of this chapter is to discuss methodologies by which it will be possible to evaluate the benefits derived from the implementation of information systems. In achieving this, it will be necessary to consider inter alia how it is possible to convert the benefits generated by systems into measurable values, as well as how it will be possible to place specific values on individual systems.

Before such an exercise can be contemplated, it is essential to establish a framework in which the value of systems may be assessed. *The Shorter Oxford English Dictionary* states that:

> *Value is the amount of some commodity, medium of exchange, etc., which is considered to be an equivalent for something else; a fair or adequate equivalent or return.*

In business terms, a rough and ready definition of value is generally accepted to be the amount of money which exchanges hands when a willing buyer trades a good or service with a willing seller. Paul Strassman expresses this succinctly by stating *'A computer is worth only what it can fetch at an auction'* (Strassman, 1990). Although this quick definition is frequently used, it does not reflect the often complex nature of associating a value to a business asset. Not all goods or services have to be traded or auctioned in order to establish their value. Fixed assets in balance sheets are regularly evaluated without any intention of selling them. Sometimes these fixed assets are revalued in terms of what they would sell for, other times fixed asset evaluation is based on what they earn for the business.

Of course, it is generally recognised that the balance sheet value of a business asset is in no way related to its earning capability. It is the earning capability of the firm's information systems which must be addressed in this chapter. Therefore, although the value of an information system could be seen at least in one sense as the amount which an organisation would be prepared to pay for the system, in actual fact the value to the firm represents not so much the purchase price, but rather an amount which the organisation believes it earns from the use of the system.

## 4.2   VALUE AS A FUNCTION OF CONTEXT AND PERCEPTION

Value is always determined by both context and perception. This is well illustrated by considering how the price of listed shares behave on stock markets. A share in the public listed company Rowntree in 1988 cost about 450. After a bid for the Rowntree company had been made by Nestlé the same share commanded a price of approximately 700. No change had occurred inside of Rowntree, nor to the market in which it functioned, yet its value had profoundly changed. The context in which the shares then traded, ie of an imminent potential takeover, was quite different, and the market therefore perceived these equities to have a much higher value. Another example is the way in which the oil price has behaved in the second half of 1990. On 2 August 1990 the cost of a barrel of oil on the Rotterdam spot market was about $16. Within a few weeks, and without any interruption to the oil supply, nor any material increase in demand, the oil price had increased to over $30 per barrel. Then, within a few weeks the oil price, when war appeared to be less imminent, dramatically dropped. Figure 4.1 is an extract from *The Economist* magazine dated December 22 1990, showing the behaviour of the oil price from January to the end of that year. Both of these situations are characterised by perceptual shifts which cause major changes in the viewpoint of buyers and sellers.

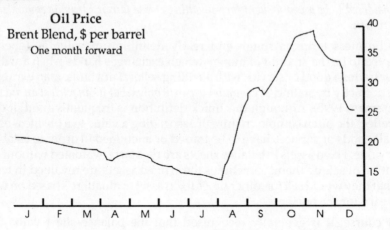

Figure 4.1     Variation of oil price throughout 1990

On a less dramatic note, the value of the assets in a firm's balance sheet is entirely dependent on the management view or perception of whether the firm will remain a going concern, and the expected economic life of the individual items owned by the company. Again, the numbers associated with the individual assets are entirely a function of context and perception.

Changes in value may also occur without any change to context, and thus be entirely a result of a change in perception. There are many examples of this, the most important of which is perhaps the work undertaken by the advertising industry. Advertisers, especially those who concentrate on luxury goods, spend the greater part of their time and efforts trying to enhance the value of the goods or services offered by their clients by raising and maintaining the market's perception of these firms and their products or services.

Translating this into the information systems arena means that identical firms with identical systems generating identical benefits (if such a situation could actually exist), may well have entirely different views of the values of their systems. The yardstick used to measure the value of a system is without doubt an elastic device, but then so are all yardsticks used to measure business performance. In fact, the precision and robustness of business measuring technology is most frequently overstated and this applies no less to the efforts in measuring the performance in information systems.

## 4.3 MEASURING BUSINESS PERFORMANCE

Before embarking on the discussion of how IT effectiveness may be measured and the role of cost benefit analysis in this process, it is appropriate to consider some of the general issues related to the matter of assessing business performance.

There is a very deep need in Western industrial culture to regularly measure business performance. There are several reasons for this, including the need to enhance performance as well as ensure growth. Both performance and growth enhancement are required to meet stakeholding expectations or increased salaries, wages, profits, dividends, etc. Although these business performance measurements take a large variety of forms and are therefore difficult to describe in generalities, it may be said that business performance assessment frequently focuses on the issues of liquidity, activity, profitability and potential. In assessing these dimensions, standard ratios are produced such as NP%, GP%, Stockturn, ROI, ROE, Administration Costs/Turnover, etc. The number and type of ratios used varies enormously from firm to firm, and reflects the nature of the industry and size of organisation as well as management style. Organisations regularly change their performance measurement indices or ratios as they attempt to perfect the measures they use. The more useful measures are kept and the less useful discarded.

### 4.3.1 What constitutes good performance?

This is a question which is asked regularly. For example, is a net profit (NP) of 10% good? Is an ROI of 20% satisfactory or is a stockturn of 5 poor? The question of good performance cannot be answered in isolation. To be able to assess performance it is necessary to know in what industry the firm is functioning, the size of the firm, and, especially, the approach and the goals of management. For example, an ROI of 15% might be exceptionally good for a firm in the iron and steel market, and absolutely terrible for an organisation in the electronics industry. A large firm in a highly concentrated industry might require a net profit of 10%, whereas a small firm may be quite content with a net profit of 5%. However, perhaps the most important issue with regard to the question of good performance, is the expectation of management. If management has set an ROI of 10% as one of its objectives, then good performance is the realisation of this target, ie an ROI of 10% or better. Poor performance is then an ROI of less than 10% (all other things being equal).

### 4.3.2   Ratios

A common approach to the use of these ratios is to consider them over a period of time in order to establish a trend. Thus, if over the past 5 years the ROI has been steadily increasing then it is probably true to say that performance has been improving, although it may not yet be at a stage where it could be considered good. In using this longitudinal approach to ratio analysis, it is necessary to be aware of possible changes in accounting practices which can affect the basis of the way the ratios are calculated, and thus produce apparent movements in the ratios without there being any substantive change in business circumstances. Also, if a measure such as ROI is used and if the firm is not continually replacing its assets, especially its fixed assets, routine depreciation policy may generate increasing percentages without any improvement occurring.

### 4.3.3   Inflation

Another difficulty which must be addressed when using financial ratios is the deterioration caused to the value of money by inflation. Inflation plays havoc on the generally accepted accounting system. It can cause profits to be overstated and assets to be undervalued in the firm's accounts. As a result of inflation, ratios may become significantly distorted and reflect a seriously untrue picture. Figure 4.2 is a table showing the effect of inflation on specific commodities in the United Kingdom from 1900 through 1930, 1960 and 1990. One of the key aspects of ratio analysis as a business performance measuring device is that although it is an imperfect system, the results which it produces are good enough for most purposes and in a wide variety of business situations.

It is most important to stress that the measurement of business performance is not a science but rather an art. Two different financial analysts may take diametrically opposed views of the health of a business, and these opinions may be based on the same data set. In the final analysis only future performance can be the arbitrator.

# Prices in Britain 1900–1990

| Actual and (in bold) revalued to 1990 prices, £ | 1900 | 1930 | 1960 | 1990 |
|---|---|---|---|---|
| Railway fare | 1.66 | 5.00 | 8.40 | 59.00 |
| London to Glasgow 2nd class, return | **66.40** | **156.25** | **84.00** | **59.00** |
| Atlantic crossing by ship, (to New York) | 12.33 | 16.00 | 67.00 | 970.00 |
| Cheapest Cunard ticket available | **674.00** | **516.80** | **670.00** | **970.00** |
| Atlantic crossing by air, (to New York) | n/a | n/a | 154.35 | 323.00 |
| Cheapest Cunard ticket available | | | **1,543.50** | **323.00** |
| London to Nairobi by air (return) | n/a | 178.20 | 199.30 | 642.00 |
| Cheapest ticket available | | **6,562.50** | **1,993.00** | **642.00** |
| Bottle of Whisky | .18 | .71 | 1.95 | 8.80 |
| Including tax | **6.74** | **20.31** | **19.31** | **8.80** |
| Car | 225 | 170 | 494 | 6,180 |
| Ford, cheapest model | **10,238** | **5,313** | **4,940** | **6,180** |
| Monet painting of Waterloo Bridge | 793 | 1,744 | 20,000 | 4,000,000 |
| "Effet de Soleil" (oil on canvas, 1903) | **34,496** | **67,144** | **200,000** | **4,000,000** |
| English dinner at the Savoy | .38 | .78 | 2.38 | 28.75 |
| Soup, main course, pudding, coffee | **15.20** | **24.38** | **23.80** | **28.75** |
| Top of the range camera | 20.00 | 18.60 | 145.00 | 1,200 |
| Sanderson, Leica, Nikon | **880.00** | **581.25** | **1,450.00** | **1,200** |
| Telephone call, 3 minutes | .25 | .33 | .13 | .41 |
| London to Glasgow | **8.93** | **10.31** | **1.30** | **.41** |
| Telephone call, 3 minutes | n/a | 15.00 | 3.00 | 2.33 |
| London to New York | | **468.75** | **30.00** | **2.33** |
| Opera Ticket at Covent Garden | .13 | .33 | .18 | 3.00 |
| Least expensive | **5.20** | **10.31** | **1.80** | **3.00** |
| Household coal, | 1.18 | 1.24 | 4.22 | 120.66 |
| per short ton | **47.20** | **38.75** | **42.20** | **120.66** |
| The Economist | .03 | .05 | .08 | 1.60 |
| | **1.20** | **1.56** | **.75** | **1.60** |
| Gold | 4.24 | 4.25 | 12.56 | 209.16 |
| per oz | **169.60** | **132.81** | **125.60** | **209.16** |
| Men's suit | n/a | 4.20 | 30.00 | 269.00 |
| Dak's 2-piece | | **99.62** | **300.00** | **269.00** |

*Source: The Economist, 1990*

Figure 4.2    Effects of inflation on prices of selected commodities

## 4.4   WHEN IS PERFORMANCE MEASURED

As a general rule, there are certain circumstances in which performance is either not measured or is measured with less care and attention. These circumstances include, but are not limited to:

- Where the amount of funds involved are not substantial.
- Where the performance or value is taken for granted.
- Where the organisation classifies the activity in terms of an ongoing expense rather than as a capital investment.

These three business variables to a substantial extent dictate a firm's attitude to the performance measurement issue. The table in Figure 4.3 indicates how different business functions relate to the above three variables.

|                   | Finance | Personnel | Manuf. | Marketing | R&D | IS |
|-------------------|---------|-----------|--------|-----------|-----|-----|
| Size              | L       | L         | G      | G         | G   | G   |
| Agreed Value      | A       | A         | A      | A         | A   | ?   |
| Expense/ Capital  | E       | E         | C      | E         | E   | C   |
| Risk              | L       | L         | M      | M         | H   | VH  |
| Measure           | L       | L         | H      | L         | M   | ?   |

| | | | |
|---|---|---|---|
| L  Low | G  Great | A  Agreed | N  Not Agreed |
| E  Expense | C  Capital | ?  Undecided | M  Medium |
| | H  High | VH High | |

Figure 4.3    Approaches to funding by business function

Funds spent on the finance division, other than for DP or IS purposes are generally not analysed too closely. This is because the sums are relatively low, the need is commonly agreed, and the accounting treatment does not usually require the amount to be capitalised. Exactly the same argument applies to the personnel division. In the manufacturing environment the size of the investment is typically much bigger and the expenditure is treated as capital. This leads to a more analytical approach being taken.

Although the size of marketing spend is considerable, as it is usually regarded as a necessary expenditure, the concern about the measurement of its effectiveness is not always expressed in an interest for detailed metrics. The time span of marketing effort being relatively short, it is treated as an ongoing expense. Also, because of the closeness of marketing to the survival of the business itself, expenditure may not be questioned in the amount of detail that might otherwise be the case. R&D expenditure is frequently treated similarly.

### 4.4.1 Why IS expenditure is heavily scrutinised

The IS function qualifies for detailed analytical scrutiny for several reasons:

- The amounts of money are frequently quite substantial.

- Because many IS investments are not always close to the revenue or profit making aspects of the business, there is not always agreement as to its need, value or performance.

- Much of IS expenditure, especially on hardware, has traditionally been capitalised.

To these three dimensions must be added the question of risk. IS projects have traditionally been seen as high risk. This is due to the fact that there have been a number of IS failures, many of which have involved large amounts of funds and have received quite a lot of visibility. In addition top management frequently has little or no understanding of the IS function and therefore considers all IS activity to carry the highest risk profile.

All these factors have led to management requiring a detailed and analytical approach to the assessment and evaluation of IS investment. It is frequently argued by IS professionals that top management are too rigorous in their demands of estimates and projections. It is said that other functions are not hindered in the same way as the ISD.

### 4.5 THE ASSESSMENT OF IT EFFECTIVENESS

The assessment or evaluation of IT, and especially IT effectiveness, is a difficult task which must be undertaken with considerable care. In addition, attention must be paid to the reasons why the assessment is being undertaken, as the approach to the evaluation depends on the purpose for which it will be used. In practice an important consideration is the individual who commissions the IT effectiveness study.

If the question of effectiveness is being asked by the accountant, then the answer is probably required in terms of ROI, the formula for which is described in Appendix 4. The calculated ROI number on its own is generally regarded as being of little value. This statistic becomes much more valuable when the IT ROI is compared to either the organisation's cost of capital or perhaps to the ROI for the firm's total assets. A standard such as an industry average would also be considered very useful in this respect.

If the question of effectiveness is being asked by the operating management, the focus of the question is probably directed at the issue of whether the organisation is getting the most from the IT investment. This question cannot be answered by simple reference to an ROI measure, as the investment may be showing quite an acceptable ROI, but may not yet be realising its full potential. Here, what can be achieved must be known and the performance of the system to this standard is the essence of the answer to the question. What can be achieved can only be ascertained by comparison to some other installation, either in another department or in another firm.

If the question of effectiveness is being asked by the Board of directors, then the focus is probably on the issue of whether the computers are enhancing the general performance of the business as a whole. This sort of question is often couched in strategic terms such as: are the systems contributing to the firm's ability to realise its corporate strategy? This means that a much more general position must be considered as it is possible for a computer to enhance departmental effectiveness at the expense of the overall corporate strategy.

### 4.5.1 How well is the ISD doing?

Some firms feel the need to ask this question in order to assure themselves that their IT budget is being well spent. There is, however, no simple answer to this question. Some firms are content with establishing whether their objectives are being met. This is relatively easy, especially if business objectives and key performance indicators were specified in the original specification of requirements.

However, other firms want a more absolute evaluation. There are basically only two ways of approaching this type of evaluation. In the first place the firm can compare themselves to their competitors. Firms may often obtain a significant amount of information about the way competitors are using IT and they can obtain a rough idea of how much such IT activity costs. The firm may interview clients and also the clients of competitors to establish their relative performance. This type of evaluation is, at the end of the day, even more subjective than most.

The second approach to answering the question of how well the ISD is doing is to compare current performance with historic performance which requires the existence of a database of detailed measurements of performance and IT expenditure. This is the most satisfactory way of answering the question. Unfortunately, not many firms have the required statistical history to be able to perform this type of analysis.

## 4.6  PURPOSE OF THE IT INVESTMENT

The purpose of the investment is most critical to the process of defining the approach to its evaluation and to its performance measurement. As mentioned in the previous section, IT investment which is used to improve efficiency requires efficiency measuring techniques such as work study or cost benefit analysis. IT investment which has been implemented to enhance management effectiveness requires value added analysis, value chain assessment, etc. IT investment for business advantage or business transformation requires measuring techniques such as strategic analysis, relative competitive performance, etc. The table in Figure 4.4 suggests how different investment types may be treated.

| Investment Purpose | Investment Type | Evaluate/Measure |
|---|---|---|
| Business survival | Mandatory | Continue/Discontinue business |
| Improving efficiency | Vital | Cost benefit |
| Improving effectiveness | Critical | Business analysis |
| Competitive leap | Strategic | Strategic analysis |
| Infrastructure | Architecture | Very broad terms |

Figure 4.4    Investment purposes, types and evaluation techniques

## 4.7  MATCHING THE ASSESSMENT EFFORT TO STRATEGY

It is important to focus assessment efforts, especially when dealing with systems which have the potential to generate a competitive advantage. Specifically, strategic IT investment may be seen as having an impact on the firm's ability to function as a low cost leader or as a differentiator.

### 4.7.1  A strategy of differentiation

If the organisation's strategy is one of differentiation then the following are the issues on which the IT's performance should be measured:

- Does IT lead to adding information to the product?
- Does the IT application make it easier for the clients to order, buy and obtain delivery of the goods or service?
- Are there less errors in processing the business?
- Has the after sales service aspects of the business been enhanced?

### 4.7.2   A strategy of cost leadership

If the strategy is one of low cost leadership then the following are the issues on which the IT's performance should be measured.

- Will the IT application result in direct cost reductions?
- Will there be labour reductions?
- Will the time to market improve?
- Will there be greater utilisation of equipment?
- Will Just-In-Time manufacturing be possible?

The matching of benefits to systems purpose is really a key aspect to understanding and managing IT benefits.

### 4.8   DIFFERENT APPROACHES TO MEASUREMENT

There are two generic approaches to measurement. These approaches are common to all forms of measurement, whether the measurement relates to speed, obesity, water flow, beauty contests, weighing potatoes or assessing information systems. Measurement may be based on:

- Physical counting.
- Assessment by ordering, ranking or scoring.

Whether the contents of a tanker, the weight of a boxer or the speed of a jet plane is being measured, units are being counted. When it is difficult or impossible to count the assessment is made by ordering, ranking or scoring.

Both of these fundamental approaches are used as the basis of a variety of techniques such as cost benefit analysis or strategic match analysis. These are discussed in detail later in this book.

A first approach to measurement of IT effectiveness is to compare the system's objectives to the actual achievements of the system. For such an exercise to work the system's objectives must have clearly been stated with key performance indicators (KPI) having been specified. Objectives without KPI are of little value, as objectives which are set without attention as to how the business will know if they are achieved, are frequently too vague to be meaningful. Figure 4.5 shows some satisfactory and some poor objectives. The definition of the objectives and the KPIs should be clearly laid out in the system specification. Unfortunately this is not always done.

Also, even when the objectives and the KPIs have been properly defined, it is not always possible to measure the actual impact of an information technology application, simply because the effects may be indirect, or rendered invisible by surrounding noise in the system.

| Satisfactory Objectives | Poor Objectives |
|---|---|
| 1  To reduce inventories by 5% by value and 10% by volume within the next 180 days | 1  To improve profitability |
| | 2  To reduce errors |
| 2  To increase the firm's ROI by 1% by the end of the financial year | 3  To improve staff morale |
| | 4  To enhance cash flow |
| 3  To reduce the amount invested in debtors so that the debtors days decline from 80 to 68 | 5  To obtain a competitive advantage |
| 4  To improve staff acceptance of the new IT system as reflected by their attitudes expressed in regular satisfaction surveys | |
| 5  To deliver detailed proposals of typeset quality to clients within 48 hours of being given leave to present such documents | |

Figure 4.5    Examples of satisfactory and poor systems objectives

## 4.9   INTANGIBLE BENEFITS

Where it is hard to directly observe the effect of the IS, the following methodology may be used to help assess the nature of the benefits of the system. (This method is fully described by Dr David Silk, 1990 (a).)

### 4.9.1   Steps involved in measuring intangible benefits

1   conceptualise the chain of cause and effect events which may result from the introduction of the system.

2   Identify how it will be possible to establish the changes which are likely to occur as a result of the introduction of the information system. Here the focus is on the direction of the changes, ie will the inventories rise or fall? will more phone calls be taken? etc.

3   Consider how the size of the change may be measured.

Where the effect of the system is clear, the analyst may proceed with the next three steps.

4   Measure the size of the change.

5   Put a monetary value on the changes which have been observed.

6   Use techniques such as payback, ROI, NPV, IRR, etc, to assess whether the information system investment will produce an adequate return to justify proceeding.

This six step methodology is a useful framework for approaching IT evaluation studies, even where it is hard to identify benefits. The following is an example of how the method is used:

### 4.9.2   A new billing system as an example of the conceptual approach

1   A new billing system will reduce errors, get out invoices in less time, etc, by checking prices, discounts and business terms. Month end statement runs will be two days instead of 10.

2   Changes:
    1   few customer queries
    2   few journal entries
    3   less reconciliations
    4   more cash

3   1   keep a register of queries
    2   count journal adjustments
    3   record time on reconciliations

4   Check interest paid on overdraft, and interest earned on cash available

5   Time released multiplied by the salary paid, or where overdraft is eliminated, interest not paid

6   Use standard calculations

### 4.9.3   Things that can go wrong with the above analysis

The above six step approach to measuring IT benefits is susceptible to a number of problems of which the following three are the most frequently encountered.

#### 4.9.3.1   *Noise*

Noise refers to the fact that the effect of the IT investment may be masked by other events in the environment. Thus, although the inventory levels should have risen or fallen due to the new system, circumstances in the economy produced an effect which overwhelmed the benefits of the system.

### 4.9.3.2   Fluctuations in the short term

Sometimes IT benefits are hidden behind short term fluctuations due to seasonal changes in demand, cost or prices. To make sure that such fluctuations do not obscure the presence of IT benefits, measurements must be taken at regular intervals over a period of time.

### 4.9.3.3   Lies, damn lies and statistics

All measurement techniques are based on assumptions and these assumptions may often be manipulated to show the required results.

## 4.10   SPECIFIC METHODOLOGIES

There are several different methodologies available to assess the performance of IT. The following are a few of the most commonly used:

1.   Strategic match analysis and evaluation

2.   Value chain assessment (firm and industry)

3.   Relative competitive performance

4.   Proportion of management vision achieved

5.   Work study assessment

6.   Economic assessment - I/O analysis

7.   Financial cost benefit analysis

8.   User attitudes

9.   User utility assessment

10.   Value added analysis

11.   Return on management

12.   Multi-objective multi-criteria methods

### 4.10.1   Strategic match analysis and evaluation

This is a ranking or scoring technique which required all the primary IT systems to be assessed in terms of whether or not they support the firm's generic corporate strategy. The two main generic strategies are differentiation and cost reduction. If a system helps improve customer service it generally helps the firm differentiate itself in the market, while if it helps to reduce costs it is generally supportive of a cost reduction strategy.

Figure 4.6 shows a list of the more important applications in a large firm and this list may be used to assist in the categorisation of the systems.

| Function | Low Cost | Differentiation |
|---|---|---|
| Product design & development | Product engineering systems<br>Project control systems<br>CAD | R&D databases<br>Professional workstations<br>Electronic Mail<br>CAD<br>Custom engineering systems<br>Integrated systems to manufaturing |
| Operations | Process engineering systems<br>Process control systems<br>Labour control systems<br>Inventory management systems<br>Procurement systems<br>CAM<br>Systems to supplies | CAM for flexibility<br>Quality assurance systems<br>Systems to suppliers<br>Quality monitoring systems for suppliers |
| Marketing | Streamlined distribution<br>　　systems<br>Centralised control systems<br>Economic modelling systems<br>Telemarketing | Sophisticated marketing systems<br>Market databases<br>IT display & promotion<br>Competition analysis<br>Modelling<br>High service level distribution systems |
| Sales | Sales control systems<br>Advertising monitor systems<br>Systems to consolidate sales<br>　　function<br>Strict incentive monitoring system | Differential pricing<br>Office-field communications<br>Sales support<br>Dealer support<br>Systems to customers |
| Administration | Cost control systems<br>Quantitative planning and<br>　　budgeting systems<br>Office automation for staff<br>　　reduction | Office automation for integration of<br>　　functions<br>Environmental scanning & non-quantitative<br>　　planning systems |

Figure 4.6  Key business applications

Weights may be associated with the more important systems and a score may be given on the basis of the degree to which these systems have been implemented and are achieving their objectives. Figure 4.7 shows a strategic match evaluation form used with simple unweighted scores.

Such an evaluation technique is useful if applied each year so that the firm may obtain a feel for the direction in which the IS function is progressing.

### 4.10.2  Value chain assessment (firm and industry)

This is another scoring or ranking system. In this case the Michael Porter value added chain is used as the basic checklist to which the firm's application systems are compared. This process may be conducted in terms of the firm's internal value activities as well as the industry value activities. For a thorough

| Function | Low Cost Possibilities | Actual Systems | Rating |
|---|---|---|---|
| Product design & development | Project control systems | Project control systems | 6 |
| Operations | Process control systems<br>CAM | Process control systems<br>CAM | 3<br>7 |
| Marketing | Telemarketing | Telemarketing | 5 |
| Sales | Sales control systems<br>Systems to consolidate<br>    sales function | Systems to consolidate<br>    sales function | 4 |
| Administration | Cost control systems<br>Office automation for<br>    staff reduction | Cost control systems<br>Office automation for<br>    staff reduction | 8<br>4 |

Figure 4.7    Completed evaluation form

analysis, both approaches should be used. In a similar way to the strategic match analysis, evaluation weights may be associated with the more important systems and scores may be given on the basis of the degree to which these systems have been implemented and are achieving their objectives. In applying the value chain assessment technique Figure 1.5 and Figure 1.7 may be used as a basis of the two checklists required.

### 4.10.3   Relative competitive performance

Some firms assess their performance by comparing themselves to their competition. This requires monitoring their competitors acquisition of IT, the way they use it to achieve their corporate strategy as well as being able to estimate their costs. These are quite difficult processes and frequently rely on very subjective evaluations involving ranking and scoring.

### 4.10.4   Proportion of management vision achieved

This is another ranking and scoring technique which has a very high degree of subjectivity. Managers are asked to assess the current systems in terms of what their original plans were. When there is a large number of managers involved a questionnaire or survey approach may be used. Although this is a highly subjective approach it may be applied in a relatively objective way by conducting regular assessments on a six or twelve monthly basis.

### 4.10.5   Work study assessment

The work study approach to IT benefit evaluation requires regular reviews of how the work in the department is being performed. During these reviews the volume of work is carefully recorded as well as the time required to perform all the necessary tasks. Work study assessment can be relatively objective particularly if it is conducted by work study professionals. The results of a work study appraisal may be used as input to subsequent cost benefit analysis.

### 4.10.6 Economic assessment

An economic assessment is a theoretical approach to IT benefit evaluation. It requires the development of a model expressed in mathematical terms in which the relationship of input and outputs are expressed. Although expressed in apparently rigorous mathematical terms this method also relies on very subjective views of the nature of the relationships between the input and output variables.

### 4.10.7 Financial cost benefit analysis

There are a number of quite different approaches to financial cost benefit analysis. Several of these are described in detail in Chapter 5.

### 4.10.8 User attitudes

User attitudes may be used to assess how IT is performing within the firm. Here a survey method is used to extract attitudes towards the importance of IT to individual users, as well as how the ISD is performing in its delivery of IS. This issue is fully explored in Chapters 7 and 12.

### 4.10.9 User utility assessment

It may be argued that systems which are heavily used are more successful than those which are not. By establishing the frequency of use of a system it is believed that it is possible to assess its value to the firm. This technique involves counting the amount of activity sustained by the system, measured in terms of its input, processing and output. However, excellent systems have been known to fail for trivial reasons, while poor systems have survived for years and therefore this approach leaves many questions unanswered.

### 4.10.10 Value added analysis

Using this technique the value of the system rather than its cost is firstly assessed. Once the value or benefit has been agreed then a cost is calculated. The system is then developed on a prototyping basis at a relatively low cost. Once this has been completed an assessment is made to decide whether the benefits derived have justified the cost. If the decision is that the investment is justified then the firm proceeds to the next stage in the IT applications development.

### 4.10.11   Return on management

Return on management is a concept proposed by Paul Strassman initially in his book *Information Payoff* (Strassman, 1985) and again in *The Business Value of Computers* (Strassman, 1990). The return on management (ROM) method is a valued added approach which isolates the management added value and then divides this by the management cost.

Strassman is convinced that IT must be assessed by its impact on management and thus proposes that ROM be used to evaluate this technology. Strassman is also adamant that management is the key to successful IT as the following quote demonstrates:

"A computer is worth only what it can fetch in an auction. It has value only if surrounded by appropriate policy, strategy, methods for monitoring results, project control, talented and committed people, sound relationships and well designed information systems."

When expressed as a formula:

$$\text{ROM} = \frac{\text{Management value added}}{\text{Management cost}}$$

Management value added is the residue after every contribution to a firm's inputs are paid. If management value added is greater than management cost then management efforts are productive in the sense that their outputs exceed their inputs.

This approach attributes surplus value to management rather than capital and as such, it is a departure from classical economics. It is based on the philosophical notion that in contemporary society, the most scarce resource is not capital, raw materials nor technology, but rather management. In Strassman's view 'good' management makes all the difference between success and failure and ROM recognises this fact.

The method used for calculating management value added may be demonstrated by considering the diagram shown in Figure 4.8. In it revenue is described as being composed of purchases and taxes and business value added. In turn the business value added consists of:

1. Shareholders value added

2. Operations costs

3. Management costs

4. Management value added

The calculation procedure is an exhaust method. Firstly the purchases and

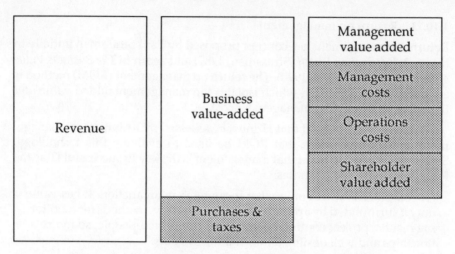

Figure 4.8     Calculating management value added

taxes are subtracted from the revenue to derive the business value added. The business value added is then decomposed by firstly, subtracting the shareholders value added, which is the dividend, then, secondly, subtracting the operations costs, which are all the direct and overhead costs. At this stage only management cost and management value added remain in the figure. When management costs are subtracted only the management value added remains.

Strassman claims that the ROM method is a superior measure because it combines both financial statement and balance sheet entries, it is self indexing, it isolates the productivity of management, and it makes possible diagnostic evaluations.

### 4.10.12   Multi-objective multi-criteria methods

Multi-objective multi-criteria methods are subjective methods for appraising the value of different outcomes in terms of the decision makers own preferences. It assumes that the value of a project or an IT investment may be determined or measured in terms other than money. Therefore, preferences are used instead of ROI etc.

The philosophy behind multi-objective multi-criteria methods is that different stakeholders may have different ideas about the value of different aspects of an IT investment and that these may not be strictly comparable in money terms. This technique allows different views and values to be investigated and assists in exposing potential conflicts at the decision making stage.

Multi-objective multi-criteria methods are most useful when strategic choices have to be made between quite different alternatives.

## 4.11   CLASSIFICATION OF METHODOLOGIES

Each of these methodologies leads to the development of a measure or metric which allows the IS to be evaluated. Sometimes the metric is compared to a corporate or industry standard or sometimes relative metrics are compared, for competing systems. However, in most cases a single measure is not sufficient to make an evaluation. Two or three metrics will usually be required but six or seven measures should be avoided. These methodologies may be categorised as primarily objective or subjective in nature. However, even in the more objectively oriented approaches the calculation of the metric will almost invariably be based on subjective criteria and any suggestion that the method is totally objective should be resisted. Figure 4.9 categorises these measures in terms of their relative subjectivity/objectivity. The key to using these metrics is to attempt to maintain as high a level of consistency between the evaluation of different systems.

| Classification | Evaluation Approach |
|---|---|
| Partially Objective | Cost Benefit Analysis<br>Economic Analysis<br>System Usage<br>Quality Assurance<br>Relative Competitive Performance<br>Work Study Assessment |
| Fully Subjective | User Attitudes<br>Management Vision<br>Value Chain Assessment<br>Strategic Match Analysis |

Figure 4.9   Classification of evaluation approaches

Before directly addressing any of these techniques themselves there are several philosophical questions or issues which must be raised. These include the following:

### 4.11.1   To what extent are costs and benefits a question of definition?

There are several different aspects to this question which must be addressed.

–   What assumptions underlie the cost and the benefit calculation? What goes into the investment? Most commentators would agree that the hardware cost should be included, but there is considerable disagree-

ment as to the amortisation policy for the hardware. Some firms capi-
talise their software, while others insist that it must be treated as an
expense. With some systems, training can represent a substantial proportion of the total costs and this is seldom capitalised. Should it
perhaps not be treated as an investment cost? Few firms bother to
attempt to account for staff time, especially management time, while
this is known to frequently represent a sizable element in the development cost of many systems.

–  It is not always clear what costs should be attributed to a system. Direct
   costs are relatively easy to identify. Although those associated with end
   user computing may be difficult to identify. However, overheads or
   corporate burden often represent a major issue which is not easily
   resolved. Should the ISD carry part of the cost of the International
   Headquarters and the Chairman's Rolls Royce? In addition the notion
   of being able to state the cost of a system implies a final date which can
   be fixed in time. Systems typically do not behave like this as they
   generally evolve and, therefore, do not lend themselves easily to a cut
   off date.

–  What benefit streams have been identified and for how long? How far
   into the future can the continued viability of the system be assumed to
   last? Does the firm have a rigidly controlled policy on investment
   horizons?

–  How are future benefit streams adjusted for inflation? What measure
   of inflation has been used? Are different estimates of inflation being
   used for different factors of production?

–  In the case of international firms, how are multi-currency situations to
   be handled and how are future exchange rates accommodated?

Hardly any of these questions can be answered by simple objective facts.
Each one is loaded with opinion, subjectivity and value judgments. Therefore
the problem of producing sound, objective, unbiased IT evaluations is considerable.

### 4.11.2  Further issues relating to some of the major approaches to benefit assessment

All approaches to IT benefit assessment have significant conceptual or practical flaws. This does not mean that they cannot be or should not be used, but
practitioners should be aware of their limitations.

### 4.11.2.1   Strategic analysis and evaluation

1.  Highly subjective.
2.  Issues not well understood.
3.  All but top management may be unaware of strategy.

### 4.11.2.2   Value chain assessment

1.  Very subjective.
2.  Difficult to obtain hard data.
3.  Not well understood by management.

### 4.11.2.3   Relative competitive performance

1.  Information available may be sketchy.
2.  Difficult to compare benefits of different systems.
3.  Uncertainty about competitors plans.

### 4.11.2.4   Proportion of management vision achieved

1.  No hard data.
2.  Virtually no objectivity in this approach to assessment.
3.  It is sometimes not easy to get top management to admit to failure.

### 4.11.2.5   Work study assessment

1.  Objectivity may be relatively superficial.
2.  Changes in work patterns may drastically alter the assessment.
3.  Most managers are not familiar with these techniques.

### 4.11.2.6   Economic assessment - I/O analysis

1.  Requires an understanding of economic analysis.
2.  It is relatively abstract.
3.  It attempts to avoid detailed quantification of monetary terms.
4.  Most managers are not familiar with these techniques.

### 4.11.2.7   Cost benefit analysis based on financial accounting

1.  This approach is subject to manipulation.
2.  Accounting requires a sound infrastructure which many firms do not have.

3.  Financial accounting cannot extend beyond simple monetary terms and thus many issues of value are omitted.

4.  However this approach has a long established acceptance in business.

### 4.11.2.8  User attitudes

1.  Requires statistical analysis.
2.  Not many practitioners available.
3.  Has credibility gap problems.

### 4.11.2.9  User utility assessment

1.  Users may not tell the truth or simply exaggerate.
2.  Users may have vested interests in presenting a particular viewpoint.
3.  Corporate culture may colour users views and the interpretation of the outcome.

### 4.11.2.10  Value added analysis

1.  Very practical approach.
2.  Keeps costs under control.
3.  Encourages prototyping.

### 4.11.2.11  Return on management

1.  A major break with classical economics.
2.  Not easy to operationalise.
3.  Useful to stimulate re-thinking.

### 4.11.2.12  Multi-objective multi-criteria methods

1.  A very unquantifiable method.
2.  Not useful as a post implementation tool.
3.  Useful to stimulate debate.

## 4.12  CHOICE OF EVALUATION METHODOLOGY

There is in fact a bewildering choice of evaluation methodologies available to management. Each methodology is designed to assess the firms IT effectiveness in a different way. The critical skill is to be able to select the methodology most appropriate for the firm's particular circumstances.

## 4.13   SUMMARY

There is a wide range of IS assessment techniques available. Each approach has some strengths and weaknesses. In order to choose one which is appropriate, it is necessary to focus on the objective of the assessment and what decisions the evaluator intends to make with the results of the assessment. It is essential to always bear in mind that all measurement techniques, by their very nature, have some element of subjectivity built in, and where possible allowances should be made for this.

# 5     Cost Benefit Analysis

## 5.1   INTRODUCTION

Having decided, at a strategic level, the general direction of the firm's IT investment, it is now usually necessary to perform some detailed analysis of the impact on the business of the proposed investment. This usually implies the conducting of a detailed feasibility study which would normally involve cost benefit analysis.

There are many different categories of both costs and benefits and it is essential that all the appropriate elements are generally addressed in the analysis. Unlike IT benefits, the concept of IT costs are well understood and therefore do not need elaborate definition. However, in connection with IT the term *hidden cost* is sometimes encountered. A hidden cost is a non-obvious cost of IT which may in fact appear in another department or function as a result of computerisation. According to Willcocks (1991) operations and maintenance costs are sometimes considered to be hidden and these may amount to as much as 2.5 times the development and installation costs over the first four years of the life of an IT project. As the impact of IT has become more and more understood there is less and less scope for costs to be hidden.

The term *opportunity cost* is also sometimes used. The opportunity cost of an investment or project is the amount which the firm could earn if the sum invested was used in another way. Thus the opportunity cost of a computer system might be the amount which would be earned if the funds were invested in the core business, or if the funds were placed in an appropriate bank account.

## 5.2   DIFFERENT TYPES OF COSTS

The following is a fairly comprehensive list of all the major costs that a system may incur:

- Direct costs of hardware and software purchased, hired or leased.
- Costs of communications media, notably telephones and digital lines.
- Support and maintenance costs, either due to in-house specialists or third-party vendors.

- Consumables such as disks, floppy diskettes, magnetic tape, printer ribbons, toner cartridges.

- Ancillaries and accessories such as new furniture for computer work-stations, acoustic hoods for printers, uninterruptable power supplies, cabling.

- Bureau charges for access to hardware and software.

- Costs incurred by IS planning, management, development, analysis, programming.

- IS specialist staff costs, including recruitment and training as well as salaries.

- Consultants, analysts and contractors costs from third party firms.

- Training and tutoring costs incurred by non-IS staff when learning to use the new system.

- Time spent by non-IS staff and management for developing, introducing and evaluating the system.

- Time spent by non-IS staff and management in sorting out problems on the new system.

- Modifications to the site, buildings and offices necessary to accommodate the new system.

- Transition costs when converting to the new system, for activities such as rewriting software, setting up files and databases, converting existing data, parallel operation of new and old systems, use of temporary staff during the transitional phase, etc.

- Suppliers' charges for installation and delivery of system components.

- One-off staff payments to encourage transition to the new system, or redundancy payments if applicable.

- Insurance charges for loss or damage to the equipment, and also consequential loss of income if the equipment is out of service for a significant period.

- Charges for provision of backup equipment or services, to cater for the possibility of system failure.

- Documentation costs, both for initial development and for ongoing updates at regular intervals.

- Costs involved in upgrading software and hardware.

- Costs due to having a system with a limited growth capacity, or due to having a non-standard system requiring special attention.

- Costs due to inefficient operation, such as those due to poor cash flow, lack of accurate information for planning and decision making.
- Costs due to delays in system implementation, thereby losing the benefits that may have possibly been gained in that period.
- The cost of failure if the system proves ineffective, or is constantly out of action due to hardware or software problems.
- The costs, in both human and financial terms, of failing to take account of the working conditions and environment during the transitional phase, and once the new system is operational.

The above list includes both hard and soft costs.

Hard costs are those which are readily agreed by everyone as being attributable to the IS and which are easily captured by the firm's accounting system. Amongst hard costs are payments to vendors for hardware and software and IS staff salaries as well as the costs for site modification, consultants, etc.

Soft costs are those costs which may not be readily agreed as being attributable to the IS effort and which are not easily identifiable in the firm's accounting records. Soft costs include items such as users' time in learning systems, users' time in sorting out problems, reduced productivity encountered during the learning experience of a new system by operators, etc. The dis-benefits referred to in Chapter 3 are sometimes referred to as soft costs.

It is interesting to note that the costs of implementing new IT systems has changed dramatically over the past 20 years. According to Bjorn-Anderson (1986) the organisational costs have increased from about 20% to 50%. This is clearly shown in Figure 5.1.

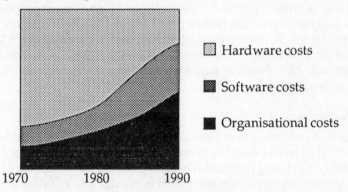

**Figure 5.1    Increase in organisational costs incurred during IT implementation**

## 5.3   COST BENEFIT ANALYSIS

Cost benefit analysis may be defined as the process of comparing the various costs of acquiring and implementing an information system with the benefits which the organisation derives from the use of the system. In general cost benefit analysis should be performed on a marginal costing basis. This means that only additional costs incurred by the new system should be included. Likewise only marginal benefits, ie new or additional benefits, should be compared to the costs.

It is often thought that only benefits are difficult to estimate. As most IT projects over-run their cost, this is clearly not so. Considerable care must be given to cost estimation, especially where software development is concerned. Also on-going costs are regularly undetected and therefore these must be carefully scrutineered.

Different approaches to benefit analysis are required for automate, informate and transformate investments. The following are among the most important.

### 5.3.1   Cost displacement

Cost displacement considers the cost of the investment and compares this to the other costs which the system has saved. This is typically used in the more traditional data processing environments where computers are used to replace clerical workers or even sometimes blue collar workers. It is not really appropriate for situations where the IT system will add value rather than reduce costs. A cost displacement justification is a classical automate situation, although it may also have informate implications. Figure 5.2 shows an example of cost displacement analysis.

This cost displacement approach to assessing an IT investment proposition is an *ex-ante* analysis of what the firm hopes to achieve. It is nothing more than a statement of intent. To ensure that these intentions are carried out, a list of details about the system and the environment in which it will function must also be supplied. This detail is supplied in Figure 5.3 for the above cost displacement proposal.

### 5.3.2   Cost avoidance

A cost avoidance analysis is very similar to cost displacement but in this case no cost has been removed from the system because the introduction of IT has prevented cost from being incurred. This is typically used in the more traditional data processing environments and is generally less relevant to more modern IT applications. Thus, cost avoidance is most appropriate in automate systems. Figure 5.4 shows an example of cost avoidance analysis.

| Using IT to automate clerical jobs (All Numbers in 000's) | |
|---|---|
| Investment Costs | |
| Hardware | 185 |
| Software | 98 |
| Commissioning | 32 |
| **TOTAL** | **315** |
| | |
| Monthly On-going Costs | |
| Staff | 9 |
| Maintenance | 20 |
| General | 8 |
| Amortisation | 8 |
| **TOTAL** | **45** |
| | |
| Monthly Benefits | |
| Reduction in Clerical Salaries | 39 |
| Reduction in Supervisory Salaries | 8 |
| Reduction in Other Staff Costs | 4 |
| Office Space Released | 2 |
| Other Office Expenses Saved | 1 |
| **TOTAL** | **54** |
| | |
| Improvement per Month | 9 |
| Annual Net Benefit | 108 |
| | |
| ROI | 34.29% |

**Figure 5.2   The cost displacement approach**

The cost avoidance statement of intent should be accompanied by the list of points shown in Figure 5.5 which will help ensure that the proposal is achieved.

### 5.3.3   Decision analysis

Decision analysis attempts to evaluate the benefits to be derived from better information which is assumed to lead to better decisions. In turn, better decisions are believed to lead to better performance. As it is hard to define good information, let alone good decisions, cost benefit analysis performed using this method is difficult.

Decision analysis is a classic informate situation which requires a financial value to be associated with information. In some cases, it is relatively easy to

1.   List of the jobs which will be affected by the new system. Against each job a date by which the change will occur should be stated.

2.   List of individuals, by name, whose work will change.

3.   List of supervisors and managers, by name, who will be affected.

4.   An indication, by name, of the staff which will no longer be required in their functions after the system is fully operating.

5.   Plans for staff transfer or staff redundancy.

6.   List the office space which will be released by the reduction in staff.

7.   Indicate which other departments require the released space.

8.   Indicate how the space can be relet to other enterprises.

9.   Indicate which leases are coming up for review and may therefore be terminated.

10.   A timetable for the occurrence of each of the above.

Responsibility for the above Mr J.J. Jones

**Figure 5.3      Supporting details for the cost displacement approach**

measure the effect of information, although there will frequently be considerable noise in the environment which will obscure the effects of the system. The key to decision analysis is to perform rigorous business analysis of the situation before the introduction of the proposed technology. The types of business relationships at work and their effects on each other must be understood. Also how the proposed IT will disrupt these business relationships, hopefully in a positive way, must be explained. Figure 5.6 shows an example of decision analysis. This case relies on understanding how the firm's credit control works, how the cash flow functions, and how investment availability impacts sales.

The actions required to ensure the success of the above proposal are listed in Figure 5.7.

### 5.3.4   Impact or time release analysis

Impact analysis attempts to quantify the effect which IT can have on the physical performance of employees. Impact analysis may have elements of automate, informate and even transformate, depending on the exact circumstances involved.

The primary benefit of time release is that staff may do other work, and

| Using IT to avoid employing more staff (All Numbers in 000's) Investment Costs - | |
|---|---|
| Hardware | 432 |
| Software | 187 |
| Commissioning | 220 |
| **TOTAL** | **839** |
| Monthly On-going Costs | |
| Staff | 34 |
| Maintenance | 65 |
| General | 12 |
| Amortisation | 23 |
| **TOTAL** | **134** |
| Monthly Benefits | |
| Clerical Staff not Required | 120 |
| Management Staff Not Required | 7 |
| Accommodation not Require | 15 |
| Other Costs Avoided | 3 |
| **TOTAL** | **145** |
| Improvement per Month | 11 |
| Annual Net Benefit | 132 |
| ROI | 15.73% |

Figure 5.4  The cost avoidance approach

1. A forecast of activities which will increase the need for staff and resources or a statement of a change in policy which would require additional resources.

2. A precise list of the current work involved in these processes. This should be compiled as a result of detailed work study.

3. A detailed statement of how the IT application will prevent the need for these new resources.

4. A plan for the measurement of the performance of the department after the new IT application has been commissioned.

5. A timetable for the occurrence of each of the above.

Responsibility for the above Mr S.S. Smith

Figure 5.5    Supporting details for the cost avoidance approach

| Using IT to improve performance through more information | |
|---|---|
| All Numbers in 000's | |
| Investment Costs - | |
| Hardware | 876 |
| Software | 89 |
| Commissioning | 23 |
| **TOTAL** | **988** |
| Monthly On-going Costs | |
| Staff | 5 |
| Maintenance | 88 |
| General | 6 |
| Amortisation | 27 |
| **TOTAL** | **126** |
| Monthly Benefits | |
| Reduction in Bad Debts | 14 |
| Interest Earned by Faster Receipts | 8 |
| Reduction in Obsolete Inventories | 43 |
| Increased Sales due to better availability | 111 |
| **TOTAL** | **176** |
| Improvement per Month | 50 |
| Annual Net Benefit | 600 |
| ROI | 60.73% |

**Figure 5.6  The decision analysis approach**

1. A statement of why the application will produce a benefit.

2. A statement of how this benefit will be realised.

3. Details of current performance in the function at present.

4. How the situation will differ after the introduction of the IT application.

5. A plan for the measurement of the performance of the department after the new IT application has been commissioned.

6. A timetable for the occurrence of each of the above.

Responsibility for the above Mr A.A. Adams

**Figure 5.7    Supporting details for the decision analysis approach**

when this involves acquiring extra sales it may contribute to transforming the business. Figure 5.8 shows an example of impact analysis.

The time release should be accompanied by a list such as that shown in Figure 5.9.

### 5.3.5   Nominal breakeven analysis

This nominal breakeven analysis asks decision makers to determine subjectively how much the various services offered by the IT systems is worth to them. Once the cost of the system is covered by these subjective estimates then the systems is given a go-ahead. This approach to cost benefit analysis is used when the benefits are very intangible. Figure 5.10 shows an example of nominal breakeven analysis.

The supporting document for the nominal breakeven analysis proposal is shown in Figure 5.11.

All of these *ex-ante* investment proposals must be used on the basis of an *ex-post* evaluation. These financial statements may be regarded as budgets, and actual costs and benefits may be recorded against them. Variances are then easily calculated as shown in Figure 5.12.

There are two distinct sets of difficulties with the *ex-post* statement in Figure 5.12 which refer to the accounting system's ability to deliver the required figures. The first difficulty is whether the cost numbers have been recorded in such a way that they can be presented under the titles suggested in the budget. The second difficulty relates to whether the amount of the benefits can be extracted from the accounting data. With regards the costs, new accounting procedures and codes may have to be established in order to group the costs in the required way. The issue of the benefits is more complex and requires considerable thought and analysis in order to establish the measurability of the benefits, as well as to make provision for a number of different types of noise which may be present.

### 5.3.6   How to evaluate an intangible benefit

A typical intangible IT benefit is the ability of management to perform what-if analysis on financial plans and budgets. More information of this type is clearly advantageous and valuable to management but it is very difficult to associate a particular financial amount with this type of benefit.

One approach to evaluating this type of benefit is to ask the managers who are using this facility to place a value on it. This may be done by asking a series of questions such as: Would you pay £10 for this report? If the answer is yes then the next question would be: Would you pay £10000 for this report? If the

| | |
|---|---|
| Using IT to improve salesmen's productivity | |
| All Numbers in 000's | |
| Investment Costs for 5 systems - | |
| Hardware | 30 |
| Software | 23 |
| Commissioning | 75 |
| **TOTAL** | **128** |
| | |
| Monthly On-going Costs | |
| Staff | 2 |
| Communications Costs | 2 |
| Maintenance | 3 |
| General | 1 |
| Amortisation | 12 |
| **TOTAL** | **20** |
| | |
| Monthly Benefits | |
| Average No. of Sales Calls per Day | 6 |
| Average Value of Sales per Call | 2 |
| | |
| Reduction in Av. Sales Call Time | |
| from 35 to 15 minutes | 20 minutes |
| Reduction in Time required for daily | |
| form filling from 60 to 10 minutes | 50 minutes |
| **TOTAL TIME RELEASE** | **170 minutes** |
| | |
| Av. Travel Time required between | |
| Sales Calls 25 minutes | |
| | |
| Therefore IT provides the opportunity | |
| for 4 more Sales Calls per Day | |
| | |
| Resulting Additional Revenue | 8 |
| Net Profit % | 10.00% |
| | |
| Daily Benefit from 5 systems | 3 |
| Monthly Benefit from 5 systems | 60 |
| **ANNUAL NET BENEFIT** | **40** |
| | |
| ROI | 31.25% |

Figure 5.8  The impact analysis approach

1. A statement of why the application will produce a benefit, and how this benefit will be realised.

2. Details of current performance in the function at present, and how the situation will differ after the introduction of the application.

3. If new business is expected to be generated as a result of the application, then a forecast (and justification) of activities which will increase.

4. A plan for the measurement of the performance of the department after the new IT application has been commissioned.

5. A timetable for the occurrence of each of the above.

Responsibility for the above Mr B.B. Bloggs

**Figure 5.9      Supporting details for the time release approach**

| | |
|---|---:|
| Using IT to improve office worker's productivity | |
| All Numbers in 000's | |
| Investment Costs for 5 systems - | |
| Hardware | 205 |
| Software | 45 |
| Commissioning | 59 |
| **TOTAL** | **309** |
| | |
| Monthly On-going Costs | |
| Staff | 5 |
| Communications Costs | 2 |
| Maintenance | 3 |
| General | 1 |
| Amortisation | 4 |
| **TOTAL** | **15** |
| | |
| Monthly Benefits | |
| Improvement in Secretarial Efficiency | 4 |
| Figure Work Improvements | 5 |
| Better Presentation of Proposals and Reports | 3 |
| Better Communications through E-Mail | 2 |
| Better Administration with databases | 2 |
| **TOTAL** | **16** |
| | |
| Improvement per Month | 1 |
| Annual Net Benefit | 12 |
| ROI | 3.88% |

**Figure 5.10      The nominal breakeven analysis approach**

1.  List any tangible benefits and state how the achievement of these may be measured.

2.  Establish the key performance indicators for these tangible benefits.

3.  A detailed statement of how the value of the intangible benefits were assessed.

4.  A list of suggestions as to how the intangible benefits may be evaluated after implementation.

5.  A plan for the measurement of the performance of the department after the new IT application has been commissioned.

6.  A timetable for the occurrence of each of the above.

Responsibility for the above Mr C.C. Cluff

**Figure 5.11     Supporting details for the nominal breakeven approach**

FINANCIAL REPORT AFTER ONE YEAR'S USE
Using IT to automate clerical jobs

| Investment Costs | Budget | Actual | Variance |
|---|---|---|---|
| Hardware | 185 | 196 | −11 |
| Software | 98 | 120 | −22 |
| Commissioning | 32 | 38 | −6 |
| **TOTAL** | **315** | **354** | **−39** |
| Monthly On-going Costs | | | |
| Staff | 9 | 6 | 3 |
| Maintenance | 20 | 18 | 2 |
| General | 8 | 9 | −1 |
| Amortisation | 8 | 9 | −1 |
| **TOTAL** | **45** | **42** | **3** |
| Monthly Benefits | | | |
| Reduction in Clerical Salaries | 39 | 40 | 1 |
| Reduction in Supervisory Salaries | 8 | 9 | 1 |
| Reduction in Other Staff Costs | 4 | 5 | 1 |
| Office Space Released | 2 | 2 | 0 |
| Other Office Expenses Saved | 1 | 1 | 0 |
| **TOTAL** | **54** | **57** | **3** |
| Improvement per Month | 9 | 15 | 6 |
| **ANNUAL NET BENEFIT** | **108** | **180** | **72** |
| ROI | 34.29% | 50.85% | 16.56% |

**Figure 5.12     Ex-post cost benefit analysis**

answer is no then a binary search may be conducted to find the value of the facility to the user. The value so derived may be considered as the size of the intangible benefit. Of course, this approach produces a very subjective evaluation of the benefit. However, it does result in a number as opposed to a simple comfort statement, and the number may be used in a cost benefit analysis calculation to see if the investment makes sense. This approach may be considered to be semi-hard or semi-soft analysis and is sometimes referred to as benefit negotiation.

Figure 5.13 shows an example of a cost benefit analysis using intangible benefits. In this case there are two benefits which cannot easily be quantified.

---

**Intangible Benefits**

Using IT to improve selection of appropriate consultants
All numbers in 000's

| | |
|---|---|
| Hardware 386-PC etc | 15 |
| Software | 8 |
| Commissioning | 6 |
| **TOTAL** | **29** |

Monthly On-going Costs

| | |
|---|---|
| Staff | 1.00 |
| Maintenance | 0.20 |
| General | 0.20 |
| Amortisation | 0.10 |
| **TOTAL** | **1.50** |

Monthly Benefits

| | |
|---|---|
| Senior Management Time | 1.00 |
| Clerical Time | 0.50 |
| Better Proposals | X |
| Better Consulting Work | Y |
| **TOTAL** | **1.50** |

Firms Cost of Capital                    25.00%

Therefore values of intangible benefits of X and Y together
must be at least £7250 per annum.
However the benefit to the firm could be much larger.
If the monthly benefits cannot be estimated then the total
benefits can be stated as being at least £8750 per annum.

---

Figure 5.13      Analysis of intangible benefits

If benefit negotiation does not work then it is possible to impute a benefit value. An imputed benefit value is one which is derived by calculating the amount a system must be worth to the firm if it is to proceed with the investment and earn its required rate of return. This of course assumes that the firm remains economically rational.

### 5.3.7  Transformate analysis

The type of analysis which is used to assess a transformate opportunity is the same as that analysis employed for any strategic investment. Strategic investments often involve many considerations which are particularly difficult to quantify. Issues such as competitive advantage, market share, new product development are just a few examples. Strategic investments are frequently considered so important that a full *ex-ante* cost justification may not be undertaken, or if it is the results of the analysis may simply be ignored. Statements such as "it's too important to ignore" or "the cost of not doing it will be crippling" are frequently heard in association with strategic investments. Therefore, strategic investment appraisal studies will often contain more words than numbers. The descriptive part of the proposal will contain words such as those shown in Figure 5.14.

---

1.   This investment represents an extremely attractive opportunity for the firm to penetrate a new and profitable market.

2.   The demand in the new market is likely to increase at a compound rate of 25% pa for the rest of the decade.

3.   The new production facility will reduce our costs so substantially that we will be able to undercut both our nearest competitors.

4.   Client service will improve substantially.

---

**Figure 5.14  Strategic considerations**

Good practice, however, requires some numeric analysis to be performed. As transformate or strategic investments will have a longer time implication than efficiency or effectiveness investments, the simple ROI and payback methods are not adequate. The time value of money based techniques such as discounted cash flow need to be used.

For discounted cash flow techniques more data and assumptions are required. This technique is shown in Figure 5.15. An explanation of the financial techniques is supplied in Appendix 4.

**A proposal to use IT to transformate the business**

All figures in 000's

| | |
|---|---:|
| Hardware | 1987 |
| Software | 765 |
| Commissioning | 411 |
| **TOTAL** | **3163** |

Annual On-going IT Costs

| | |
|---|---:|
| Staff | 340 |
| Maintenance | 172 |
| General | 38 |
| Amortisation | 645 |
| **TOTAL** | **1 195** |

| Annual Benefits | Year-1 | Year-2 | Year-3 | Year-4 |
|---|---:|---:|---:|---:|
| Sales | 997 | 2998 | 3421 | 6675 |
| Cost of sale | 1444 | 1945 | 2050 | 2864 |
| Net profit | –447 | 1054 | 1371 | 3811 |
| Tax | 0 | 347 | 452 | 1257 |
| After Tax Profit | –447 | 707 | 919 | 2554 |
| Amortisation | 645 | 645 | 645 | 645 |
| Net Cash Flow | 198 | 1352 | 1564 | 3199 |

| | |
|---|---:|
| Firm's Cost of Capital | 20.00% |
| Tax Rate | 33.00% |
| Economic Life of the project | 4 |
| | |
| Net Present Value | 389 |
| Profitability Index | 1.16 |

Figure 5.14     A cost benefit analysis for a transformate proposal

## 5.4   DETERMINISTIC Vs STOCHASTIC EVALUATION PROCESSES

In this section traditional cost benefit analysis is undertaken using discounted cash flow techniques involving estimates of the investment amount, the annual benefits and the cost of capital. All these variables are difficult to estimate. However, the cost of the firm's capital is frequently considered the most difficult variable to determine. The rate of interest which the firm pays on its debt or an arbitrarily chosen hurdle or discount rate is sometimes used as a surrogate for the cost of capital.

IT systems evaluation may be undertaken in several different ways using a variety of measures and at least two different processes. The two processes discussed here are the deterministic approach using single point estimates for the input values and generating a single estimate for the result, and the stochastic approach which uses ranges as input and generates a range of results. The stochastic method is sometimes referred to as Simulation or Risk Analysis.

Deterministic analysis assumes a certain world where the exact value of input variables can be known. Once the values of these inputs are entered a unique result, determined by the logic of the algorithm and the precise data, is calculated.

Risk analysis, on the other hand, attempts to accommodate the inherent variability in the input estimates and produces a result which more closely reflects the level of uncertainty frequently experienced in the real world.

### 5.4.1   Deterministic analysis

Figure 5.16 shows the data input form for a deterministic model in a spreadsheet, and Figure 5.17 shows the data entered.

**Figure 5.16     The input form for a deterministic spreadsheet model**

The use of discounted cash flow techniques requires that all figures used actually represent cash dispensed or received by the firm. Therefore, profit

```
           A          B      C       D      E      F       G
1  ------------------------------------------------------------
2  Capital Investment Appraisal System
3  ------------------------------------------------------------
4                        Cash-Out Cash-In  Net Cash Movement each year
5
6  Amount Invested - Year 0  350000                 -350000
7  Cash Flows        Year 1          60000           60000
8                    Year 2          95000           95000
9                    Year 3         120000          120000
10                   Year 4         180000          180000
11                   Year 5         200000          200000
12 ------------------------------------------------------------
13 Fixed Rate of Interest    20.00%
14                                    Y1      Y2      Y3      Y4
15 Inflation Adjusted Interest Rates 25.00% 29.00% 30.00% 35.00%
16
17 ------------------------------------------------------------
18
19
```

Figure 5.17    Completed input form for the deterministic model

figures which include non-cash items such as depreciation or reserves should not be used. Figure 5.18 shows the results which use a number of different investment measures including payback, NPV, PI, IRR, etc. Explanations of these measures together with their formulae are supplied in Appendix 4.

```
           A        B      C      D      E      F      G      H
21 ------------------------------------------------------------
22 Investment Reports
23 ------------------------------------------------------------
24 Payback in years & months              3 years    5 months
25 Rate of return(%)              37.43%
26 N P V Fixed Discount Rate (FDR)  2598
27 Profitability Index FDR (PI)     1.01
28 Internal Rate of Return (IRR)   20.28%
29
30 ------------------------------------------------------------
31
32 Variable Discount Rates
33 N P V Variable Discount Rates (VDR) -71754
34 Profitability Index VDR (PI)     0.79
35
36 ------------------------------------------------------------
37
38 Discounted Payback FDR in years and months  4 years  11 months
39
```

Figure 5.18    Results produced by the deterministic model

An important feature of this spreadsheet is the use of variable costs of capital or interest rates. These interest rates may be used to reflect either anticipated rates of inflation, or more generally, to adjust for an increasing risk profile. The further into the future the estimated benefit the greater the degree of uncertainty or risk, and therefore the higher the discount or interest rate which is normally associated with the investment. The high interest rate has the effect of reducing the future value of the benefit.

The results shown in Figure 5.18 are, of course, highly dependent upon the assumptions made concerning the cost of capital, the investment amount and the annual cash flows. As these future estimates are always uncertain it is appropriate to perform what-if analysis on these assumptions. Figure 5.19

Sensitivity Analysis varying Fixed Interest Rate

|         | NPV     | PI   |
|---------|---------|------|
|         | 2598    | 1.01 |
| 20.00%  | 2598    | 1.01 |
| 21.00%  | -6710   | 0.98 |
| 22.00%  | -15656  | 0.96 |
| 23.00%  | -24258  | 0.93 |
| 24.00%  | -32533  | 0.91 |
| 25.00%  | -40496  | 0.88 |
| 26.00%  | -48162  | 0.86 |
| 27.00%  | -55545  | 0.84 |
| 28.00%  | -62658  | 0.82 |
| 29.00%  | -69514  | 0.80 |
| 30.00%  | -76124  | 0.78 |
| 35.00%  | -105861 | 0.70 |

Figure 5.19     Variation in cost of capital and NPV

Sensitivity Analysis on NPV varying Investment and Fixed Interest Rate

| Investment | Interest Rates | | | | | |
|--------|--------|--------|--------|--------|--------|--------|
| 2598   | 20.00% | 21.00% | 22.00% | 23.00% | 24.00% | 25.00% |
| 40000  | 86244  | 82880  | 79645  | 76533  | 73539  | 70656  |
| 45000  | 81244  | 77880  | 74645  | 71533  | 68539  | 65656  |
| 50000  | 76244  | 72880  | 69645  | 66533  | 63539  | 60656  |
| 55000  | 71244  | 67880  | 64645  | 61533  | 58539  | 55656  |
| 60000  | 66244  | 62880  | 59645  | 56533  | 53539  | 50656  |
| 65000  | 61244  | 57880  | 54645  | 51533  | 48539  | 45656  |
| 70000  | 56244  | 52880  | 49645  | 46533  | 43539  | 40656  |
| 75000  | 51244  | 47880  | 44645  | 41533  | 38539  | 35656  |
| 80000  | 46244  | 42880  | 39645  | 36533  | 33539  | 30656  |
| 85000  | 41244  | 37880  | 34645  | 31533  | 28539  | 25656  |
| 90000  | 36244  | 32880  | 29645  | 26533  | 23539  | 20656  |
| 95000  | 31244  | 27880  | 24645  | 21533  | 18539  | 15656  |
| 100000 | 26244  | 22880  | 19645  | 16533  | 13539  | 10656  |
| 120000 | 6244   | 2880   | -355   | -3467  | -6461  | -9344  |

Figure 5.20     Effect of variation in cost of capital and
investment amount on NPV

shows a what-if table indicating the way in which the NPV is related to the cost of capital. Against each cost of capital estimate there is the resulting NPV.

Figure 5.20 shows the effect of different investment amounts and different costs of capital on the project. As the investment amounts are shown vertically, and the costs of capital are shown horizontally, the resulting NPV may be read from the intersection of the chosen row and column. Thus, with an investment of 70000 and a cost of capital of 21% the resulting NPV will be 52880.

### 5.4.2   Risk analysis

As mentioned previously, the risk of an investment is the potential of input/output variables to fluctuate from their original estimates. As in the vast majority of cases input/output variables do fluctuate, and risk analysis accommodates this by allowing ranges, rather than single point estimates, to be used. It is generally much easier to confidently state that an investment will be between 200,000 and 300,000 than it will be 250,000.

There are a variety of techniques available which assist management in assessing the extent and the size of the risk inherent in a particular investment. There are at least three generic approaches to identifying and assessing risk. These are:

– Group brainstorming

– Expert judgement

– Assumption analysis

Group brainstorming uses group interaction to identify the variables which carry the most exposure to variability. Once the variables have been identified, the group then attempts to quantify the limits of the variability as well as the probability associated with the range of possible inputs and outputs. Brainstorming groups may meet several times before the estimates of the variables are finalised.

Expert judgement uses experienced individuals who are aware of the factors causing the investment potential to vary. This is the quickest and easiest way of identifying risk, but considerable care must be given to choosing the expert.

Assumption analysis requires the detailed questioning of each assumption. This analysis requires each assumption to be modified in such a way that circumstances will be evaluated which are disadvantageous to the investment. The effect of the changes in assumptions are then used as part of the range of variable specification.

A useful tool in assessing different types of risk is the influence diagram.

An influence diagram is a perceptual map showing concepts or issues to illustrate how different aspects of a proposed investment may interact with each other, causing variability in the input/output estimates.

### 5.4.2.1   Influence diagrams

An influence diagram allows all the related concepts and issues to be mapped showing the interconnections between them. Such perceptual mapping may be used to quickly identify areas of high variability, which are those with a high number of interconnections. This technique is especially useful for facilitating creative thinking in the search for the identification and quantification of risk. Figure 5.21 shows an influence diagram illustrating the nine factors which directly or indirectly effect sales volumes.

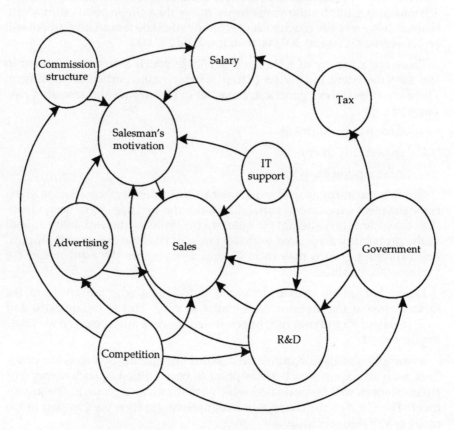

**Figure 5.21   An influence diagram**

However, after the perceptual map has been developed it is then necessary to debate the size of the potential fluctuations in the variables. This may only be done by bringing together a group of experienced managers and discussing the likely value of each factor. At the conclusion of such a debate, maximum and minimum values should be established for sales, costs, prices, assets, cash flows, etc.

Figures 5.22, 5.23 and 5.24 show the input form and results screens for the risk analysis calculations performed for the IRR, and Figures 5.25 and 5.26 show the results produced for risk analysis of the NPV.

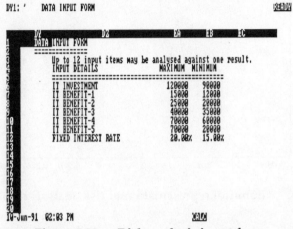

Figure 5.22      Risk analysis input form

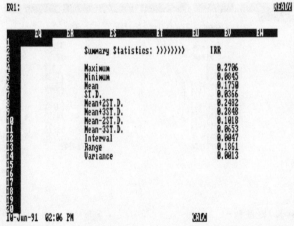

Figure 5.23      Results screen for risk analysis on IRR

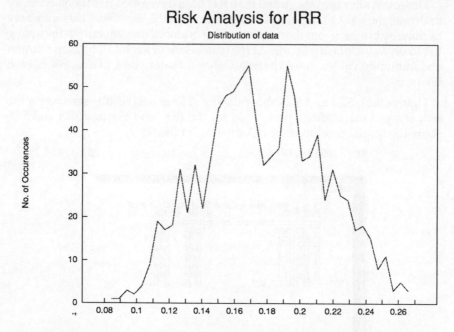

**Figure 5.24    Graphical representation of risk analysis results for IRR**

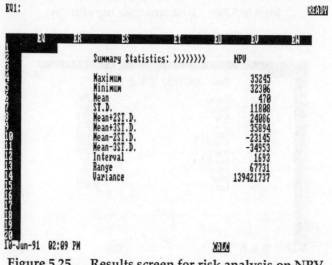

**Figure 5.25    Results screen for risk analysis on NPV**

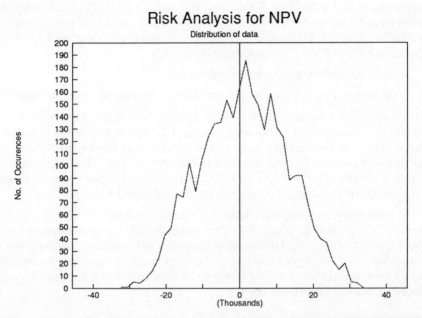

**Figure 5.26    Graphical representation of risk analysis results on NPV**

Figure 5.22 shows that the initial investment amount is not certain, but it is known that it will be between £120,000 and £90,000. Similarly the IT benefits for years 1 to 5 are also specified as ranges, for example in year 1 the maximum benefit is estimated at £15,000 and the minimum value of the benefit is stated at £12,000. Similarly, the exact rate of interest is not known and it is estimated at between 20% and 15% per annum.

### 5.4.3    The results of risk analysis

The example used to produce the results in Figures 5.22 and 5.23 would be regarded as being of relatively low risk. The reason for this is that the most likely outcome is a return of 17.5% with a standard deviation of 3.6%. This means that even if all the most unfavourable estimates occur, ie maximum investment costs, lowest benefits and highest cost of capital, this investment will still be expected to produce an IRR of 6%. On the positive side, if the investment is kept low and the highest benefits are achieved etc, then this investment could produce a return as high as 28%.

The example used to produce the results shown in Figures 5.25 and 5.26 would be regarded as a relatively high risk. The most likely outcome of this investment is an NPV of 470. Although this is in itself satisfactory, the investment also has the potential of making a substantial loss, ie as much as an NPV of -34953. Of course if all goes well this investment could return a positive NPV of 3598. This variability is the risk.

A basic question which is frequently asked is:

*Is the benefit to be derived from IT evaluation or assessment worth the effort?*

In some respects this question is now obsolete. There are many who would argue that information technology is so clearly a basic requirement for business that it is unnecessary to perform regular cost benefit analysis. Such arguments say that IT is as essential to the firm as is an adequate telephone system. On the other hand, IT still does not represent trivial amounts to most organisations and, therefore, should not be compared to telephones.

In reality, unless some measurement is done, management will never know how it is performing. And, therefore, even though the measurement of IT performance is imperfect it is essential to perform these calculations to obtain some sort of indication. However, whatever method or metric is chosen it must be realised that it is very likely to be no more than a subjective assessment with a very low level objectivity.

## 5.5  SUMMARY

There are a number of different approaches to cost benefit analysis which range from fairly simple single point estimate techniques to rather sophisticated risk analysis. It is important to choose the appropriate level of sophistication and not to over work the numbers. In some cases, where the amounts are small, it may not be necessary to perform any cost benefit analysis at all.

# 6 Establishing Measures of Benefits

## 6.1 MEASURING BENEFITS

The focus of this chapter is to describe how management may get the most out of a systems' implementation. This could either be a new system or it could be an already established one. The chapter is aimed at providing guidelines to those who are responsible for achieving benefits.

The main point of classifying benefits is to assist in measuring and monitoring them, with a view to controlling and maximising the positive effects of the change. The techniques of measuring and monitoring will vary depending on the benefits sought and the details of the system. However, there is one general rule which is all too often ignored; there has to be history of measurement dating back to some time before the system was implemented if any meaningful analysis of the effects of the change is to be undertaken. Without an appropriate amount of historical statistics it is quite difficult to comment on the benefits derived from IT.

Starting to measure some benefit such as improved productivity from the time of implementation is a meaningless exercise, of no use except possibly to provide the historical data for the next time a change is planned. This point will be repeated and expanded several times below.

### 6.1.1 Established business measures

Ideally, the benefits monitoring should be based on business measures that are already in common use in the firm. These will presumably have been chosen to reflect important aspects of the firm's performance. Additionally, there will be a history of these measures and an understanding of seasonal fluctuations or other trends. However, if these measures are not appropriate for the system under consideration, or do not exist at all, special monitoring will have to be undertaken. This is of course a cost in itself and, like all measurement, runs the risk of distorting the process being measured.

The measures which will be used should be decided as part of the original specification of requirements and should be discussed in some detail in the feasibility study or outline system specification. This is not a common practice

117

with many systems analysts. However, the sole point of introducing any system is to improve some aspect of the firm's operations, to deliver a benefit. It is difficult to see how a thorough system specification can be drawn up, or agreed by the customer, unless consideration has been given to the present level of performance, which is presumably considered to be inadequate, and a target level established for future performance after the new system has been implemented.

Thus, the base level of performance is established during the initial system specification. If the measure is not one which the firm monitors as a matter of course, monitoring of this performance must start as soon as the project has been approved and design work is under way, in order to give as much historical information as possible before the change.

### 6.1.2   Timing of measurement

How frequently such monitoring will be undertaken will vary enormously. The timing will depend on the variability of the process, and how quickly changes can be effected. Because of this variability, there is little point in attempting to generalise on this matter, the best people to judge are usually the operational managers who are responsible for the process concerned.

In this less than perfect world the idea of measuring just what benefit the firm is gaining from its investment often does not occur to anyone until after the system has been installed. The historical information has not been col- lected but the Board are insisting on a report justifying the expenditure. What should be done in response to this unexpected demand? In most situations, unless standard business measures can be used to monitor the system, it is impossible to accurately reconstruct any meaningful information.

If the measure used to assess the benefit is not one regularly recorded as part of the firm's performance monitoring we are reliant on reconstructing it some time, maybe months or years, after the system has been introduced; and are reliant on the memory of people working in the department.

Attempting to ask managers, months after the event, to recollect some aspect of their department's performance which has not been formally recorded is doomed to failure and will inevitably produce confusion and bad feeling. Some will have moved on. Others will apply different interpretations to the questions. All will feel that their time is being wasted. After all, what will the firm do if the answer is unfavourable? Certainly the system will not now be taken out. As a result, the information gathered will be of little real use.

### 6.1.3   Measurement noise

If standard business measures can be used the position is more hopeful, but only just. The historical figures will be available, but they will show apparently random variations which may mask the effect being sought. The variations were almost certainly not random, but the opportunity to discover the real reason has passed with the moment. This "noise" in the measurements can be filtered out if the reasons are known, as they generally are at the time. They will be forgotten in a surprisingly short time, especially if there is a high turnover in the department concerned. Something not unknown at a time of system changes.

Having laboured the point that monitoring must predate the implementation by as long as possible, it is necessary to consider what should be monitored, and how the results should be interpreted.

## 6.2 PRODUCTIVITY AND FINANCIAL SAVINGS

Financial savings and productivity changes are reasonably easy to monitor. However, the raw data has to be corrected for changes in volume and background improvements before it can be used.

The following example is based on changes in productivity, but the principle applies to most of the benefits under consideration.

### 6.2.1 Productivity

The object is to measure the improvement in productivity that has occurred because of the new system. The point of comparison should be the base figure quoted in the original outline system specification, but any time before implementation got under way will probably do. If the business is of a cyclical nature similar parts of the cycle should be compared.

If the system has been implemented in a number of similar work groups each group should be monitored individually and the results aggregated at a later stage. The different levels of performance for each work group will give valuable information.

#### 6.2.1.1 *Establishing the variables*

The following is an approach to establishing the variables for the formula to calculate change in productivity.

Call the number of staff employed in the group under study before implementation as "Staff before". At that time the group had an output, call it "Volume before". The choice of volume measures will be discussed in more detail later.

After the system has been implemented the work group will have some other number of staff, "Staff now". Their volume will now be "Volume now".

These numbers may of course be the same as the numbers before implementation, which makes the mathematics easy even if it does not give much productivity improvement.

We can therefore see that the number of staff that would be needed to cope with present volume of work, at the level of productivity which was the norm before implementation, will be:

$$\frac{\text{Staff before * Volume now}}{\text{Volume before}}$$

The difference between this figure and the staff actually employed now is the raw productivity change:

$$\frac{\text{Staff before * Volume now}}{\text{Volume before}} - \text{Staff now}$$

Expressing this as a percentage:

$$\% \text{ Change} = \left\{ \frac{\text{Staff before * Volume now}}{\text{Volume before}} - \text{Staff now} \right\} * \frac{100}{\text{Staff before}}$$

These calculations should be carried out on all the raw data collected, that is for each of the work groups. Clearly they are best carried out with the aid of a good spreadsheet.

However, we cannot yet claim this change as proof that the system has paid for itself. Most firms experience an automatic, or systematic, increase in productivity. This results from a number of factors, such as the accumulation of small ideas to do the job better (ie the learning curve effect), or a growing customer base. This effect can be very small but in some industries it can be 5% or 10% per annum. One of the reasons for requiring a base of historical information is to enable a measurement of this trend before system implementation. It is unlikely that this effect will have ceased during the time between the before and after measures and thus a correction needs to be made to the percentage change calculated above.

The correction involves subtracting an appropriate multiple of the annual systematic productivity improvement from the percentage change calculated above. These calculations are rough and ready, and there is little justification in attempting sophistications such as compounding the annual rate or correcting for the fact that the two percentage figures are calculated to different bases.

There may be other reasons for productivity improvements which need to be taken into account, that is, subtracted from the percentage change calculated above. However, claims from the operational managers need to be treated with some caution. Many line managers will be quite convinced that most of the good things that have happened in their group are the result of good management, not the result of the new system. A particularly frequent claim is that the improvement is due to the reorganisation that the manager has carried out, something he has been planning to do for some time. Investigation of this claim often proves that the change in question would have been impossible without the flexibility offered by the new system. Indeed often, the ability to make the change has been part of the original system justification.

The only way of establishing the truth of some of these claims is to study the detail and the trends; this will require some understanding of the operational issues involved. A question to which we shall return.

The "after" measures should not be taken until after the confusion surrounding implementation has subsided. For a large system or change this will generally take at least three months. At that stage, it is unlikely that much productivity improvement will be noticeable. They will not happen until the operational managers become more familiar with the new system and start to make changes that take advantage of its different strengths and weaknesses. Thereafter, monitoring should take place at regular intervals for at least a couple of years, by which time the next change will probably be in the offing.

Obviously the times quoted above will differ depending on the size and nature of the change.

The value of the productivity improvement in monetary terms should be relatively easy to calculate, using average pay rates.

### 6.2.2 Cost savings

Reduced costs should be easy to calculate from the firm's financial control systems. The raw figures should be corrected for volume and price changes in a similar way to that described above. Again, the ability to compare the savings made in a number of similar work groups will give much valuable information.

### 6.3 VOLUME MEASURES

There remains the question of what volume measures should be used to monitor individual work groups. In many cases this will be fairly straightforward, depending on the work of the group.

However, when the group has a number of outputs, or no obvious single measure, the position is more difficult. This is often the case with clerical groups. When there is a choice of measures one should be chosen that most directly relates to the function that is being automated.

It should be realised that once a group of workers knows that they are being monitored they will usually work to improve the measure, whatever it is. Care must therefore be taken to chose a measure which does reflect the desired output. For example, a telephone sales office might be monitored on call handling times (lower is good) or number of calls handled (higher is good). But, whilst these objectives are certainly important, if they are reached at a cost of curtness, or of releasing the call before a real attempt to add value has been made, the effects will be counterproductive. In this case a more useful measure would probably involve value of orders taken per person per day. Note that this measure would give a systematic improvement at least equal to the inflation rate without any improvement in productivity.

It must again be emphasised that the decision about what volume measures should be used must be made at the earliest stages of the system design and planning.

## 6.4   QUALITY OF SERVICE IMPROVEMENTS

Much of what has already been said also applies to monitoring quality of service benefits. The measures must be chosen as part of the original system design, and allowance must be made for changes in quality attributable to other factors such as the learning curve.

Whilst internal measures of quality are never as reliable or truthful as external measures (asking the customers "how was it for you?") they are quite adequate for this purpose. Any bias is unlikely to change significantly in the period under review.

It is probably not necessary to value the improvement in quality of service, or in customer perception. The original investment appraisal decision was to spend a certain amount of money in order to obtain certain benefits. The decision implies that the benefits detailed are worth the expense to the firm. Therefore, the object of the exercise is to ensure that those benefits are achieved, not to second guess the capital approvals committee by attempting to value them against the system cost.

However, if a value is required there are two different approaches:

 −   The first is to calculate how much it would have cost the firm to achieve the improvement without the system. For example, quality of service can usually be improved by employing more staff, so that they have more time to spend with a customer, or are free to attend to a fault immediately it is reported. This sort of calculation is generally fairly easy in a service company which has been operating for more than a couple of years.

However, the accuracy of the estimate is often viewed with some, understandable, scepticism by senior mangers who suspect the operational managers of using the exercise to seek an increase in resource instead of thinking through deficiencies in their own management.

In addition, the approach can fall to the argument that "if the improvement cost that much we would never contemplate doing it". In other words the estimate produced is so high that there was no realistic possibility that the firm would have spent so much money, and therefore the benefit is not really worth that much in "real life".

—   The second approach is to estimate what value the improvement has to the firm, usually in terms of increased business or added premium. A firm which offers a better service should be able to charge a higher price and retain customers.

This is an obvious benefit to set against the cost of the change, but it is not usually an easy one to monitor. The level of business will be affected by a large number of factors, many of them outside the firm's control.

But if the firm is large, and the implementation or change is phased in the different areas, the effect of the change can be separated from the environmental changes. This is another benefit of measuring the effect of the change in as small work groups as possible.

## 6.5   CUSTOMER PERCEPTION AND INTERNAL BENEFITS

These were referred to as intangible benefits. There are a number of definitions of intangible benefits. Essentially, these are the effects of a new system which either cannot be directly measured, cannot be valued or cannot be directly related to the change. Perhaps more formally, intangible benefits are those which do not readily translate into money values, but which nonetheless clearly have significant value to the firm.

They are thus more difficult to monitor or control. It is also difficult to draw general conclusions about effects which may vary from changes in workers' morale to a perception amongst the general public or even from an internal point of view, the quality of decisions taken. Possibly the most that can be said is that they often involve changing attitudes.

There are techniques to assign monetary values to such benefits, but these are not generally adopted in industry. In any event, it would be difficult to write them to the asset register or balance sheet, except maybe as goodwill.

The techniques used fall into three main classes: how much it would cost to achieve the benefit in some other way, how much additional business or price premium the benefit achieves, or by establishing a subjective value.

The first two techniques are essentially the same as those described in the discussion about quality of service. It is worth commenting that many firms add a considerable price premium simply on the basis of their higher quality image. The price premium of a heavily advertised brand of coffee increased from 5% to 25% over the last couple of years of the eighties, purely as the result of a highly successful advertising campaign which associated it with luxury and a desirable life style; the actual product was not changed at all.

The third class of techniques rely on averaging out a number of subjective views, answers to the question "how much would you pay for this?" The actual techniques used are a little more sophisticated than the bald description above, generally involving a style of questioning resembling a binary chop.

For example:

"Would you pay £10 for this car?"          Yes

"Would you pay £10,000 for the same car?"   No

The value is thus somewhere between £10 and £10,000 and further questioning will narrow the gap. Obviously such a brief description cannot do justice to the technique.

Subjective techniques such as the above are often viewed with disdain in industry. However, most allocations of value involve an element of subjectivity; even the hallowed and audited company accounts.

However, firms do frequently spend money to achieve intangible benefits. Most public relations or advertising falls into this category. The fact that it is difficult to value the benefit does not mean that the effect cannot be measured. The effects of advertising is usually monitored, often by using a control area of the country. Many firms do conduct regular surveys of customers' perceptions of the product or the firm itself. Similarly workers' attitudes can be monitored.

It may be difficult to sort out the underlying systematic change, eliminate the effects of noise in the environment, or to relate changes with the system, but the only way forward in these cases is to study the trends over some years and look for step changes. Internal debate within the firm sparked off by a study can be very useful. It may also be helpful to study other, non IT decisions, the firm has made to gain an intangible benefit and consider how the firm has justified those decisions; that is, consider the values implicit in those decisions.

As with most benefit analysis, all this can only be carried out with any degree of success if the process starts well before the change. Many firms do nowadays conduct regular surveys of customer and staff attitudes. A history of such surveys is essential if any meaningful conclusions are to be possible.

## 6.6 UNEXPECTED BENEFITS

Many systems give rise to improvements which were not intended or anticipated. These can be quite difficult to identify and measure. Many systems also lead to dis-benefits which were not intended but we can normally rely on the line managers to complain about these. Not so much fuss may be made about unexpected benefits.

The best way of discovering such happy and unexpected occurrences is to spend time talking to staff using the system. As the benefit was not intended it is unlikely that there are any meaningful measures which will enable the effect to be monitored or accurately valued. But it should be documented as fully as possible. If it is completely unexpected it is likely to have only occurred to a few of the groups using the system and the idea will need exporting to other groups.

### 6.6.1 Analysis of results

Having measured the benefits of an IT implementation, the next step is to analyse these measures and interpret their meanings.

Three basic questions need to be answered:

- Were the system objectives met? If not, why not?
- What can be done to improve the system performance?
- What lessons were learnt for next time?

The system objectives were those set out in the original capital approval; or as subsequently modified. Reasons for not achieving all the objectives are clearly important for question three.

Question two should be addressed whether or not the stated objectives were met. There is much to be learnt from the way the system is being used in practice, unexpected benefits may be discovered, new modifications to the system suggested.

"The past is another land, they do things differently there." Even if the system has gone in exactly as planned it is unlikely that it is now the perfect solution it appeared to be when the original design specification was drawn up. In the time since then, both the IT view of the world, and the core business itself, will have changed. Once the system is in and running, and achieving the original design benefits, numbers of improvements will be suggested. These suggestions need justifying in the usual way. How much will they cost? What benefits will they bring? How will we measure those benefits? A mechanism is needed to control and vet these suggestions, and apply a reasonableness test to the claims.

Learning the lessons is clearly important for the long term health of the firm. Some firms produce a list of "Lessons Learnt" which are passed on to subsequent implementation teams. It may be considered doubtful whether anyone takes much notice of these pearls of wisdom. Most firms have found that lessons learnt are only absorbed and used if they are built into the organisation. The simplest way of achieving this seems to be to use the same group, with substantially the same people, for subsequent implementations or changes. This is another reason for setting up a benefits monitoring group.

### 6.6.2   Using the results

Most large implementations will affect a number of work groups. It was stated above that these groups should be monitored separately. The principal reason for this advice is that the most useful information about underlying trends, about potential benefits and dis-benefits and about unexpected benefits comes from an analysis of the different results from the different groups.

Figures 6.1 to 6.6 show the numeric results from the implementation of a major new system in a large UK firm during the late 1980s, and Figures 6.7 to 6.13 show the graphical representations of the same results. The system affected a number of different functions in each of about two dozen geographically diverse offices, and implementation was phased over a couple of years. For this firm, the systematic productivity improvement varies between five and eight percent per annum in the different functions. There are few significant seasonal variations.

A large number of measures were taken every six months. The examples reproduced here only relate to productivity but the system was intended to improve many aspects of the firm's business, including quality of service, customer perception, cash flow, staff morale as well as productivity. Relevant measures were collected for a period of years enabling the firm to produce a complete time series from which scatter diagrams were produced. The data set in the diagrams relates to about three months after the last local office implementation.

Figure 6.7 relates to a telephone sales function. The calculated productivity change is plotted against number of months since implementation. The solid line represents the systematic productivity change. This is an alternative, graphical, way of taking into account the systematic change. In effect, the line

| | District One | | | | District Two | | | | |
| --- | --- | --- | --- | --- | --- | --- | --- | --- | --- |
| | North | South | West | Total | Central | South | North | City | Total |
| **General Info** | | | | | | | | | |
| Conversion Date | 25-10-88 | 1-4-89 | 1-4-89 | | 26-11-88 | 2-1-89 | 2-3-89 | 18-5-89 | |
| Elapsed Months | | | | | | | | | |
| At 31-3-89 | 5 | 0 | 0 | 0 | 4 | 3 | 2 | -2 | -2 |
| At 30-9-89 | 11 | 6 | 6 | 6 | 10 | 9 | 8 | 4 | 4 |
| At 31-3-90 | 17 | 12 | 12 | 12 | 16 | 15 | 14 | 10 | 10 |
| **New Installations** | | | | | | | | | |
| Month end 31-3-88 | 3598 | 2407 | 1856 | 7861 | 3345 | 2399 | 2211 | 3912 | 11867 |
| Month End 30-9-88 | 3467 | 2591 | 2134 | 8192 | 3321 | 2446 | 2267 | 3945 | 11979 |
| Month End 31-3-89 | 3441 | 2564 | 2113 | 8118 | 3361 | 2366 | 2309 | 3876 | 11912 |
| Month End 30-9-89 | 3367 | 2544 | 2235 | 8146 | 3278 | 2310 | 2388 | 3812 | 11788 |
| Month End 31-3-90 | 3215 | 2789 | 2108 | 8112 | 3308 | 2267 | 2467 | 3756 | 11798 |
| **Installed Base** | | | | | | | | | |
| At 31-3-88 | 255876 | 199639 | 150876 | 606391 | 188021 | 155612 | 150412 | 201557 | 695602 |
| At 30-9-88 | 275234 | 214552 | 158660 | 648446 | 205883 | 167331 | 161278 | 220944 | 755436 |
| At 31-3-89 | 294094 | 229876 | 169554 | 693524 | 222583 | 178297 | 170237 | 241556 | 812673 |
| At 30-9-89 | 315661 | 245124 | 178996 | 739781 | 240612 | 191458 | 180567 | 262725 | 875362 |
| At 31-3-90 | 332690 | 260665 | 189001 | 782356 | 255387 | 201256 | 191004 | 283245 | 930892 |
| **% Bill Defaults** | | | | | | | | | |
| At 31-3-88 | 0.047 | 0.044 | 0.041 | | 0.045 | 0.041 | 0.041 | 0.051 | |
| At 30-9-88 | 0.047 | 0.045 | 0.041 | | 0.046 | 0.041 | 0.042 | 0.054 | |
| At 31-3-89 | 0.049 | 0.046 | 0.041 | | 0.045 | 0.041 | 0.042 | 0.055 | |
| At 30-9-89 | 0.048 | 0.047 | 0.040 | | 0.044 | 0.040 | 0.041 | 0.056 | |
| At 31-3-90 | 0.050 | 0.049 | 0.041 | | 0.045 | 0.040 | 0.041 | 0.055 | |

Figure 6.1    System implementation results – general information

| Numbers of Staff | District One | | | | Central | District Two | | | |
| --- | --- | --- | --- | --- | --- | --- | --- | --- | --- |
| | North | South | West | Total | Central | South | North | City | Total |
| **Tele Sales** | | | | | | | | | |
| At 31-3-88 | 60 | 42 | 34 | 136 | 58 | 49 | 47 | 65 | 219 |
| At 30-9-88 | 75 | 41 | 34 | 150 | 65 | 48 | 45 | 63 | 221 |
| At 31-3-89 | 65 | 53 | 41 | 159 | 57 | 52 | 57 | 68 | 234 |
| At 30-9-89 | 59 | 47 | 33 | 139 | 55 | 49 | 48 | 62 | 214 |
| At 31-3-90 | 55 | 41 | 31 | 127 | 56 | 47 | 44 | 57 | 204 |
| **Sales Backup** | | | | | | | | | |
| At 31-3-88 | 12 | 8 | 8 | 28 | 11 | 8 | 9 | 22 | 50 |
| At 30-9-88 | 23 | 8 | 8 | 39 | 18 | 12 | 12 | 25 | 67 |
| At 31-3-89 | 21 | 12 | 12 | 45 | 12 | 13 | 16 | 23 | 64 |
| At 30-9-89 | 20 | 8 | 7 | 35 | 11 | 10 | 11 | 18 | 50 |
| At 31-3-90 | 18 | 6 | 5 | 29 | 10 | 8 | 7 | 17 | 42 |
| **Sales Force** | | | | | | | | | |
| At 31-3-88 | 15 | 11 | 8 | 34 | 14 | 11 | 11 | 24 | 60 |
| At 30-9-88 | 15 | 11 | 8 | 34 | 14 | 11 | 11 | 24 | 60 |
| At 31-3-89 | 14 | 11 | 8 | 33 | 13 | 11 | 11 | 25 | 60 |
| At 30-9-89 | 15 | 10 | 9 | 34 | 14 | 11 | 10 | 25 | 60 |
| At 31-3-90 | 15 | 10 | 8 | 33 | 14 | 12 | 11 | 25 | 62 |
| **TOTAL SALES** | | | | | | | | | |
| At 31-3-88 | 87 | 61 | 50 | 198 | 83 | 68 | 67 | 111 | 329 |
| At 30-9-88 | 113 | 60 | 50 | 223 | 97 | 71 | 68 | 112 | 348 |
| At 31-3-89 | 100 | 76 | 61 | 237 | 82 | 76 | 84 | 116 | 358 |
| At 30-9-89 | 94 | 65 | 49 | 208 | 80 | 70 | 69 | 105 | 324 |
| At 31-3-90 | 88 | 57 | 44 | 189 | 80 | 67 | 62 | 99 | 308 |
| **Installation Staff** | | | | | | | | | |
| At 31-3-88 | 70 | 52 | 39 | 161 | 68 | 44 | 43 | 87 | 242 |
| At 30-9-88 | 71 | 51 | 39 | 161 | 68 | 45 | 42 | 88 | 243 |
| At 31-3-89 | 69 | 52 | 39 | 160 | 67 | 45 | 41 | 88 | 241 |
| At 30-9-89 | 70 | 53 | 39 | 162 | 68 | 45 | 41 | 88 | 242 |
| At 31-3-90 | 69 | 52 | 38 | 159 | 68 | 45 | 42 | 89 | 244 |

Figure 6.2    System implementation results – staff numbers

| BILLING | | | | | | | | | |
|---|---|---|---|---|---|---|---|---|---|
| **Customer Query Staff** | | | | | | | | | |
| At 31-3-88 | 44 | 34 | 28 | 106 | 34 | 31 | 32 | 41 | 138 |
| At 30-9-88 | 56 | 33 | 27 | 116 | 46 | 30 | 31 | 49 | 156 |
| At 31-3-89 | 48 | 41 | 34 | 123 | 38 | 44 | 38 | 43 | 163 |
| At 30-9-89 | 40 | 33 | 29 | 102 | 38 | 37 | 32 | 42 | 149 |
| At 31-3-90 | 35 | 28 | 24 | 87 | 37 | 32 | 31 | 40 | 140 |
| **Invoicing Staff** | | | | | | | | | |
| At 31-3-88 | 12 | 10 | 9 | 31 | 11 | 10 | 10 | 18 | 49 |
| At 30-9-88 | 22 | 9 | 8 | 39 | 16 | 11 | 12 | 24 | 63 |
| At 31-3-89 | 18 | 18 | 15 | 51 | 14 | 15 | 14 | 28 | 71 |
| At 30-9-89 | 16 | 12 | 11 | 39 | 11 | 13 | 11 | 22 | 57 |
| At 31-3-90 | 10 | 11 | 9 | 30 | 13 | 13 | 11 | 19 | 56 |
| **Debt Chasing** | | | | | | | | | |
| At 31-3-88 | 5 | 3 | 3 | 11 | 3 | 3 | 4 | 12 | 22 |
| At 30-9-88 | 6 | 3 | 3 | 12 | 3 | 4 | 4 | 11 | 22 |
| At 31-3-89 | 4 | 3 | 3 | 10 | 3 | 3 | 4 | 11 | 21 |
| At 30-9-89 | 5 | 3 | 3 | 11 | 3 | 3 | 4 | 11 | 21 |
| At 31-3-90 | 5 | 3 | 3 | 11 | 3 | 3 | 5 | 12 | 23 |
| **TOTAL BILLING** | | | | | | | | | |
| At 31-3-88 | 61 | 47 | 40 | 148 | 48 | 44 | 46 | 71 | 209 |
| At 30-9-88 | 84 | 45 | 38 | 167 | 65 | 45 | 47 | 84 | 241 |
| At 31-3-89 | 70 | 62 | 52 | 184 | 55 | 62 | 56 | 82 | 255 |
| At 30-9-89 | 61 | 48 | 43 | 152 | 52 | 53 | 47 | 75 | 227 |
| At 31-3-90 | 50 | 42 | 36 | 128 | 53 | 48 | 47 | 71 | 219 |
| **TOTAL STAFF** | | | | | | | | | |
| At 31-3-88 | 218 | 160 | 129 | 507 | 199 | 156 | 156 | 269 | 780 |
| At 30-9-88 | 268 | 156 | 127 | 551 | 230 | 161 | 157 | 284 | 832 |
| At 31-3-89 | 239 | 190 | 152 | 581 | 204 | 183 | 181 | 286 | 854 |
| At 30-9-89 | 225 | 166 | 131 | 522 | 200 | 168 | 157 | 268 | 793 |
| At 31-3-90 | 207 | 151 | 118 | 476 | 201 | 160 | 151 | 259 | 771 |

**Figure 6.3    System implementation results – staff numbers**

| RATIOS | District One | | | | Central | District Two | | City | Total |
|---|---|---|---|---|---|---|---|---|---|
| | North | South | West | Total | | South | North | | |
| **Instals/tele staff** | | | | | | | | | |
| At 31-3-88 | 60 | 57 | 55 | 58 | 58 | 49 | 47 | 60 | 54 |
| At 30-9-88 | 46 | 63 | 63 | 55 | 51 | 51 | 50 | 63 | 54 |
| At 31-3-89 | 53 | 48 | 52 | 51 | 59 | 46 | 41 | 57 | 51 |
| At 30-9-89 | 57 | 54 | 68 | 59 | 60 | 47 | 50 | 61 | 55 |
| At 31-3-90 | 58 | 68 | 68 | 64 | 59 | 48 | 56 | 66 | 58 |
| **Instals/Sales backup** | | | | | | | | | |
| At 31-3-88 | 300 | 301 | 232 | 281 | 304 | 300 | 246 | 178 | 237 |
| At 30-9-88 | 151 | 324 | 267 | 210 | 185 | 204 | 189 | 158 | 179 |
| At 31-3-89 | 164 | 214 | 176 | 180 | 280 | 182 | 144 | 169 | 186 |
| At 30-9-89 | 168 | 318 | 319 | 233 | 298 | 231 | 217 | 212 | 236 |
| At 31-3-90 | 179 | 465 | 422 | 280 | 331 | 283 | 352 | 221 | 281 |
| **Instals/Salesman** | | | | | | | | | |
| At 31-3-88 | 240 | 219 | 232 | 231 | 239 | 218 | 201 | 163 | 198 |
| At 30-9-88 | 231 | 236 | 267 | 241 | 237 | 222 | 206 | 164 | 200 |
| At 31-3-89 | 246 | 233 | 264 | 246 | 259 | 215 | 210 | 155 | 199 |
| At 30-9-89 | 224 | 254 | 248 | 240 | 234 | 210 | 239 | 152 | 196 |
| At 31-3-90 | 214 | 279 | 264 | 246 | 236 | 189 | 224 | 150 | 190 |
| **Instals/Total Sales** | | | | | | | | | |
| At 31-3-88 | 41 | 39 | 37 | 40 | 40 | 35 | 33 | 35 | 36 |
| At 30-9-88 | 31 | 43 | 43 | 37 | 34 | 34 | 33 | 35 | 34 |
| At 31-3-89 | 34 | 34 | 35 | 34 | 41 | 31 | 27 | 33 | 33 |
| At 30-9-89 | 36 | 39 | 46 | 39 | 41 | 33 | 35 | 36 | 36 |
| At 31-3-90 | 37 | 49 | 48 | 43 | 41 | 34 | 40 | 38 | 38 |
| **Instals/Installer** | | | | | | | | | |
| At 31-3-88 | 51 | 46 | 48 | 49 | 49 | 55 | 51 | 45 | 49 |
| At 30-9-88 | 49 | 51 | 55 | 51 | 49 | 54 | 54 | 45 | 49 |
| At 31-3-89 | 50 | 49 | 54 | 51 | 50 | 53 | 56 | 44 | 49 |
| At 30-9-89 | 48 | 48 | 57 | 50 | 48 | 51 | 58 | 43 | 49 |
| At 31-3-90 | 47 | 54 | 55 | 51 | 49 | 50 | 59 | 42 | 48 |

Figure 6.4 System implementation results – ratios (1)

| BILLING | | | | | | | | | |
|---|---|---|---|---|---|---|---|---|---|
| Bills/Query Staff | | | | | | | | | |
| At 31-3-88 | 5815 | 5872 | 5388 | 5721 | 5530 | 5020 | 4700 | 4916 | 5041 |
| At 30-9-88 | 4915 | 6502 | 5876 | 5590 | 4476 | 5578 | 5203 | 4509 | 4843 |
| At 31-3-89 | 6127 | 5607 | 4987 | 5638 | 5857 | 4052 | 4480 | 5618 | 4986 |
| At 30-9-89 | 7892 | 7428 | 6172 | 7253 | 6332 | 5175 | 5643 | 6255 | 5875 |
| At 31-3-90 | 9505 | 9309 | 7875 | 8993 | 6902 | 6289 | 6161 | 7081 | 6649 |
| Bills/Invoice Staff | | | | | | | | | |
| At 31-3-88 | 21323 | 19964 | 16764 | 19561 | 17093 | 15561 | 15041 | 11198 | 14196 |
| At 30-9-88 | 12511 | 23839 | 19833 | 16627 | 12868 | 15212 | 13440 | 9206 | 11991 |
| At 31-3-89 | 16339 | 12771 | 11304 | 13599 | 15899 | 11886 | 12160 | 8627 | 11446 |
| At 30-9-89 | 19729 | 20427 | 16272 | 18969 | 21874 | 14728 | 16415 | 11942 | 15357 |
| At 31-3-90 | 33269 | 23697 | 21000 | 26079 | 19645 | 15481 | 17364 | 14908 | 16623 |
| Default/debt chasers | | | | | | | | | |
| At 31-3-88 | 2405 | 2928 | 2062 | 2454 | 2820 | 2127 | 1542 | 857 | 955 |
| At 30-9-88 | 2156 | 3218 | 2168 | 2425 | 3157 | 1715 | 1693 | 1085 | 4135 |
| At 31-3-89 | 3603 | 3525 | 2317 | 3194 | 3339 | 2437 | 1787 | 1208 | 6255 |
| At 30-9-89 | 3030 | 3840 | 2387 | 3076 | 3529 | 2553 | 1851 | 1338 | 1221 |
| At 31-3-90 | 3327 | 4258 | 2583 | 3378 | 3831 | 2683 | 1566 | 1298 | 1190 |
| Bills/Billing Staff | | | | | | | | | |
| At 31-3-88 | 4195 | 4248 | 3772 | 4097 | 3917 | 3537 | 3270 | 2839 | 3328 |
| At 30-9-88 | 3277 | 4768 | 4175 | 3883 | 3167 | 3718 | 3431 | 2630 | 3135 |
| At 31-3-89 | 4201 | 3708 | 3261 | 3769 | 4047 | 2876 | 3040 | 2946 | 3187 |
| At 30-9-89 | 5175 | 5107 | 4163 | 4867 | 4627 | 3612 | 3842 | 3503 | 3856 |
| At 31-3-90 | 6654 | 6206 | 5250 | 6112 | 4819 | 4193 | 4064 | 3989 | 4251 |
| Customers/Staff | | | | | | | | | |
| At 31-3-88 | 1174 | 1248 | 1170 | 1196 | 945 | 998 | 964 | 749 | 892 |
| At 30-9-88 | 1027 | 1375 | 1249 | 1177 | 895 | 1039 | 1027 | 778 | 908 |
| At 31-3-89 | 1231 | 1210 | 1115 | 1194 | 1091 | 974 | 941 | 845 | 952 |
| At 30-9-89 | 1403 | 1477 | 1366 | 1417 | 1203 | 1140 | 1150 | 980 | 1104 |
| At 31-3-90 | 1607 | 1726 | 1602 | 1644 | 1271 | 1258 | 1265 | 1094 | 1207 |

Figure 6.5    System implementation results – ratios (2)

| % IMPROVEMENTS | District One | | | | District Two | | | | |
|---|---|---|---|---|---|---|---|---|---|
| | North | South | West | Total | Central | South | North | City | Total |
| **Tele Sales** | | | | | | | | | |
| At 31-3-89 | -13% | N/A | N/A | N/A | 2% | -7% | N/A | N/A | N/A |
| At 30-9-89 | -5% | -6% | 23% | 1% | 3% | -4% | 6% | 2% | 2% |
| At 31-3-90 | -2% | 18% | 22% | 10% | 2% | -1% | 18% | 8% | 6% |
| **Total Sales** | | | | | | | | | |
| At 31-3-89 | -19% | N/A | N/A | N/A | 2% | -13% | N/A | N/A | N/A |
| At 30-9-89 | -14% | -1% | 22% | -1% | 2% | -7% | 5% | 3% | 1% |
| At 31-3-90 | -12% | 22% | 26% | 8% | 3% | -4% | 19% | 7% | 6% |
| **Installers** | | | | | | | | | |
| At 31-3-89 | -3% | N/A | N/A | N/A | 2% | -4% | N/A | N/A | N/A |
| At 30-9-89 | -6% | 4% | 20% | 3% | -2% | -6% | 13% | -4% | -1% |
| At 31-3-90 | -9% | 16% | 16% | 4% | -1% | -8% | 14% | -6% | -1% |
| **Bill Query Staff** | | | | | | | | | |
| At 31-3-89 | 6% | N/A | N/A | N/A | 7% | -27% | N/A | N/A | N/A |
| At 30-9-89 | 32% | 26% | 15% | 26% | 16% | 4% | 20% | 28% | 18% |
| At 31-3-90 | 50% | 48% | 40% | 47% | 27% | 26% | 30% | 43% | 32% |
| **Invoice Staff** | | | | | | | | | |
| At 31-3-89 | -35% | N/A | N/A | N/A | -9% | -35% | N/A | N/A | N/A |
| At 30-9-89 | -10% | 3% | -4% | -4% | 28% | -7% | 10% | 8% | 10% |
| At 31-3-90 | 47% | 21% | 25% | 32% | 18% | -1% | 17% | 35% | 20% |
| **All Billing Staff** | | | | | | | | | |
| At 31-3-89 | 15% | N/A | N/A | N/A | 15% | 33% | N/A | N/A | N/A |
| At 30-9-89 | -0% | 3% | 8% | 3% | 10% | 21% | 3% | 7% | 10% |
| At 31-3-90 | -29% | -16% | -14% | -20% | 13% | 11% | 3% | 0% | 6% |
| **Customers/Staff** | | | | | | | | | |
| At 31-3-89 | 5% | N/A | N/A | N/A | 16% | -3% | N/A | N/A | N/A |
| At 30-9-89 | 20% | 19% | 17% | 19% | 27% | 15% | 19% | 31% | 24% |
| At 31-3-90 | 35% | 36% | 34% | 35% | 35% | 27% | 30% | 44% | 35% |

**Figure 6.6    System implementation results – % improvements**

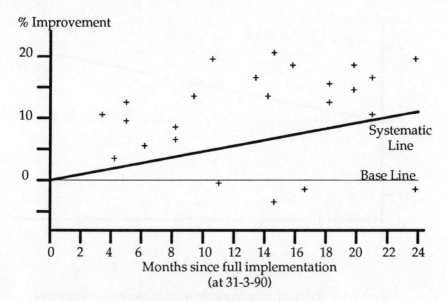

**Figure 6.7    Productivity improvement in the telephone sales
function after full implementation**

shows the improvement that the firm could have expected if it had not
implemented the system. Offices below the systematic line are showing an
effective productivity reduction as a result of the new system. The systematic
line is referred to in some organisations as the learning curve.

The function concerned had previously been mainly paper based and the
conversion to a completely screen based system was not without its difficulties.
However, once the initial difficulties were overcome quite large savings were
made. Thus, the overall trend was a dip below the systematic line for the first six
months or so, followed by a rapid improvement. The original dip is not well
represented in Figure 6.7 because the firm learnt the lessons from the earlier
implementations and managed to guide later offices more quickly through the
early problems. Figure 6.8 shows the same function, but after only eight offices
had converted (ie it is data from eighteen months earlier).

Figure 6.7 also shows other characteristics which are typical of such situations. A few offices stand out as performing particularly well, and a few are
clearly in trouble. Some of the very good results will be due to incorrect
information, local staff misunderstanding the data collection exercise, sharp
pencils and other distortions. But they may be due to a particularly good local
team and may point to some of the unexpected benefits mentioned above.

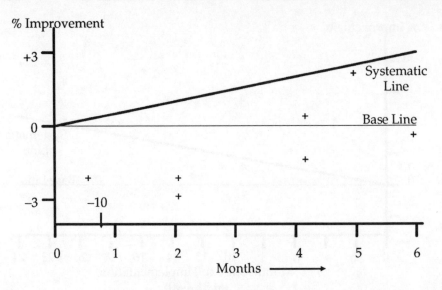

**Figure 6.8     Productivity improvement in the telephone sales
function after partial implementation**

In any event, investigation of the reasons is necessary. To undertake these investigations the firm used experienced operational managers, who had been well trained in the new system. In such circumstances by far and away the best source of information is direct contact with the staff in the functional office.

Some of the bad results might also be due to incorrect data, but this is less likely. The publication of scatter diagrams such as these leads to intense competitive pressure amongst the managers concerned and, especially after the first issue, few managers were careless enough to make mistakes which showed their office in a worse light than strictly necessary.

In practice, the offices showing bad results were genuinely in trouble. To help these offices improve, their staff were encouraged to make exchange visits with staff from paired offices which were performing well. The pairing was generally arranged by the central monitoring team.

Figure 6.9 shows similar information from the invoicing function. These staff had been used to sophisticated computer systems for some time and the introduction of another one made little difference to their work or performance. However, a couple of local offices found ways of using the new system to reorganise their work groups and give a large improvement. These show quite clearly in Figure 6.9. The firm was still investigating the possibility of implementing these ideas in all offices when this data was collected.

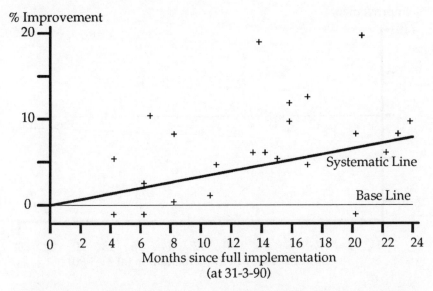

**Figure 6.9    Productivity improvement in the invoicing function**

The data was also used to calculate an overall improvement, across all functions, for each office (not reproduced here). However, not all lunches are free. The system had some drawbacks, and Figure 6.10 shows the performance in a function that was adversely affected by dis-benefits produced by the change. The reasons for this poor performance were understood and the need for extra staff had been foreseen. What was not expected was the wide variation between offices. Figures 6.11 and 6.12 show two attempts to analyse this aspect, neither very successful. Figure 6.11 analyses performance by size of local office, Figure 6.12 by the software level of the displaced old system.

The new system almost completely automated one function, staff numbers per local office fell from about a dozen to one or two. However, over the period, the volume of work in this function increased and the result was calculated, with productivity savings of over 100%. Figure 6.13 shows the results. This was quite difficult to explain to some managers. But the calculation outlined above is sensitive to changes in volume, deliberately so. Thus, a group which experiences a reduced volume can show a negative productivity change even though the number of staff has reduced; also difficult for some managers to accept.

The publication of these series of scatter diagrams to the senior managers in the firm, including the local office managers, had a pronounced effect.

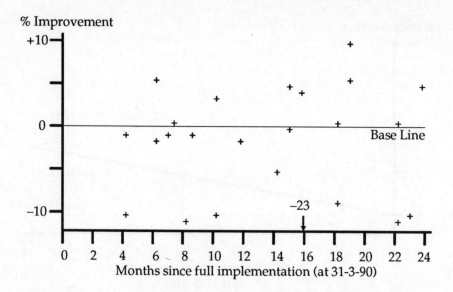

**Figure 6.10    Productivity change in a function which suffered from dis-benefits due to the new system**

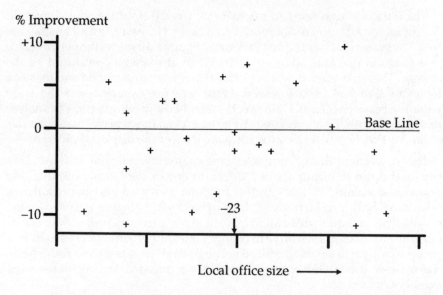

**Figure 6.11    Analysis of variations between offices by size**

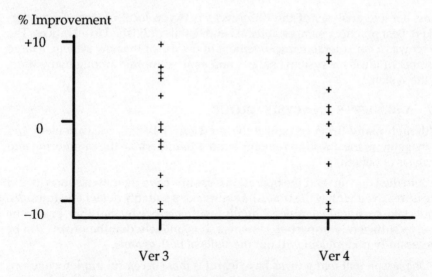

**Figure 6.12    Analysis of variations between offices by software level of the displaced system**

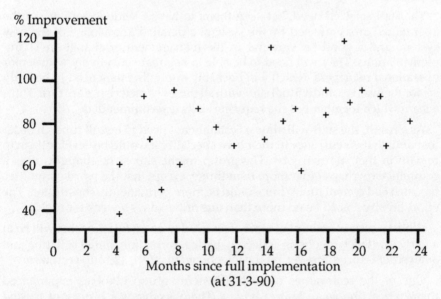

**Figure 6.13    Productivity improvements in a function almost totally automated by the new system**

Considerable analysis of the differences between local offices was undertaken. Best practices were established and details published to all offices. The
effect was a considerable improvement in the use of the new system, a large
number of ideas for system changes and a raised morale among many users
of the system.

## 6.7   A BENEFITS ANALYSIS GROUP

Although many firms recognise the need for IT benefit measurement and
management, the question remains: who is to undertake the monitoring and
analysis of benefits?

Both the IT group and the operational groups have their own concerns and
pressures. Neither has the time, the ability nor a suitably detached attitude to
undertake such analysis alone. Equally, neither is seen by the other, or anyone
else, as sufficiently impartial. However, it is unlikely that the project can be
successfully undertaken without the skills of both groups.

One lesson that many firms have learnt is that successful implementations
are a result of a team approach combining the best from the IT group and the
operational group. This approach is also recommended for a benefits analysis
and monitoring group.

The staff selected need, between them, to have a wide experience of the
operational areas affected by the system, a detailed knowledge of the new
system, and a good background in the management of change or IT implementations. They will need to be able to negotiate effectively with senior
operational managers, which will probably imply that they need to be fairly
senior themselves. Individual staff with all these characteristics are rare. Thus,
a team which together has the requisite skills is recommended.

As a result, the staff will almost certainly not need to be full time. In order
to maintain their currency in their own speciality it would be best for them to
remain in their normal jobs. The group might almost be thought of as a
committee (perhaps of no more than three), except that the word committee
has such bad connotations, but should be more permanently constituted. The
effort involved need be no more than one or two days a week for each.

Whilst a certain amount of work does need to go on full time this will be at
a fairly low level, involving collecting basic information, initial collating and
analysis of returns, answering the telephone. In effect, a group secretary.

One of the real values of such a benefits group involves experienced
managers acting as an honest broker. The objective is a history of trusted
analysis showing benefits gained from past systems, leading to sensible
claims for new systems. An important additional benefit of the group, which

will more than pay its costs, is the maximising of benefits from every system. By ensuring that the firm knows just what is going right, and wrong, with any system, and knowing which groups are gaining maximum, and minimum, benefit from it, help can be directed to the right place. Further system development can be targeted sensibly. Much of this work would be done by fairly junior staff working under the guidance of the part time managers.

Different firms will find their own solutions to this question. But, whatever group or committee is set up, it will only be effective if the senior management of the firm take seriously the concept that no major change, or implementation of a computer system, is contemplated without a statement of the objectives for the change. The achievement of these objectives needs to be monitored, managed and maximised.

## 6.8 SUMMARY

In order to control and eventually manage the effect of IT investment, the following steps should be taken:

1. Start the preparation for IT benefit measurement as early as possible. Where possible, measure the performance of the department before the introduction of the system.

2. Agree the targets which the new system is expected to achieve.

3. Establish the measures which will be used to determine if these targets are being achieved.

4. Research how the measure or metric is likely to behave. Will it be cyclical? What other factors other than the new system are likely to affect the chosen measure?

5. The history the firm has in measuring IT benefits. Are there any historical trends which may be useful? What mistakes have been made before and what may be learnt from them?

6. Using the chosen targets and metrics, begin measurement. Ensure that a reasonable time period has elapsed, ie 3 to 6 months, before measurement begins.

7. Select small groups, wherever possible, to measure. Small groups are preferable because:

   a) they may be compared

   b) they are relatively resilient to organisational changes

   c) serendipitous benefits are easier to observe in smaller groups than in larger groups.

8.  Consolidate the individual group results and present them where appropriate graphically.

9.  Publish these results to all levels of management and operatives. Discuss the results with a wide range of individuals with a view to discovering causes for variation and reasons for serendipitous benefits.

10. Encourage weaker groups to copy the winners.

# 7 How to Evaluate the Success of the IT Function

## 7.1 A HOLISTIC APPROACH TO IT FUNCTION EVALUATION

This chapter addresses a holistic approach to the evaluation of the performance of the IT function.

The IT function of an organisation is involved in the development, implementation and maintenance of numerous information technologies/systems. These systems aim to meet needs at all levels within the organisation. In evaluating the success or effectiveness of the IT department it is necessary to evaluate the performance of the individual systems, and then use the aggregate of the performances on the individual systems as an overall measure of the success or effectiveness of the IT department. In organisations where there is a high degree of decentralisation of the IT function, the evaluation is not focused so much on the IT department but rather on the users of the information systems.

For the organisation's IT function to be managed successfully, management will need to have appropriate instruments whereby it can measure the effectiveness of IT within the organisation. In fact, recent surveys reveal that general management consider measurement of IT effectiveness a key issue (Silk, 1990 (b)). Unfortunately, there is little agreement on how to measure effectiveness.

The measurement problem is exacerbated by the many ways in which one can view effectiveness. For example, an IT department can be considered effective when it:

- is meeting its objectives
- operates within its budgets
- delivers on time
- is a major catalyst in directing the firm's use of IT
- ensures that the firm is using IT competitively
- its role in the organisation is clearly understood
- it is generally perceived to be an ally

141

- its internal efficiency is at least equivalent to the industry average
- it can deliver systems for no greater cost than they can be purchased in the open market
- it is perceived by top management to be value for money and users believe that IT is being deployed in a way which supports their pursuit of excellence.

There is, however, one thing on which there is agreement, which is that success is not necessarily reflected in the level of investment in information technologies.

Despite the obvious difficulty in measuring the effectiveness of the IT function, the fact that it is competing for resources with other functions, such as marketing, finance, production and so on, means it is essential that we do have credible ways not only of identifying the benefits of the IT function, both 'hard' and 'soft', but also a means of measuring them.

## 7.2   GOAL CENTRED VS SYSTEMS' RESOURCES

There are basically two general views with respect to measuring IT effectiveness. These are the goal centred view and the system resource view (Hamilton and Chervany, 1981 (a) and (b)). In the goal centred view we focus on the outcomes of the IT function. We determine the task objectives of the system and then establish the criteria for measuring whether these objectives have been achieved. In the systems' resource view we focus on the process or functional aspects of the system. In this case effectiveness is measured against such things as user job satisfaction, communication between IT staff and users, and quality of service.

Where the firm's task objectives or system resources are relatively obvious, and where intangible benefits play a relatively small role, direct physical measurements may be used to assess the effectiveness of the system. However, where complex situations are involved, simple techniques are no longer appropriate and perceptions become a critical part of the process for measuring the overall effectiveness of an information system (IS).

In this chapter some recent significant contributions to the problem of measuring the effectiveness of management information systems (MIS) are reviewed. User information satisfaction (UIS) is recognised as an important indicator (surrogate) of MIS effectiveness. It is on this approach to the measurement problem that we now concentrate, and in particular on perceptual measures of UIS. This involves incorporating user feelings, beliefs, opinions and attitudes towards IT into the evaluation procedure.

In the context of IS effectiveness, it is generally believed that if users declare themselves to be satisfied with the system then the system may be said to be effective. Clearly, such satisfaction measurement is at best an indirect and relative measure which must be used with considerable care. In some organisations users could be happy with inadequate systems. However, trends are the most important aspect.

## 7.3  TANGIBLE VS INTANGIBLE BENEFITS

Thirty or so years ago the evaluation of the IT function was relatively straightforward. At this time computers were used to automate well understood, well structured office systems, thereby increasing efficiency through cost savings. These systems were used by operational staff to perform time consuming accounting, stock control and wages tasks. Traditional cost benefit and work study methods for calculating the effectiveness of the IT function were adequate. The techniques used to perform cost benefit analysis included *cut-off period, payback period, discounted cash flow (DCF)* and *return on investment (ROI)*.

Since then, new technology, particularly the advent of the microcomputer, has resulted in information technologies having progressed from the basic cost reduction and control type applications to the provision of decision support at the strategic level (Money et al, 1988). The influence of new technologies is, therefore, increasingly being felt at top management level.

This upward penetration of new information technologies raises issues which previously did not exist. In evaluating IS effectiveness we have to consider both the MIS and the environment within which it operates. Thus, broader organisation-wide issues have to be considered, and this includes behavioural aspects. A consequence is that there is a certain 'invisibility' associated with the contributions of the information systems to the effectiveness of the organisation as a whole. This invisibility is usually expressed by reference to intangible benefits. The traditional cost benefit approaches to evaluating effectiveness are now generally regarded as inadequate, especially when a holistic view of the firm is required.

More recent approaches account for the intangible benefits which tend to be overlooked by traditional cost benefit analysis (see Chapter 5). These approaches incorporate user perceptions on a number of criteria relating to IS into an overall measure of satisfaction with the IS. These include perceptions on numerous variables related to such things as input procedures, output procedures, computer processing capabilities, speed of response, quality of service, IS staff quality, availability of training, quality of documentation, and organisational factors such as top management involvement and user participation. These issues, considered holistically, represent a framework which may be used to measure effectiveness.

## 7.4   USER INFORMATION SATISFACTION (UIS)

User satisfaction is generally considered to result from a comparison of user expectations (or needs) of the IS with the perceived performance (or capability) of the IS on a number of different facets of the IS. This is considered to be a holistic approach to systems effectiveness as it addresses the whole IS function rather than individual systems.

More specifically, overall attitude to the IS function can be considered to be influenced by the size and direction of the discrepancies (or gaps) between expectations and performance. A positive (negative) gap results when perceived performance exceeds (is below) expectation. A 'large' gap implies dissatisfaction with the IS capabilities. A 'large' positive gap can be interpreted as indicating that IS resources are being wasted, whereas a 'large' negative gap indicates a need for improved performance.

A variant to the above approach is to use the correlation between expectations and performance scores as a measure of 'fit'. The correlations provide a means for assessing the overall effectiveness of the IS function, where high positive correlations can be taken to imply 'consensus' of views.

Of the many published papers on UIS two will be discussed in more detail below, namely, the Miller and Doyle (1987), and the Kim (1990) papers. Both these studies propose conceptual models to explain UIS, thereby adding credence to the instruments developed from them. These models have their roots in the theory of organisational and consumer behaviour. This is easy to comprehend if one accepts that the IS function impacts on the whole organisation and is aimed at satisfying the user (ie customer) who can be both internal as well as external to the organisation.

## 7.5   A GAP APPROACH TO MEASUREMENT

### 7.5.1   The Kim model

A feature of Kim's model is that UIS is considered to be influenced not only by post implementation experience with the IS but also by pre-implementation expectations of the IS. The latter is captured through the user's initial expectations of the IS.

In this approach, UIS is measured by the discrepancy between the user's perception score of the IS performance and the user's expectation score of the IS. Further, the model describes how UIS is influenced by the discrepancies that arise during the developmental and service delivery processes. The developmental stage comprises two sub-stages, namely, the determination of the IS requirements and the design and installation of the IS. These various stages give rise to three gaps which influence the UIS. These gaps may in turn be influenced by various organisational factors. Examples include: user participation in defining the IS requirements; top management support which may take the form of increased investment in IS, thereby influencing the gap between the design specifications and the quality of the IS installed; and the extent of user training which is likely to impact on the gap between the actual quality of the IS installed and what the user perceives the quality to be through use of the system. There may also be other organisational factors which directly impact the IS, rather than indirectly through the gaps. The Kim model is represented diagrammatically in Figure 7.1.

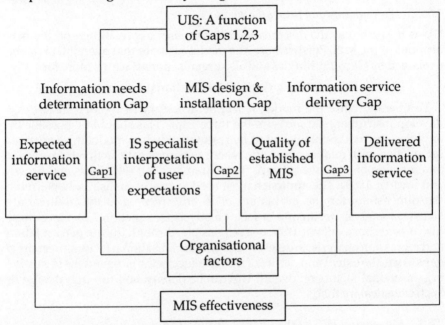

**Figure 7.1        A UIS model**

## 7.5.2   Interpreting the model

### 7.5.2.1   Interpretation of the gaps

– *Gap 1* This is the discrepancy between the users' expectations of the IS and the systems designers' interpretations of these expectations.

– *Gap 2* This is the discrepancy between the IS specialist's interpretation of the users' needs and the quality of what is actually installed for the user.

– *Gap 3* This is the discrepancy between the quality of what is actually installed and what the user experiences when interacting with the MIS.

### 7.5.2.2    Incorporation of organisation factors

The model postulates that the three gaps can be affected by organisational factors. For example, Gap 1 could be influenced in a positive way by encouraging user participation in the design stage. This involves determining the information requirements desired from the MIS. On the other hand, top management support for MIS, exhibited through, say, the provision of enough resources, should be positively correlated with Gap 2. Finally the provision of proper training should be positively correlated with Gap 3.

### 7.5.2.3    Formulating and fitting the model

UIS is measured as the discrepancy between user expectations and the perceptions of the MIS. Furthermore, the model assumes that overall UIS can be explained by Gaps 1 through 3 and also organisational factors. More formally:

$$UIS = f(Gap1, Gap2, Gap3, Organisational Factors)$$

To operationalise the model, it will be necessary in the first instance to develop instruments to measure the three gaps. This should be possible by applying the methodologies used by researchers when modelling consumer satisfaction with quality of service, where consumer satisfaction is expressed as a function of a number of gaps (Parasuraman et al, 1985, 1988, and Brown and Swartz, 1989). The approach most used to conceptualise and determine the dimensions for the evaluation of IS effectiveness is the multivariate statistical analysis technique of factor analysis (see section 7.6). Once these instruments are available it should be possible, through the use of correlation and regression analysis, to determine which organisational factors affect these gaps. Also, the extent and nature of the influence of the gaps and the identified organisational factors on overall UIS can be determined through the use of such statistical methods.

### 7.5.3    Measuring UIS of the overall IS function

Of the many instruments proposed for measuring, through perception, user satisfaction with information systems, the one due to Miller and Doyle is described here (Miller and Doyle, 1987). It is, in spirit, similar to the conceptual model described above. The instrument has been extensively used in many different firms, in many different sectors, and the results provide convincing evidence of the instrument's reliability and validity.

### 7.5.3.1    Description of the instrument

The instrument is designed to measure the perceived effectiveness of the overall IS function and involves the use of a questionnaire. The questionnaire comprises five parts labelled Part A through Part E.

Part A consists of 34 questions which measure the extent to which certain facets of the IS are perceived to be important in ensuring the organisation's IS will be effective and successful. The attitudes are rated on a semantic differential scale of 1 – (irrelevant) to 7 – (very critical). Part B consists of four questions on the future needs for IS; Part C consists of the same 34 questions as Part A but in this case the respondent is asked to rate the 34 questions with respect to the actual performance achieved within their organisation. Again a 7-point scale is used but in this case the levels of perceived importance go from 1 – (very poor) to 7 – (excellent); Part D consists of four questions relating to the organisation's performance in developing new systems; Part E consists of four questions which capture certain demographic data. There is also a question which asks for a rating of the organisations overall IS performance on a scale of 1 – (complete failure) to 7 – (very successful).

The importance ratings in Parts A and B capture perceptions on the business needs, while the performance ratings in Parts C and D capture perceptions of the organisation's IS capabilities.

A factor analysis of the 38 performance ratings revealed that there were seven dimensions of user satisfaction underlying the responses to these 38 questions. These are:

- Functioning of existing transaction/reporting systems
- Linkage to strategic processes of the firm
- Amount and quality of user involvement
- Responsiveness to new systems needs
- Ability to respond to end user computing needs
- IS staff quality
- Reliability of services

See Appendix 5 for an abridged list of the original 38 questions. The full questionnaire is given in Miller and Doyle (1987). Also see section 7.6 for a description of the factor analysis method.

### 7.5.3.2   Interpreting the results

The mean of the performance responses to each of the 38 questions can be taken as a measure of the perceived performance on each of the 38 facets.

Overall user attitude to the IS function is measured by a composite score derived from the user performance mean ratings on the 38 questions, by calculating their mean value. This gives the user an overall assessment of the organisation's IS capabilities.

The fit between importance and performance ratings can be measured by the square of the correlations between these scales, and/or by the discrepancies (gaps) between these scales. Miller and Doyle recommend the use of correlation as the preferred measure of success of the MIS.

Importance and performance ratings are obtained from both IS specialists and users. This results in six correlation measures of fit. These are shown in Figure 7.2 (Miller, 1989).

| Measure of Fit | IS Specialist | | User | | Significance of $R^2$ Implies |
|---|---|---|---|---|---|
| | Imp | Perf | Imp | Perf | |
| 1 | X | X | | | IS staff satisfaction |
| 2 | X | | X | | Agreement on what is important for the business |
| 3 | X | | | X | IS provides capabilities that are highly rated by users |
| 4 | | X | X | | IS staff aware of organisational needs and are meeting these |
| 5 | | X | | X | Agreement on how IS is performing |
| 6 | | | X | X | User satisfaction |

Figure 7.2     Measures of fit

These correlations between the 38 items mean importance and mean performance scores provide a quick and reliable method for assessing the overall effectiveness of the IS function. High positive correlations imply a consensus of views. Firms in which the IS function is successful tend to demonstrate high squared correlations for, in particular, measures 1, 3 and 6.

Further analysis is possible. The instrument can be used to assess the IS function on each of the seven critical areas for success. Also, an analysis of responses on individual items can provide useful information. For example, a count of item non-responses can identify those items on which respondents can provide an opinion, and those for which they have difficulty in expressing an opinion. The variability in responses, as measured by the standard deviation, can also provide useful information. Should the standard deviation of both the importance and performance ratings be greater for IS specialists than users, this may imply that users are less able to discriminate in their responses to the questionnaire than the specialists. This in turn may suggest a need for education in IS. There are many other possibilities of very basic, but worthwhile, analyses of the responses to this questionnaire.

Research in this area is still in its early stages. Use of the approach described does make it possible to quickly obtain a reliable and valid assessment of the IS function and thereby identify those areas where effort is required to improve the chances of success. The questionnaire does appear to offer significant advantages over the traditional approaches of cost benefit and economic analysis.

## 7.6   FACTOR ANALYSIS

Factor analysis is a mathematical procedure which can assist the researcher in conceptualising a problem.

According to Kerlinger (1969) factor analysis is a method for determining the number and nature of the underlying dimensions (or factors) among large numbers of measures of the concept being evaluated. Factor analysis is a technique used to locate and identify fundamental properties underlying the results of tests or measurements and which cannot be measured directly (a factor is a hypothetical entity that is assumed to underlie the results of the tests). It is therefore a technique which can be used to provide a parsimonious description of a complex multi-faceted intangible concept such as UIS.

Factor analysis is a multivariate statistical technique which is available on many statistical software packages. In this book it was performed using the SPSS/PC+ software package. In using factor analysis there are traditionally four steps to be performed with the computer results which are:

1.  Consult the Kaiser-Meyer-Olkin (KMO) measure of sampling adequacy. The rule for the use of this statistic is that if the KMO is less than 0.50 there is no value in proceeding with the technique. The greater the value of the KMO the more effective the factor analysis is likely to be.

2.    Examine the eigen values. Only factors with an eigen value of greater than one are used in the analysis.

3.    Study the rotated factor matrix. Examine each factor one at a time, looking for the input variables that influence the factor, which have a loading of 0.5 or more.

4.    Attempt combining the meaning of the variables identified in 3 above into a super-variable which will explain the combined effect of these individual variables, and will become the invisible factor the analysis attempts to isolate.

### 7.6.1    A gap model applied to an office automation/network system

The effectiveness of a computer network system of a leading business school is investigated. The focus is on users of the system which include academics, secretarial and administration staff, and MBA students.

The study involved the use of a self completion questionnaire, which is shown in Figure 7.3. The questionnaire comprised four sections. The first section captured background information relating to the individual's position in the Business School, years of work/study experience, years of work experience with a PC, and finally years of work experience with a PC network. This is followed by three parts labelled A, B and C. Parts A and B use the same set of 24 questions, where these questions capture information on various facets of the system.

– Part A measures the extent to which the attributes are perceived to be important to the effectiveness of the system. Expectation was measured on a 4-point scale from 1 – irrelevant to 4 – critical.

– Part B uses the same items but now the respondent was asked to rate the performance of the Information Systems Department on a 4-point scale from 1 – very poor to 4 – excellent.

– Part C involves a general question about the individual's overall satisfaction with the computer network system.

There were 86 questionnaires available for analysis. Of these 76 were completed by the MBA students. The analysis that follows was performed on the MBA responses.

### 7.6.1.1    Basic results

A basic analysis of the expectation and performance perceptions was intially performed. Averages and standard deviations (SD) for the expectation and performance scores appear in Figure 7.4. Also in Figure 7.4, for each of the questions, are the mean perceptual gap scores, as well as their standard

# The Measurement of IS Effectiveness in a Business School Environment.

The following questionnaire has been designed to help assess the effectiveness of the computer network system used by academics, secretarial and administration staff as well as students in your business school. This is part of an academic initiative at the UK business school, Henley - The Management College, where a number of the staff are working in the area of measuring and managing IT benefits.

The questionnaire has been divided into three parts. Parts A and B use the same set of 24 questions. Part C is one open ended question.

Your answers to the questions in Part A refer to the system's attributes which you believe are important to the effectiveness of the system. Your answers to the second set of 24 questions in Part B refer to how the Information Systems Department of the business school performs in terms of these systems attributes.

Finally in Part C we would welcome any comments that you would like to make concerning your own experience with the computer network and/or with the Information Systems Department in respect of its effectiveness.

The questionnaire uses a four point scale.

| First set of 24 questions: | Second set of 24 questions: |
|---|---|
| Critical | Excellent |
| Important | Good |
| Not important | Poor |
| Irrelevant | Very poor |

For example, you might think that ease of access to computer facilities is critical, and therefore your rating in the first set of questions will be:

| Irrelevant | Not Important | Important | Critical |
|---|---|---|---|

If you feel that the performance of the Information Systems Department in providing these facilities is good, this will mean your rating in the second set of questions will be:

| Very poor | Poor | Good | Excellent |
|---|---|---|---|

The Questionnaire should not take more than 15 minutes to complete. All information supplied by respondents will be treated with the utmost confidence.

Please supply the following information about your position in the Business School:

Are you Academic, Secretarial/Administration or Student:

| Acacdemic | Sec/Admin | Student |
|---|---|---|

How many years have you been working and/or studying at the Business School: [ ]

How many years experience have you had working with a PC: [ ]

How many years experience have you had working with a PC network: [ ]

Thank you very much for your assistance in this research. Please return your completed questionnaire to Miss Lucy Vieira.

Dr. Dan Remenyi
Information Management Department
Henley - The Management College

Figure 7.3     User satisfaction questionnaire - Page 1

## PART A

Answer the first set of questions by ticking the box which corresponds to your opinion of the importance of the following 24 attributes in ensuring the effectiveness of your system.

1.    Ease of access for users to computing facilities.

| Irrelevant | Not Important | Important | Critical |
|---|---|---|---|

2.    Up-to-dateness of hardware.

| Irrelevant | Not Important | Important | Critical |
|---|---|---|---|

3.    Up-to-dateness of software.

| Irrelevant | Not Important | Important | Critical |
|---|---|---|---|

4.    Access to external databases through the system.

| Irrelevant | Not Important | Important | Critical |
|---|---|---|---|

5.    A low percentage of hardware and software down time.

| Irrelevant | Not Important | Important | Critical |
|---|---|---|---|

6.    A high degree of technical competence of systems support staff.

| Irrelevant | Not Important | Important | Critical |
|---|---|---|---|

7.    User confidence in systems.

| Irrelevant | Not Important | Important | Critical |
|---|---|---|---|

8.    The degree of personal control users have over their systems.

| Irrelevant | Not Important | Important | Critical |
|---|---|---|---|

9.    Systems responsiveness to changing users needs.

| Irrelevant | Not Important | Important | Critical |
|---|---|---|---|

10.    Data security and privacy.

| Irrelevant | Not Important | Important | Critical |
|---|---|---|---|

11.    System's response time.

| Irrelevant | Not Important | Important | Critical |
|---|---|---|---|

12.    Extent of user training.

| Irrelevant | Not Important | Important | Critical |
|---|---|---|---|

Figure 7.3    User satisfaction questionnaire - Page 2

13. Fast response time from systems support staff to remedy problems.

| Irrelevant | Not Important | Important | Critical |
|---|---|---|---|

14. Participation in planning of the systems requirements.

| Irrelevant | Not Important | Important | Critical |
|---|---|---|---|

15. Flexibility of the system to produce professional reports, e.g. graphics and desktop publishing

| Irrelevant | Not Important | Important | Critical |
|---|---|---|---|

16. Positive attitude of information systems staff to users.

| Irrelevant | Not Important | Important | Critical |
|---|---|---|---|

17. User's understanding of the system.

| Irrelevant | Not Important | Important | Critical |
|---|---|---|---|

18. Overall cost-effectiveness of information systems.

| Irrelevant | Not Important | Important | Critical |
|---|---|---|---|

19. Ability of the system to improve personal productivity.

| Irrelevant | Not Important | Important | Critical |
|---|---|---|---|

20. Ability of the system to enhance the learning experience of students.

| Irrelevant | Not Important | Important | Critical |
|---|---|---|---|

21. Standardisation of hardware.

| Irrelevant | Not Important | Important | Critical |
|---|---|---|---|

22. Documentation to support training.

| Irrelevant | Not Important | Important | Critical |
|---|---|---|---|

23. Help with database or model development.

| Irrelevant | Not Important | Important | Critical |
|---|---|---|---|

24. Ability to conduct computer conferencing with colleagues.

| Irrelevant | Not Important | Important | Critical |
|---|---|---|---|

**Figure 7.3    User satisfaction questionnaire - Page 3**

## PART B

Answer this set of questions by ticking the box which corresponds to your opinion of the performance of the Information Systems Department in terms of the following 24 attributes.

1.  Ease of access for users to computing facilities.

| Very Poor | Poor | Good | Excellent |
|-----------|------|------|-----------|

2.  Up-to-dateness of hardware.

| Very Poor | Poor | Good | Excellent |
|-----------|------|------|-----------|

3.  Up-to-dateness of software.

| Very Poor | Poor | Good | Excellent |
|-----------|------|------|-----------|

4.  Access to external databases through the system.

| Very Poor | Poor | Good | Excellent |
|-----------|------|------|-----------|

5.  A low percentage of hardware and software down time.

| Very Poor | Poor | Good | Excellent |
|-----------|------|------|-----------|

6.  A high degree of technical competence of systems support staff.

| Very Poor | Poor | Good | Excellent |
|-----------|------|------|-----------|

7.  User confidence in systems.

| Very Poor | Poor | Good | Excellent |
|-----------|------|------|-----------|

8.  The degree of personal control users have over their systems.

| Very Poor | Poor | Good | Excellent |
|-----------|------|------|-----------|

9.  Systems responsiveness to changing users needs.

| Very Poor | Poor | Good | Excellent |
|-----------|------|------|-----------|

10. Data security and privacy.

| Very Poor | Poor | Good | Excellent |
|-----------|------|------|-----------|

11. System's response time.

| Very Poor | Poor | Good | Excellent |
|-----------|------|------|-----------|

12. Extent of user training.

| Very Poor | Poor | Good | Excellent |
|-----------|------|------|-----------|

Figure 7.3    User satisfaction questionnaire - Page 4

13. Fast response time from systems support staff to remedy problems.

| Very Poor | Poor | Good | Excellent |
|-----------|------|------|-----------|

14. Participation in planning of the systems requirements.

| Very Poor | Poor | Good | Excellent |
|-----------|------|------|-----------|

15. Flexibility of the system to produce professional reports, e.g. graphics and desktop publishing.

| Very Poor | Poor | Good | Excellent |
|-----------|------|------|-----------|

16. Positive attitude of information systems staff to users.

| Very Poor | Poor | Good | Excellent |
|-----------|------|------|-----------|

17. User's understanding of the system.

| Very Poor | Poor | Good | Excellent |
|-----------|------|------|-----------|

18. Overall cost-effectiveness of information systems.

| Very Poor | Poor | Good | Excellent |
|-----------|------|------|-----------|

19. Ability of the system to improve personal productivity.

| Very Poor | Poor | Good | Excellent |
|-----------|------|------|-----------|

20. Ability of the system to enhance the learning experience of students.

| Very Poor | Poor | Good | Excellent |
|-----------|------|------|-----------|

21. Standardisation of hardware.

| Very Poor | Poor | Good | Excellent |
|-----------|------|------|-----------|

22. Documentation to support training.

| Very Poor | Poor | Good | Excellent |
|-----------|------|------|-----------|

23. Help with database or model development.

| Very Poor | Poor | Good | Excellent |
|-----------|------|------|-----------|

24. Ability to conduct computer conferencing with colleagues.

| Very Poor | Poor | Good | Excellent |
|-----------|------|------|-----------|

**Figure 7.3     User satisfaction questionnaire - Page 5**

## PART C

Please rate your overall opinion of the computer network system.

| Very Poor | Poor | Good | Excellent |
|-----------|------|------|-----------|
|           |      |      |           |

Please supply any further comments you wish concerning the effectiveness of your computer network system.

_____

_____

_____

_____

_____

_____

_____

_____

_____

_____

## Optional

If you are prepared to discuss your comments with the researchers, please write your name below.

_____

_____

_____

Figure 7.3     User satisfaction questionnaire - Page 6

| Attributes | Importances | | | Performances | | | Perceptual | | Gap Correlation with Satisfaction |
|---|---|---|---|---|---|---|---|---|---|
| | Rank | Mean | SD | Rank | Mean | SD | Gap | SD | |
| 6 High degree of technical competence from support staff | 1 | 3.45 | 0.60 | 2 | 2.82 | 0.53 | −0.63 | 0.73 | 0.0232 |
| 11 System's response time | 2 | 3.42 | 0.50 | 19 | 2.20 | 0.83 | −1.22 | 1.05 | 0.5738*** |
| 5 Low percentage of hardware and software downtime | 3 | 3.39 | 0.54 | 10 | 2.49 | 0.60 | −0.90 | 0.90 | 0.4307*** |
| 1 Ease of access for users to computing facilities | 4 | 3.37 | 0.65 | 5 | 2.75 | 0.59 | −0.62 | 0.92 | 0.2154* |
| 13 Fast response from support staff to remedy problems | 5 | 3.34 | 0.53 | 11 | 2.47 | 0.62 | −0.87 | 0.85 | 0.0524 |
| 3 Up-to-dateness of software | 6 | 3.33 | 0.53 | 1 | 3.01 | 0.53 | −0.32 | 0.77 | 0.3794** |
| 20 Ability of the system to enhance the learning experience of students | 7 | 3.32 | 0.59 | 8 | 2.66 | 0.64 | −0.66 | 0.81 | 0.3328** |
| 15 Flexibility of the system to produce professional reports | 8 | 3.22 | 0.69 | 17 | 2.22 | 0.72 | −1.00 | 1.06 | 0.2330* |
| 7 User confidence in systems | 9 | 3.20 | 0.59 | 11 | 2.47 | 0.60 | −0.73 | 0.79 | 0.3112* |
| 19 Ability of the system to improve personal productivity | 10 | 3.18 | 0.53 | 9 | 2.62 | 0.59 | −0.56 | 0.81 | 0.4160*** |
| 16 Positive attitude of IS staff to users | 11 | 3.16 | 0.49 | 3 | 2.78 | 0.62 | −0.38 | 0.77 | 0.0945 |
| 22 Documentation to support training | 12 | 3.11 | 0.56 | 22 | 1.96 | 0.62 | −1.15 | 0.95 | 0.3165** |
| 9 Systems responsiveness to changing users needs | 13 | 3.05 | 0.49 | 11 | 2.47 | 0.64 | −0.58 | 0.77 | 0.2947* |
| 12 Extent of user training | 14 | 3.04 | 0.72 | 20 | 2.14 | 0.69 | −0.90 | 0.95 | 0.0795 |
| 2 Up-to-dateness of hardware | 15 | 3.01 | 0.53 | 14 | 2.46 | 0.72 | −0.55 | 0.89 | 0.3056** |
| 17 User's understanding of the system | 15 | 3.01 | 0.62 | 16 | 2.36 | 0.56 | −0.65 | 0.84 | 0.0563 |
| 8 Degree of personal control users have over their systems | 17 | 2.95 | 0.56 | 15 | 2.37 | 0.65 | −0.58 | 0.90 | 0.2528* |
| 10 Data security and privacy | 18 | 2.80 | 0.80 | 3 | 2.78 | 0.45 | −0.02 | 0.89 | −0.1314 |
| 4 Access to external databases through the system | 19 | 2.78 | 0.62 | 18 | 2.21 | 0.55 | −0.57 | 0.79 | −0.0127 |
| 23 Help with database or model development | 20 | 2.72 | 0.69 | 21 | 2.12 | 0.65 | −0.60 | 0.90 | 0.2050* |
| 21 Standardisation of hardware | 21 | 2.63 | 0.69 | 6 | 2.74 | 0.50 | +0.11 | 0.81 | 0.0625 |
| 14 Participation in planning of systems requirements | 22 | 2.47 | 0.66 | 22 | 1.96 | 0.64 | −0.49 | 0.81 | 0.0033 |
| 18 Cost-effectiveness of IS | 23 | 2.46 | 0.74 | 7 | 2.72 | 0.51 | +0.26 | 0.96 | 0.4160*** |
| 24 Conduct computer conferencing with colleagues | 24 | 2.11 | 0.67 | 24 | 1.93 | 0.57 | −0.17 | 0.77 | 0.3204** |

\* implies correlation is significant at 5% level
\*\* implies correlation is significant at 1% level
\*\*\* implies correlation is significant at the 0.1% level

**Figure 7.4  Basic analysis of perceptions**

deviations, where the gap is determined by subtracting the expectation score from the performance score. In the last column of Figure 7.4 are the correlations between the gap scores and the overall satisfaction scores.

### 7.6.1.2  Some implications arising from the analysis

1. System's response time is ranked second in terms of expectation but nineteenth on performance.

2. Ability to conduct computer conferencing with colleagues and help with database or model development was ranked low on both expectation and performance.

3. Overall cost effectiveness of information systems, standardisation of hardware, and data security and privacy received relatively low rankings on expectation, but relatively high rankings on performance.

4. The correlation between the ranked expectation and performance item means is 0.39, which is not significant at the 5% level. This implies a lack of consensus between the perceived needs for the system to be effective and the perceived ability of the IT department to meet these needs.

5. The general evaluation of performance across all attributes was poor. Up-to-dateness of software with a mean score of 3.01, being best on performance.

6. The gaps for 15 of the 24 statements about the system are positively and significantly correlated with the overall satisfaction score, and therefore can be considered to be potentially 'good' indicators of user satisfaction. Since the gap is determined by subtracting the expectation score from the performance score, the positive correlation implies that the greater the gap, in a positive sense, the more the user satisfaction.

To visualise the gaps between the expectation and the performance scores, a *snake diagram* may be drawn. The snake diagram shown in Figure 7.5 highlights the score for both sets of questions on the same axis.

Figure 7.6 is a modified snake showing the two sets of scores as well as a graph of the gaps. In this figure, the line indicating the zero value is most important. Attributes which display a gap greater than zero, ie positive gaps, are those on which the firm is committing more resources than are perhaps required. Attributes which display a negative gap are those where the performance is less than the expectation and therefore in these respects the firm is underperforming. Where the gap is actually zero, or in other words, no gap, there is an exact match between expectations and performance.

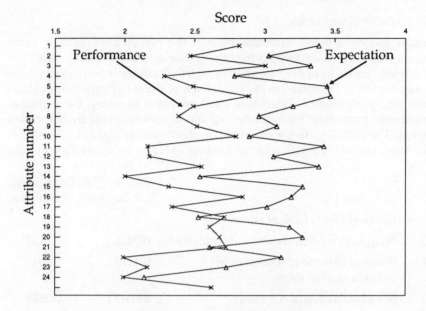

Figure 7.5      A snake diagram

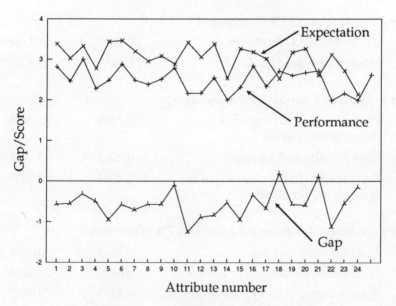

Figure 7.6      A modified snake diagram

### 7.6.1.3  Factor identification

In order to gain a better understanding of the perception scores, a factor analysis was performed on both the expectation and performance data. The underlying factors were determined through the principal component procedure of the SPSS/PC software package. Each of the set of expectation statements and performance statements were analysed by using the principal components procedure for extraction of the factors followed by a varimax rotation. The resulting factor matrices are displayed in Figures 7.7 and 7.8. Only those statements with a factor loading of 0.5 or more are listed in the tables.

|  |  | Factor loading | Gap Correlation with satisfaction |
|---|---|---|---|
| *Factor 1: Ease of Use (14.2% of variance)* | | | |
| A23. | Help with model/database development | 0.7466 | 0.2154* |
| A16. | Positive attitude of information systems staff to users | 0.6173 | 0.0945 |
| A21. | Standardisation of hardware | 0.6043 | 0.0625 |
| A22. | Documentation to support training | 0.5507 | 0.3165** |
| *Factor 2: Modernness (9.8% of variance)* | | | |
| A3. | Up-to-dateness of software | 0.8067 | 0.3794** |
| A2. | Up-to-dateness of hardware | 0.6489 | 0.3056** |
| *Factor 3: System's Control (8.0% of variance)* | | | |
| A18. | Overall cost effectiveness of information systems | 0.7746 | 0.0678 |
| A10. | Data security and privacy | 0.7092 | –0.1314 |
| A14. | Participation in the planning of the systems requirements | 0.6083 | 0.0033 |
| *Factor 4: Technical competence available (6.7% of variance)* | | | |
| A12. | Extent of user training | 0.7621 | 0.0795 |
| A17. | User understanding of the system | 0.6800 | 0.0563 |
| A6. | A high degree of technical competence | 0.5403 | 0.0232 |

**Figure 7.7    Factor analysis of student importance scores**

|  |  | Factor loading | Gap correlation with satisfaction |
|---|---|---|---|
| *Factor 1: Effective benefits (28.4% of variance)* | | | |
| B19. | Ability of the system to improve personal productivity | 0.8430 | 0.4160*** |
| B20. | Ability of the system to enhance the learning experience of students | 0.7003 | 0.3328** |
| B11. | Systems response time | 0.5745 | 0.5738*** |
| B7. | User confidence in systems | 0.5174 | 0.3112** |
| B12. | Extent of user training | 0.5118 | 0.0795 |
| *Factor 2: Modernness (7.8% of variance)* | | | |
| B9, | System's responsiveness to changing user needs | 0.7357 | 0.2947* |
| B8. | Degree of control users have over their systems | 0.6647 | 0.2528* |
| B2. | Up-to-dateness of hardware | 0.6141 | 0.3056* |
| B21. | Standardisation of hardware | 0.6091 | 0.0625 |
| *Factor 3: System access (7.3% of variance)* | | | |
| B15. | Flexibility of the system to produce professional reports | 0.7172 | 0.2330* |
| B17. | Users' understanding of the system | 0.6995 | 0.0563 |
| B22. | Documentation to support training | 0.5339 | 0.3165** |
| B5. | A low percentage of hardware and software downtime | 0.5115 | 0.4307*** |
| *Factor 4: Quality of service (6.4% of variance)* | | | |
| B16. | Positive attitude of IS staff to users | 0.7665 | 0.0945 |
| B13. | Fast response time from support | 0.6588 | 0.0524 |

**Figure 7.8     Factor analysis of student perceptions of performance**

### 7.6.1.4   Expectation scores

Eight factors with eigen values greater than 1 were extracted from the expectation data, accounting for 62.2% of the overall variance. Only the first four of these were interpretable. It could be that perceptions of what is important is not clear in the respondents' minds.

Ease of use emerged as the factor explaining most of the variance. Modernness of the system, system control, and technical competence available, in order of variance explained, were the remaining factors. These factors and the attributes loading on them are given in Figure 7.7. The KMO measure for these scores was 0.5439.

Only four of the 12 gap scores are significantly correlated with overall satisfaction. This implies that the dimensions identified by the factor analysis of expectation scores are likely to be weak measures of user satisfaction with the system.

### 7.6.1.5   *Performance scores*

Four factors, with eigen values greater than 1, were extracted from the performance data, accounting for 49.9% of the total variance. Effective benefits realisation emerged as the factor explaining most of the variance. Modernness of the system, system access and, quality of service were the remaining factors. These factors and the statements loading on them are given in Figure 7.8. The KMO for these scores was 0.7439.

Only three of the thirteen gap scores relating to statements loading on the first three factors are uncorrelated with the overall satisfaction scores. Thus, the performance factors are potentially 'good' measures of satisfaction with the system. The fourth dimension, namely, perception of the quality of the IS staff, is a weak measure of user satisfaction with the system, since for both statements loading on this factor, the gap scores are uncorrelated with overall user satisfaction.

In contrast to the analysis of the expectation data, the respondents appear to have a much clearer view of the performance of the IT department and thus the performance dimensions are likely to be more reliable measures of user satisfaction than those derived from the expectation data.

### 7.6.1.6   *Explanation of overall satisfaction scores*

Regression analysis was performed with a view to establishing which variables were important in explaining the overall satisfaction scores. The initial explanatory variable pool consisted of: the summated gap scores for each of the four perceptual performance factors, as well as the two factual variables; years of experience working with a PC; and years of experience working with a PC network. Subsequent theoretical considerations lead to a revision of the pool.

The quality of service factor shown in Figure 7.8 was excluded from the analysis as the gaps for variables loading on this factor were not correlated with the overall satisfaction scores. Also, for each of the first three factors (effective benefits, modernness and system access), those variables loading on the factor, but not correlating with overall satisfaction, were excluded from the summated gap scores. The exclusion of these variables did not change the interpretation of the factors.

In the first instance, a full regression analysis was performed using the SPSS/PC+ regression program. In this regression, the overall satisfaction scores were regressed on the *summed gap scores* for the *modified* perceptual factors, ie effective benefits, modernness and system access, as well as the two factual variables; years of experience working with a PC; and years of experience working with a PC network. The results of this regression are reported in Figure 7.9.

| | Correlation with overall opinion | Regression Coefficient | Beta Weight | Significance |
|---|---|---|---|---|
| *Gap Variables:* | | | | |
| Effective benefits | 0.548*** | 0.1021 | 0.4597 | 0.0001 |
| Modernness | 0.366** | 0.0340 | 0.1246 | 0.2389 |
| System access | 0.492*** | 0.0486 | 0.1797 | 0.1082 |
| *Non-gap Variables:* | | | | |
| PC experience | –0.058 | –0.0036 | –0.0176 | 0.8751 |
| Network experience | –0.127 | –0.0365 | –0.1190 | 0.2874 |

**     Correlation is significant at the 1% level
***    Correlation is significant at the 0.1% level

Multiple correlation $R_{Full}$ = 0.6478
Coefficient of determination $R^2_{Full}$ = 0.4196

F = 10.12       Significance = 0.0000

**Figure 7.9     Results of full regression analysis**

The results of the full regression reveal a significant regression (F=10.2, significance = 0.0000) with a multiple correlation R of 0.6478. The multiple correlation R indicates the extent of the correlation between the overall satisfaction scores and all the explanatory variables collectively. The interpretation of the $R^2$ value of 0.4196 is that the explanatory variables collectively explain 41.96% of the variation in the overall satisfaction scores. The relative impact of each explanatory variable can be inferred from the, so called, beta weights, which are standardised regression coefficients. The beta weights are used in preference to the ordinary regression coefficients as they are independent of the unit of measurement for the variable itself. In the fitted model, effective benefits with a highly significant beta weight of 0.4597 is by far the factor which has most impact on the overall opinion score. The impact of effective benefits can be considered to have approximately 2.5 times as much impact as system access which has a beta weight of 0.1797.

It is interesting to note from the second column of Figure 7.9 that while all three gap variables are significantly and positively correlated with overall satisfaction, both the PC and PC network experience variables are not significantly correlated with overall satisfaction. It is of additional interest to note that, although not significant, the correlations in the sample between overall satisfaction and both the PC and PC network experience variables, are negative. It is just possible, therefore, that overall satisfaction can be inversely related to these experience variables, which would imply that the more experienced users are more difficult to satisfy.

The regression model was re-computed using the stepwise regression procedure and the results are presented in Figure 7.10. The stepwise regression retains only two of the original five variables included in the full regression model. Despite this, the two models are very similar in terms of fit. ($R^2_{Full} = 0.4196$ versus $R^2_{Stepwise} = 0.3924$.)

| | Correlation with overall opinion | Regression Coefficient | Beta Weight | Significance |
|---|---|---|---|---|
| **Gap Variables:** | | | | |
| Effective benefits | 0.598*** | 0.1089 | 0.4890 | 0.0000 |
| Modernness | 0.366** | – | – | – |
| System access | 0.492*** | 0.0586 | 0.2167 | 0.0436 |
| **Non-gap Variables:** | | | | |
| PC experience | –0.058 | – | – | – |
| Network experience | –0.127 | – | – | – |

**   Correlation is significant at the 1% level
*** Correlation is significant at the 0.1% level

Multiple correlation $R_{Stepwise} = 0.6264$
Coefficient of determination $R^2_{Stepwise} = 0.3924$

F = 23.5721      Significance = 0.0000

Figure 7.10    Results of stepwise regression analysis

The results of the stepwise regression reveal that effective benefits and system access are significant in explaining the overall satisfaction scores. Also, a comparison of the beta weights suggests that effective benefits has about 2.25 times more impact on overall satisfaction than system assess. The full regression and stepwise regression beta weights are essentially the same.

### 7.6.1.7   Summary of findings

The gaps on the two perceptual performance factors, namely effective benefits and system access, are significant in assessing overall satisfaction with the network. The gap on effective benefits is approximately twice as important as system's access in terms of its impact on overall satisfaction. Previous PC and PC network experience do not impact significantly on overall satisfaction with the network system.

The fitted model in this case only explains about 40% of the variability in the overall satisfaction scores. Thus, there are other factors, not identified in the study, which impact on overall satisfaction. This is turn suggests that the evaluation of an office automation/network system is far more complex, involving more than just the two dimensions identified.

## 7.7   A MULTIPLE GAP APPROACH TO MEASURING UIS

A multiple gap approach to measuring UIS is currently being operationalised by IS researchers at Henley – The Management College. This original research is designed to find ways and means of offering assistance to those seeking to obtain a penetrating insight into how systems are viewed at various stages of their production, implementation, and use, and how this has an impact on UIS. Multiple gap analysis seems to be a useful instrument in this respect.

In a study presently in progress at the College, three measures of a system's benefit profiles are being studied. The first measure used related to how the system's original architects perceived the potential benefits. This information relating to potential benefits is extracted from the original specification of requirements documentation. Sixteen different benefit types were defined by the firm. These include the system's ability to:

- reduce overall costs;
- displace costs;
- avoid costs;
- provide opportunity for revenue growth;
- provide improved management information;
- provide improved staff productivity;

- provide capacity for increased volume;
- reduce error;
- provide a competitive advantage;
- catch up with competition;
- provide improved management control;
- provide improved management productivity;
- provide improved staff morale;
- provide an improved corporate image;
- provide improved customer service;
- provide improved client/supplier relationships.

During the development of the original specification of requirements, the authors of the document were required to state the relevance of each benefit type to the system by rating the benefit on a four point scale. This is a measure of the importance or need which the firm has for each of the benefit types. A questionnaire was used for this data collection which is shown in Figure 7.11.

The second measure of benefits was obtained by requesting that the project manager and other members of his or her team, on completion of the system's development, answer the same set of questions relating to the sixteen different benefit types. This data provides a second view of the potential benefits by obtaining an opinion as to what extent the project manager believes the system, as it has been developed, can actually achieve the stated benefits. This is a measure of the expectations of the IS professionals who have developed the system. Figure 7.12 shows the questionnaire required for the capture of this data.

The third measure of benefits was obtained by requesting that the users complete a similar questionnaire. However, in this instance, the questionnaire is attempting to collect data on the actual performance of the system. This questionnaire is shown in Figure 7.13. Unlike the first questionnaire, which is administered either by the researcher studying the actual specification of requirements, or by discussion with only one informant, ie the project manager, the second and third questionnaires may be administered to many users. As a result, when there are multiple users involved, summary statistics have to be calculated.

As there are three data sets collected, described in Figure 7.14, there is a potential for three distinct sets of gaps. The three different data sets collected are shown in Figure 7.15, and Figure 7.16 shows how the relative values from the different questionnaires could be presented.

## THE MEASUREMENT OF
## INFORMATION SYSTEMS BENEFITS

Answer the questions by ticking the box which corresponds to your opinion of the importance of the following types of benefit which may be achieved by the proposed system.

1.  The system's ability to reduce overall costs

| Irrelevant | Not Important | Important | Critical |
|---|---|---|---|

If you answered either IMPORTANT or CRITICAL, please give details below:

2.  The system's ability to displace costs

| Irrelevant | Not Important | Important | Critical |
|---|---|---|---|

If you answered either IMPORTANT or CRITICAL, please give details below:

3.  The system's ability to avoid costs

| Irrelevant | Not Important | Important | Critical |
|---|---|---|---|

If you answered either IMPORTANT or CRITICAL, please give details below:

4.  The system's ability to provide opportunity for revenue growth

| Irrelevant | Not Important | Important | Critical |
|---|---|---|---|

If you answered either IMPORTANT or CRITICAL, please give details below:

5.  The system's ability to provide improved management information

| Irrelevant | Not Important | Important | Critical |
|---|---|---|---|

If you answered either IMPORTANT or CRITICAL, please give details below:

6.  The system's ability to provide improved staff productivity

| Irrelevant | Not Important | Important | Critical |
|---|---|---|---|

If you answered either IMPORTANT or CRITICAL, please give details below:

7.  The system's ability to provide capacity for increased volume

| Irrelevant | Not Important | Important | Critical |
|---|---|---|---|

If you answered either IMPORTANT or CRITICAL, please give details below:

8.  The system's ability to reduce error

| Irrelevant | Not Important | Important | Critical |
|---|---|---|---|

If you answered either IMPORTANT or CRITICAL, please give details below:

1

Figure 7.11     Questionnaire used in conjunction with the
specification of requirements (Page 1)

9. The system's ability to provide competitive advantage

| Irrelevant | Not Important | Important | Critical |
|---|---|---|---|

If you answered either IMPORTANT or CRITICAL, please give details below:
_____
_____

10. The system's ability to catch up with competition

| Irrelevant | Not Important | Important | Critical |
|---|---|---|---|

If you answered either IMPORTANT or CRITICAL, please give details below:
_____
_____

11. The system's ability to provide improved management control

| Irrelevant | Not Important | Important | Critical |
|---|---|---|---|

If you answered either IMPORTANT or CRITICAL, please give details below:
_____
_____

12. The system's ability to provide improved management productivity

| Irrelevant | Not Important | Important | Critical |
|---|---|---|---|

If you answered either IMPORTANT or CRITICAL, please give details below:
_____
_____

13. The system's ability to provide improved staff morale

| Irrelevant | Not Important | Important | Critical |
|---|---|---|---|

If you answered either IMPORTANT or CRITICAL, please give details below:
_____
_____

14. The system's ability to provide an improved corporate image

| Irrelevant | Not Important | Important | Critical |
|---|---|---|---|

If you answered either IMPORTANT or CRITICAL, please give details below:
_____
_____

15. The system's ability to provide improved customer service

| Irrelevant | Not Important | Important | Critical |
|---|---|---|---|

If you answered either IMPORTANT or CRITICAL, please give details below:
_____
_____

16. The system's ability to provide improved client/seller relationships

| Irrelevant | Not Important | Important | Critical |
|---|---|---|---|

If you answered either IMPORTANT or CRITICAL, please give details below:
_____
_____

2

Figure 7.11 Questionnaire used in conjunction with the specification of requirements (Page 2)

# THE MEASUREMENT OF
# INFORMATION SYSTEMS BENEFITS

Answer the questions by ticking the box which corresponds to your opinion of the probability that the following benefits will be achieved by the proposed system.

1.   The system's ability to reduce overall costs

| Unlikely | Possibly | Probably | Certainly |
|----------|----------|----------|-----------|

If you answered either PROBABLY or CERTAINLY, please give details below:

2.   The system's ability to displace costs

| Unlikely | Possibly | Probably | Certainly |
|----------|----------|----------|-----------|

If you answered either PROBABLY or CERTAINLY, please give details below:

3.   The system's ability to avoid costs

| Unlikely | Possibly | Probably | Certainly |
|----------|----------|----------|-----------|

If you answered either PROBABLY or CERTAINLY, please give details below:

4.   The system's ability to provide opportunity for revenue growth

| Unlikely | Possibly | Probably | Certainly |
|----------|----------|----------|-----------|

If you answered either PROBABLY or CERTAINLY, please give details below:

5.   The system's ability to provide improved management information

| Unlikely | Possibly | Probably | Certainly |
|----------|----------|----------|-----------|

If you answered either PROBABLY or CERTAINLY, please give details below:

6.   The system's ability to provide improved staff productivity

| Unlikely | Possibly | Probably | Certainly |
|----------|----------|----------|-----------|

If you answered either PROBABLY or CERTAINLY, please give details below:

7.   The system's ability to provide capacity for increased volume

| Unlikely | Possibly | Probably | Certainly |
|----------|----------|----------|-----------|

If you answered either PROBABLY or CERTAINLY, please give details below:

8.   The system's ability to reduce error

| Unlikely | Possibly | Probably | Certainly |
|----------|----------|----------|-----------|

If you answered either PROBABLY or CERTAINLY, please give details below:

1

Figure 7.12      Questionnaire used by systems development
project managers (Page 1)

9. The system's ability to provide competitive advantage

| Unlikely | Possibly | Probably | Certainly |
|---|---|---|---|

If you answered either PROBABLY or CERTAINLY, please give details below:

10. The system's ability to catch up with competition

| Unlikely | Possibly | Probably | Certainly |
|---|---|---|---|

If you answered either PROBABLY or CERTAINLY, please give details below:

11. The system's ability to provide improved management control

| Unlikely | Possibly | Probably | Certainly |
|---|---|---|---|

If you answered either PROBABLY or CERTAINLY, please give details below:

12. The system's ability to provide improved management productivity

| Unlikely | Possibly | Probably | Certainly |
|---|---|---|---|

If you answered either PROBABLY or CERTAINLY, please give details below:

13. The system's ability to provide improved staff morale

| Unlikely | Possibly | Probably | Certainly |
|---|---|---|---|

If you answered either PROBABLY or CERTAINLY, please give details below:

14. The system's ability to provide an improved corporate image

| Unlikely | Possibly | Probably | Certainly |
|---|---|---|---|

If you answered either PROBABLY or CERTAINLY, please give details below:

15. The system's ability to provide improved customer service

| Unlikely | Possibly | Probably | Certainly |
|---|---|---|---|

If you answered either PROBABLY or CERTAINLY, please give details below:

16. The system's ability to provide improved client/seller relationships

| Unlikely | Possibly | Probably | Certainly |
|---|---|---|---|

If you answered either PROBABLY or CERTAINLY, please give details below:

2

Figure 7.12 Questionnaire used by systems development project managers (Page 2)

# THE MEASUREMENT OF
# INFORMATION SYSTEMS BENEFITS

Answer the questions by ticking the box which corresponds to your opinion of the performance of the system.

1.   The system's ability to reduce overall costs

| Very Poor | Poor | Good | Excellent |
|-----------|------|------|-----------|

If you answered either GOOD or EXCELLENT, please give details below:

2.   The system's ability to displace costs

| Very Poor | Poor | Good | Excellent |
|-----------|------|------|-----------|

If you answered either GOOD or EXCELLENT, please give details below:

3.   The system's ability to avoid costs

| Very Poor | Poor | Good | Excellent |
|-----------|------|------|-----------|

If you answered either GOOD or EXCELLENT, please give details below:

4.   The system's ability to provide opportunity for revenue growth

| Very Poor | Poor | Good | Excellent |
|-----------|------|------|-----------|

If you answered either GOOD or EXCELLENT, please give details below:

5.   The system's ability to provide improved management information

| Very Poor | Poor | Good | Excellent |
|-----------|------|------|-----------|

If you answered either GOOD or EXCELLENT, please give details below:

6.   The system's ability to provide improved staff productivity

| Very Poor | Poor | Good | Excellent |
|-----------|------|------|-----------|

If you answered either GOOD or EXCELLENT, please give details below:

7.   The system's ability to provide capacity for increased volume

| Very Poor | Poor | Good | Excellent |
|-----------|------|------|-----------|

If you answered either GOOD or EXCELLENT, please give details below:

8.   The system's ability to reduce error

| Very Poor | Poor | Good | Excellent |
|-----------|------|------|-----------|

If you answered either GOOD or EXCELLENT, please give details below:

1

Figure 7.13     Questionnaire used by ultimate users of systems
(Page 1)

9.   The system's ability to provide competitive advantage

| Very Poor | Poor | Good | Excellent |
|-----------|------|------|-----------|

If you answered either GOOD or EXCELLENT, please give details below:

_____

10.  The system's ability to catch up with competition

| Very Poor | Poor | Good | Excellent |
|-----------|------|------|-----------|

If you answered either GOOD or EXCELLENT, please give details below:

_____

11.  The system's ability to provide improved management control

| Very Poor | Poor | Good | Excellent |
|-----------|------|------|-----------|

If you answered either GOOD or EXCELLENT, please give details below:

_____

12.  The system's ability to provide improved management productivity

| Very Poor | Poor | Good | Excellent |
|-----------|------|------|-----------|

If you answered either GOOD or EXCELLENT, please give details below:

_____

13.  The system's ability to provide improved staff morale

| Very Poor | Poor | Good | Excellent |
|-----------|------|------|-----------|

If you answered either GOOD or EXCELLENT, please give details below:

_____

14.  The system's ability to provide an improved corporate image

| Very Poor | Poor | Good | Excellent |
|-----------|------|------|-----------|

If you answered either GOOD or EXCELLENT, please give details below:

_____

15.  The system's ability to provide improved customer service

| Very Poor | Poor | Good | Excellent |
|-----------|------|------|-----------|

If you answered either GOOD or EXCELLENT, please give details below:

_____

16.  The system's ability to provide improved client/seller relationships

| Very Poor | Poor | Good | Excellent |
|-----------|------|------|-----------|

If you answered either GOOD or EXCELLENT, please give details below:

_____

Figure 7.13     Questionnaire used by ultimate users of systems
(Page 2)

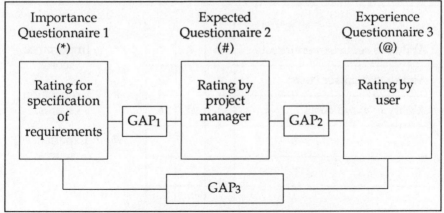

**Figure 7.14     Gap analysis concepts**

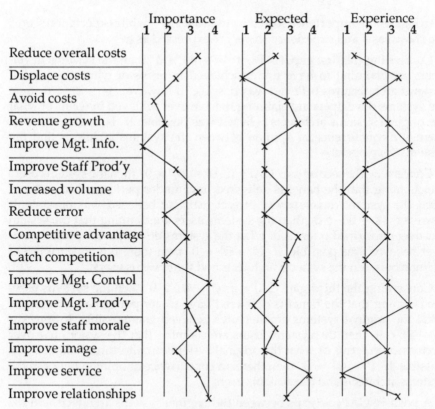

**Figure 7.15   Results showing three different data sets**

| | 1 | 2 | 3 | 4 | | |
|---|---|---|---|---|---|---|
| Ability to reduce overall costs | @ | # | * | | * | Importance scores |
| Ability to displace costs | # | * | @ | | | |
| Ability to avoid costs | * | @ | # | | # | Expectation scores |
| | | | | | | |
| | | | | | @ | Experience scores |
| | | | | | | |

**Figure 7.16    Presentation of results**

In Figure 7.16 importance scores are indicated by *, while expectation scores are shown as # and experience scores are expressed as @.

Concerning the first gap, $GAP_1$, if $(* - \#) > 0$ then the systems developers are claiming to have under achieved in terms of what the original systems architectures believed was possible. If however $(* - \#) < 0$ then the systems developers are claiming to have over achieved in terms of what the original systems architects believed was possible. If $(* - \#) = 0$ then there is a concurrence of opinion between the systems architects and the systems developers.

Concerning the second gap, $GAP_2$, if $(\# - @) > 0$ then the systems users are claiming that the benefits delivered have under performed in terms of what the systems development project manager believed was possible. If however $(\# - @) < 0$ then the systems users are claiming that the system has over performed n terms of what the systems development project manager believed was possible. If $(\# - @) = 0$ then there is a concurrence of opinion between the systems architects and the systems users.

Concerning the third gap, $GAP_3$, if $(* - @) > 0$ then the systems users are claiming that the benefits delivered have under performed in terms of what the original systems architectures believed was possible. If however $(* - @) < 0$ then the systems users are claiming that the system has over performed in terms of what the original systems architectures believed was possible. If $(* - @) = 0$ then there is a concurrence of opinion between the systems architects and the systems users.

A positive $GAP_1$, ie gaps between the original systems architects and the systems development project manager may be interpreted as an under achievement in the firm's delivery process. This under delivery may be attributed to over-enthusiasm or the lack of expected resources, or the fact that the system was not fully understood at the outset. A negative $GAP_1$ may be attributed to the reverse.

A positive $GAP_2$, ie gaps between the systems development project manager and the users, may be interpreted as an under achievement in the firm's systems realisation process. This under achievement may be attributed to the lack of training, the lack of systems documentation or the fact that the system was not fully understood or to all three such causes. A negative $GAP_2$ may be attributed to the reverse.

A positive $GAP_3$, ie gaps between the original systems architects and the systems users may be interpreted as an indication of user dissatisfaction or as an indication of the lack of effectiveness of the firm's IT. Attributing this to specific causes may be difficult and thus $GAP_1$ and $GAP_2$ may be an invaluable guide in this respect. A negative $GAP_3$ may be attributed to the reverse. This gap analysis may indentify complex relationships within the firm between users and systems people.

It is possible for there to be a positive or negative $GAP_3$ while $GAP_1$ and $GAP_2$ have different signs. For example, it is possible that there is a general user dissatisfaction with the system as shown by the positive $GAP_3$ and by a positive $GAP_2$ but there may be simultaneously a negative $GAP_1$. Such a situation would indicate a position where there were major misunderstandings between the systems professionals and the users. On the other hand there may be a very positive user view while the architectures and the systems development project manager rated the system less favourably. Both these situations suggest the need for extensive training of IS professionals and users.

The same type of analysis conducted on the results of the one gap, as has been described earlier in this chapter, may be performed on the two/three gap approach. Snake diagrams may also be drawn which are invaluable in interpreting the results. Factor analysis may also be used to explore underlying relationships in the data. As may be seen from the questionnaires shown in Figures 7.11 to 7.13 this research calls for descriptive explanations from all three types of informants. These explanations may also provide most valuable insights for management.

This type of study is longitudinal in nature. Therefore it will take at least a year or two between the time the first data set is obtained until final analysis may be conducted. However, the insight which this technique may provide will be worth the effort and the wait.

## 7.8   USING A QUESTIONNAIRE APPROACH TO MEASURE IT EFFECTIVENESS

The following is a step-by-step guide to using a survey approach to the measurement of IT effectiveness.

### 7.8.1   Obtain authorisation for the measurement exercise

This is best obtained from the highest possible level in the firm. The measurement exercise should also have the approval of the IS director.

### 7.8.2   Establish a focus group

A focus group consists of a number of IS and user executives who define the issues to be included.

### 7.8.3   Construct the questionnaire

Using information obtained from the focus group develop the measuring instrument.

### 7.8.4   Conduct a pilot survey

Produce 5 to 10 questionnaires, and complete on a face-to-face basis with prospective respondents.

### 7.8.5   Use feedback from the pilot to refine the questionnaire

The pilot survey will show those areas of the questionnaire that need enhancing and those areas that are extraneous.

### 7.8.6   Select sample

Choose an appropriate sample that is representative of the organisation as a whole. The sample should include users from all levels of the management hierarchy.

### 7.8.7   Dispatch questionnaires

Questionnaires should be dispatched to respondents. A fixed date for the return of questionnaires is essential, and respondents should be made aware of this fact.

### 7.8.8   Collect questionnaires

Depending on the distribution of the sample, the questionnaires can either be collected or returned by the respondents.

### 7.8.9   Analyse results

The results can be collated and analysed. This analysis can be time-consuming, but is essential if valuable information is to be generated.

### 7.8.10   Present report

The results of the questionnaire should be summarised in a written report, using as little technical jargon as possible.

## 7.9   SUMMARY

There is a growing trend in the utilisation of user satisfaction measurements as a surrogate for information systems effectiveness. This is a holistic approach which enables the firm to obtain an overview of the effectiveness of the IS function. Gap analysis is the most popular way of conducting these studies. It is not difficult to construct an appropriate questionnaire. There are four example questionnaires in this book. However, the analysis of the statistics which these techniques produce is not trivial and requires the assistance of a statistician.

# 8     A Ranking and Scoring Technique

## 8.1   AN OVERVIEW EVALUATION INCLUDING RISK

The first approach which a firm may wish to undertake in assessing the potential of an IT system is to perform an overview evaluation using a simple ranking and scoring technique. This procedure involves rating a system or a group of systems against a series of very general evaluation criteria. This approach is quite similar to what Parker et al (1989) refer to as Information Economics. These evaluation criteria are to do with issues such as industry attractiveness, internal value chain, industry value chain, offensive or defensive thrusts, etc. However, other issues not directly related to strategic concerns but which affect equally important dimensions of a system may also be included in this analysis and evaluation.

## 8.2   FIVE STEPS TO EVALUATION

There are five steps involved in an overview evaluation:

- Select the criteria.
- Associate weights to each criterion.
- Score individual systems in terms of how they satisfy the criteria.
- Calculate a systems rating by multiplying each score by the weight and then summing to a total.
- Select the system with the greatest total score.

The key issues of ranking and scoring addressed here are:

- Strategic Value.
- Critical Value.
- Operational Value.
- Architectural Value.
- Investment Value.
- Risk Assessment.

179

### 8.2.1   Strategic value

The strategic value refers to the system's potential to create for the firm a competitive advantage. This may be done in many ways, including effecting one or more of the five industry forces as described by Porter. Competitive advantage may also be derived by improving the firm's own value chain internally, or by changing the industry value chain. Strategic value may be derived from an offensive thrust or by a defensive reaction to other players in the market.

### 8.2.2   Critical value

The critical value of a system refers to its ability to improve the effectiveness with which the organisation competes. The attributes of the systems listed under this category will not *per se* deliver a new competitive advantage, but will generally improve the amount of basic advantage already available to the firm.

### 8.2.3   Operational value

Operational value embraces both systems which relate to efficiency issues, as well as issues which are fundamental to the firm's continued existence. These are not strictly strategic, although they are of vital importance to the firm and are, therefore, considered at the same time as the strategic issues.

### 8.2.4   Architectural value

Architectural value considers major infrastructural systems without which the information systems department probably could not function at all.

### 8.2.5   Investment value

Investment value refers to a measure of the financial benefit which a system delivers to the organisation.

### 8.2.6   Risk assessment

Risk assessment represents both conceptual and practical problems. Although it is relatively easy to define risk it is difficult to actually assess its impact on a particular information system or project. The risk of a project is the potential for the actual values of the input and output variables to fluctuate from their original estimates. For example, although the list price of a new mainframe might be £250,000, by the time the firm pays the invoice for it, the amount may be greater or less due to a price change or exchange rate fluctuation, or even a pre-installation upgrade. As original estimates may vary upward or downward, the measure of risk should reflect both the project's positive and negative potential. As most managers are averse to risk, risk is often only seen as a negative aspect of a system.

The result of this is that risky investments tend to have their benefits understated and their costs overstated. Thus, risk is treated as a cost, resulting in a reduced estimated value of the system. In general, this is not a satisfactory way of handling risk as it does not reflect the up-side potential inherent in the risk which is as intrinsic to the concept as the down-side. Entrepreneurial managers may well wish to emphasise the up-side potential of the investment, making their judgment on that evaluation rather than on the negative down-side evaluation.

The issue of risk was addressed in Chapter 5.

## 8.3   A SPREADSHEET SYSTEM FOR OVERVIEW EVALUATION

A spreadsheet has been developed in Lotus 1-2-3 for IBM compatible personal computers which will assist in the evaluation of the strategic potential of IT investment using this ranking and scoring technique.

The primary function of the spreadsheet is to offer a checklist of issues which should be considered during an IT investment evaluation process. The secondary purpose of the spreadsheet is to calculate a total score which represents the perceived value of the systems under review. The calculations involved are trivial, but the purpose of the spreadsheet is to offer a systematic approach to the ranking and scoring process.

Figure 8.1 shows the opening window of the overview evaluation spreadsheet.

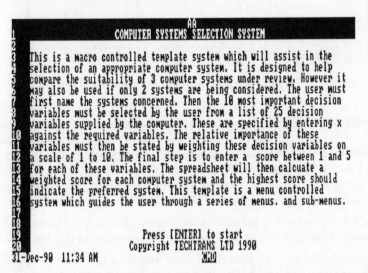

**Figure 8.1    The opening window for the overview evaluation spreadsheet**

This area of the spreadsheet is used as a message screen which explains the purpose of the spreadsheet. At the bottom of the screen the user is invited to press [Enter] to start.

On pressing the [Enter] key a menu appears on the prompt line. The user should select the input option which will lead to a sub-menu offering five new options. Figure 8.2 shows the main menu displayed at the top of the screen, together with the primary display produced by the spreadsheet system.

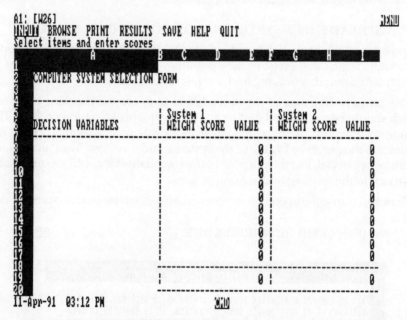

Figure 8.2    The main menu and primary spreadsheet display

The first task in using this evaluation spreadsheet is to select the evaluation criteria which are most relevant under the firm's particular circumstances. The second step is to allocate weights to each of these criteria or factors on a scale of 1 to 10. The objective of this is to effectively spell out the relative importance of the factors to the firm. The final step is to score the system or systems under review on a scale of 1 to 5 for each of the criteria chosen.

Figure 8.3 shows the full list of decision variables which are included in the spreadsheet. Additional variables could easily be added to this list.

The spreadsheet system described here requires the user to specify 10 categories or factors on which the systems are to be evaluated. A control macro

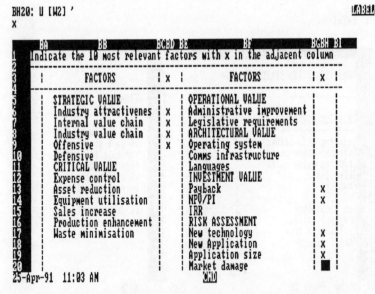

Figure 8.3   Decision variables included in the system

is built into the spreadsheet to ensure that 10 factors are chosen. Each of the 10 factors chosen from the list of 23 must be weighted on a scale of 1 to 10. Then the system sets up weighted decision variable sets which are used as checklists with which to compare competing systems. These competing systems are then individually scaled against these weighted decision variables using a scale of 1 to 5. For each competing system the weight of the decision variable is multiplied by the score and these values are then summed.

Figure 8.4 shows a window on the spreadsheet which is produced after the decision variables have been chosen and is used to enter weights, ie rank these variables in order of their importance. Figure 8.5 shows how the scores given to each decision variable by the investment analyst are entered into the spreadsheet.

In order to accommodate the risk factor the spreadsheet contains two work areas. In the first work area, the risk elements are treated as negative values. This approach reflects the risk aversion expressed by most managers. In the second work area the risk elements are calculated as positive figures. This gives the entrepreneurial manager's view of the risk inherent in the investment opportunity. This results in the system producing both a positive and negative impression of the proposed investment. The system then calculates the mid-points between these two extreme positions which it refers to as a mean value.

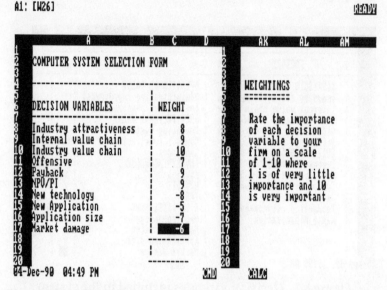

Figure 8.4    Selected criteria together with appropriate weights

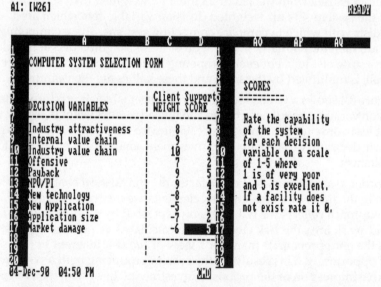

Figure 8.5    Actual scores for each of the chosen criteria

Figure 8.6 may be considered to be a work area or an interim report area in the spreadsheet. It shows all the chosen decision variables as well as the weights, scores and results for each of the systems being analysed.

```
A1: [W26]                                                               READY

         A              B C D    E     F G H     I J K     L M
 1
 2  COMPUTER SYSTEM SELECTION FORM    Risk items have been converted to
 3                                    negative values for weightings
 4
 5  ------------------------------------------------------------------
 6                                 :System 1 :System 2 :System 3
 7  DECISION VARIABLES       :WEIGHT:SCORE VALUE:SCORE VALUE:SCORE VALUE:
 8  ------------------------------------------------------------------
 9  Industry attractiveness  :  8  :  5   40 :  4   32 :  2   16 :
10  Internal value chain     :  9  :  4   36 :  4   36 :  5   45 :
11  Industry value chain     : 10  :  3   30 :  4   40 :  5   50 :
12  Offensive                :  7  :  2   14 :  4   28 :  2   14 :
13  Payback                  :  9  :  5   45 :  4   36 :  5   45 :
14  NPV/PI                   :  9  :  4   36 :  4   36 :  5   45 :
15  New technology           : -8  :  3  -24 :  2  -16 :  1   -8 :
16  New Application          : -5  :  3  -15 :  2  -10 :  2  -10 :
17  Application size         : -7  :  2  -14 :  5  -35 :  2  -14 :
18  Market damage            : -6  :  5  -30 :  5  -30 :  0    0 :
19  ------------------------------------------------------------------
20                           :     :     118 :     117 :     183 :
    ------------------------------------------------------------------
26-Apr-91  01:42 PM
```

**Figure 8.6      Calculation of results for each system**

Note that the values shown in Figure 8.6 reflect the risk-averse manager's view of different investments. Figure 8.7 shows the results of a different set of input data to those used in Figure 8.6. The interpretation of Figure 8.6 is not trivial, neither is it necessarily obvious from these values which investment will be preferred.

Broadly speaking, an entrepreneurial manager would choose the first investment opportunity as it has the best up-side potential. However, a risk-averse manager would probably ignore this and choose the second investment because it has the least downside risk. Managers looking for middle-of-the-road investing with not a great degree of risk will choose the third investment.

## 8.4   SUMMARY

In this chapter, one approach to using a ranking and scoring technique has been described. Such techniques are quite popular, and are therefore used

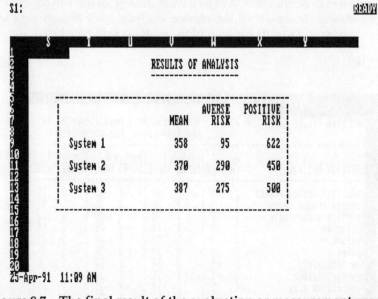

Figure 8.7    The final result of the evaluation or measurement process

extensively in business. However, the variables used and the weighting and scoring ranges employed may vary enormously. Readers are, therefore, invited to choose their own variables and use their preferred weighting and scoring measures.

# 9     Case Histories

In this chapter, a number of real situations in which both *ex-ante* and *ex-post* cost benefits, where conducted, are considered.

## 9.1    A SYSTEM TO SUPPORT A JUST-IN-TIME (JIT) PROJECT

The first case history describes the use of a system which will be a cornerstone in making a profound change to the firm's manufacturing process. The system will improve the firm's ability at materials requirements planning to such an extent that a JIT programme may be introduced. In addition, EDI will also be implemented, initially between the small number of suppliers which are essential to make the JIT programme work. The EDI will eventually be extended to enhance many other suppliers.

The effect of this system will be to substantially reduce raw materials, speed up the manufacturing process by eliminating delays due to the non availability of components, and help to reduce stocks of finished goods. Figure 9.1 shows the *ex-ante* cost justification analysis.

Projected Balance Sheet for the year ended June 30, 199X

| Fixed Assets | Before JIT: | After JIT: |
|---|---|---|
| Land & Buildings | 2543 | 2543 |
| Plant and Equipment | 986 | 986 |
| Computer Equipment | 231 | 381 |
| Furniture & Fittings | 40 | 40 |
| Total Fixed Assets | 3800 | 3950 |
| **Current Assets** | | |
| Raw Material Inventories | 654 | 164 |
| Work In Progress | 456 | 410 |
| Finished Goods | 765 | 574 |
| Cash | 211 | 211 |
| Total Current Assets | 2086 | 1359 |
| Total Assets | 5886 | 5309 |

**Figure 9.1    Case for the acquisition of a JIT system**

The emphasis here is on the effect which this system will have on the balance sheet items. The cost of the computer system has been separately itemised and from this it may be seen that the new system has been capitalised. This figure includes both the hardware and software costs. In Figure 9.2 the sales forecast and the net profit figures are quoted.

| | | |
|---|---|---|
| Sales | 5690 | 5690 |
| Net Profit | 854 | 854 |
| ROI | 14.50% | 16.08% |
| Improvement in ROI | | 10.88% |

**Figure 9.2    Forecast and net profit figures**

From these numbers it may be seen that even if there is no increase in sales the new system should produce a marked increase in the firm's ROI.

Figure 9.3 shows the situation if there is also an increase in sales. Under these circumstances there is a very significant improvement in the firm's performance as demonstrated by the ROI.

| | |
|---|---|
| Sales increase of 10% | 6259 |
| Net Profit | 939 |
| ROI | 17.69% |
| Increase in ROI | 3.18% |
| ROI performance improvement | 21.96% |

**Figure 9.3    Performance improvement after sales increase**

In Figure 9.4 the actual results reported one year after the implementation of the system are shown. From this balance sheet it may be seen that the firm managed to reduce its raw materials, work-in-progress and its finished goods stock. However, the reduction in the raw materials and work-in-progress were not as great as anticipated. On the other hand, sales performed better than planned. The net result is that there has been a substantial improvement in performance.

The un-forecast increase in sales has of course distorted the situation. This may be regarded as noise and accounted for as shown in Figure 9.5. Also in Figure 9.5, the increase in ROI which is attributable to the increase in sales is calculated. This is then subtracted from the total increase leaving a residue which may be attributable to the JIT system. The residual is then divided by the original ROI earned by the business to calculate the effect of the JIT. Thus, the firm achieved an improvement of 12.42% instead of an estimated improvement of 20.95%.

Balance Sheet as at 30 June 199X

| Fixed Assets | Budget | Actual | Variance |
|---|---|---|---|
| Land & Buildings | 2543 | 2511 | 32 |
| Plant and Equipment | 986 | 876 | 110 |
| Computer Equipment | 381 | 444 | -63 |
| Furniture & Fittings | 40 | 41 | -1 |
| Total Fixed Assets | 3950 | 3872 | 78 |

| Current Assets | | | |
|---|---|---|---|
| Raw Material Inventories | 164 | 240 | –76 |
| Work In Progress | 410 | 500 | –90 |
| Finished Goods | 574 | 431 | 143 |
| Cash | 211 | 210 | 1 |
| Total Current Assets | 1359 | 1381 | –22 |
| | | | |
| Total Assets | 5309 | 5253 | 56 |
| | | | |
| Sales | 5690 | 6213 | 523 |
| Net Profit | 854 | 932 | 78 |
| ROI | 16.08% | 17.74% | 1.66% |

**Figure 9.4    Actual report one year after implementation**

| | |
|---|---|
| Increase in sales | 523 |
| % increase in sales | 9.19% |
| % increase in ROI | 11.30% |
| Residual | 2.10% |
| JIT improvement | 12.42% |

**Figure 9.5   Adjustment for noise after sales increase**

## 9.2   AN OFFICE AUTOMATION SYSTEM

The second case history describes the introduction of an extensive office automation system which is intended to reduce the time taken to produce proposals for prospective clients, as well as reduce the time required to write the finished reports. The time savings will be realised through the use of word processing, desktop publishing and contextual databases.

Although it is believed that this system will result in the firm winning more consultancy assignments due to its ability to present proposals faster and in a much more professional way (due to the desktop publishing features of the system), these aspects of the system are regarded as too difficult to evaluate and have, therefore, been omitted from the cost benefit analysis.

Figure 9.6 shows the original proposal for the benefits which the OA system will deliver.

|  | Current<br>Without OA | Predicted<br>After OA |
|---|---|---|
| Number of proposals written per month | 42 | 42 |
| Number of reports produced per month | 9 | 9 |
| Number of management days per proposal | 3 | 2 |
| Number of management days per report | 25 | 20 |
| Number of secretary days per proposal | 5 | 3 |
| Number of secretary days per report | 35 | 30 |
| Average cost of management time | 200 | 200 |
| Average cost of secretarial time | 50 | 50 |
| Total payroll cost of producing reports | 287600 | 226050 |
| Estimated saving per month |  | 61550 |
| Estimated saving per year |  | 738600 |

Figure 9.6    Case for purchase of OA system

The benefits are all based on time savings of both management and secretarial staff. The estimates of these time savings have been based on work studies conducted by the firm using a pilot system which the organisation had functioning for 12 months before making the decision to proceed with the larger implementation of OA.

Figure 9.7 shows the costs of the investment as well as the annual on-going costs of operating the system. The Help Desk cost shown under the investment group is the cost of setting up the help group. This included recruiting and training costs. The continuing cost of the Help Desk is covered by the expense items shown in the on-going costs category.

After the system had been in place for one year, an assessment of the derived benefit was made. Figure 9.8 shows the results of this assessment. These benefits are based on a work study assessment which was conducted by the firm's experts in that field.

Set Up Costs

-------------------

| | |
|---|---|
| Hardware | 987500 |
| Software | 643100 |
| Communications | 75000 |
| Commissioning | 125000 |
| Training | 65000 |
| Help Desk | 50000 |
| | --------- |
| | 1945600 |

On-going Costs per year

-----------------------------------

| | |
|---|---|
| Staff | 145000 |
| Maintenance | 98750 |
| Amortisation | 48000 |
| Sundries | 30000 |
| | --------- |
| | 321750 |

Figure 9.7     Initial and on-going costs of the investment

| | |
|---|---|
| Number of proposals written per month | 42 |
| Number of reports produced per month | 9 |
| | |
| Number of management days per proposal | 2 |
| Number of management days per report | 15 |
| | |
| Number of secretary days per proposal | 2 |
| Number of secretary days per report | 23 |
| | |
| Average cost of management time | 200 |
| Average cost of secretarial time | 50 |
| | |
| Total payroll cost of producing reports | 174650 |
| | |
| Saving per month | 112950 |
| | |
| Estimated saving per year | 1355400 |

Figure 9.8     Results of the OA benefits assessment

Figure 9.9 shows the final assessment of the OA system incorporating the costs and the benefits. The final analysis is conducted on the basis of an ROI and a payback.

| | |
|---|---|
| Investments Costs for the OA System | 1945600 |
| On-going Costs per year | 321750 |
| Estimated saving per year | 1355400 |
| Net Benefit per year | 1033650 |
| Payback | 2 years |
| ROI | 53.13% |

**Figure 9.9    Final assessment incorporating costs and benefits**

## 9.3    A SYSTEM TO PROVIDE AFTER SALES SERVICE

The third case history relates to the use of a database systems to assist in after sales service and complaints. The database allows telephone operators to look up details of clients who phone in with queries and problems. By being able quickly to see the client history, the operator can give advice or pass on the query to an appropriate repairman for service. It is believed that the proposed database system will reduce the time taken to handle an enquiry or a complaint and thus reduce the need for operators. Also, the service offered by the firm will be improved by being able to better match the complaint to an appropriate service man.

Figure 9.10 shows the original estimation of the benefits both in time saved and in the impact this is expected to have on the salary bill. The input for this cost benefit analysis is obtained from work study data and from the personnel records which reveal the pay of the operators. Only a modest amount of improvement of 3 minutes per call is expected.

Figure 9.11 shows the estimated cost of the system both in terms of the original investment and the on-going costs. In addition, this figure shows the expected payback and the anticipated ROI.

After the system had been installed for one year, a post implementation audit was conducted which produced the results shown in Figure 9.12. The

| Estimation of Benefits | Before Database | After Database |
|---|---|---|
| Number of complaints received per day | 745 | 745 |
| Time required to deal with complaint | 10 | 7 |
| Number of hours worked per day | 7.5 | 7.5 |
| Number of complaint takers required | 16 | 11 |
| Average salary of operators per month | 865 | 865 |
| Salaries saved per month | | 4325 |
| Salaries saved per year | | 51900 |

Figure 9.10    Case for the introduction of an after sales service database

Set Up Costs

| | |
|---|---|
| Hardware | 27600 |
| Software | 14340 |
| Commissioning | 9800 |
| Training | 6400 |
| | 58140 |

On-going Costs per year

| | |
|---|---|
| Staff | 8900 |
| Maintenance | 5000 |
| Amortisation | 1200 |
| Sundries | 2500 |
| | 17600 |

| | |
|---|---|
| Investment Cost | 58140 |
| Salaries Saved pa | 51900 |
| On-going Costs pa | 17600 |
| Net Benefit pa | 34300 |

| | |
|---|---|
| Payback | 2 years |
| ROI | 59.00% |

Figure 9.11   Investment costs for after sales database

|                                          | After Database |
|------------------------------------------|:---------------:|
| Actual results                           |                |
| ------------------                       | ------------   |
| Number of complaints received per day    | 658            |
| Time required to deal with complaint     | 7              |
| Number of hours worked per day           | 7.5            |
| Number of complaint takers required      | 10             |
|                                          |                |
| Average salary of operators pm           | 865            |
| Salaries saved pm                        | 5190           |
| Salaries saved pa                        | 62280          |
|                                          |                |
| Net Benefit pa                           | 62280          |
| On-going Costs                           | 17600          |
| System Benefit                           | 44680          |
| Payback                                  | 1 year  4 months |
| ROI                                      | 76.85%         |

**Figure 9.12 Improvements after installing system**

time required to process a query/complaint had indeed been reduced to 7 minutes. However, the number of enquiries/complaints has also been reduced.

This reduction in complaints has occurred despite the fact that the firm's sales had continued to grow during this period at 11%. It is believed that the decrease in complaints received is due to the operator being able to better direct the callers to appropriate service personnel and, thus, not have to make return telephone calls with further complaints.

The improved service level implied by the reduction in complaints received has not been incorporated into the firm's analysis at this stage. A separate study will be conducted into the efficiency of the service department and an attempt will be made to isolate the influence that the computer system has on this issue.

## 9.4   A SMALL SCALE EDI SYSTEM

The fourth case history involves the use of EDI to consolidate the purchasing power of a medium sized group of companies operating in similar businesses. The group consists of 12 subsidiaries, six of which conduct very similar businesses and are encouraged to remain apart and even be competitive with each other in the marketplace.

These six firms buy their raw material from the same supplier, but none of them are large enough on their own to qualify for an additional 1.25% large volume discount which this supplier offers to its bigger customers.

It has been decided to use EDI through a VAN to consolidate the groups purchases and thus obtain the additional large volume discounts. To qualify for this discount, a firm or a group has to purchase goods in excess of £2.5 million per year.

The first step in the cost benefit analysis is to estimate the group's total purchases and thus derive the size of the potential benefit from the additional discounts. The purchases and discount calculation is performed in Figure 9.13.

|  | Sub-A | Sub-B | Sub-C | Sub-D | Sub-E | Sub-F | Total |
|---|---|---|---|---|---|---|---|
| Current purchases | 987000 | 456430 | 398999 | 187666 | 786000 | 1203452 | 4019547 |
| Forecast purchases | 1085700 | 524895 | 498749 | 375332 | 825300 | 1323797 | 4633772 |
| Estimated extra discount | 13571 | 6561 | 6234 | 4692 | 10316 | 16547 | 7922 |

Total additional benefit from the discounts          57922

**Figure 9.13    Financial case for benefits**

This system will operate through a series of personal computers which will need to be fairly powerful and which will require special software. The estimated cost of this as well as the likely on-going costs are shown in Figure 9.14.

Estimation of investment costs
-------------------------------------

| Hardware | 30000 |
|---|---|
| Software | 9000 |
| Commissioning | 2500 |
| Training | 3000 |
| | 44500 |

Estimation of on-going costs
-------------------------------------

| Staff | 6000 |
|---|---|
| Maintenance | 3000 |
| Amortisation | 15000 |
| Communications costs | 6000 |
| Sundry | 2500 |
| | 32500 |

**Figure 9.14    Estimated investment and on-going costs**

The impact of this EDI-VAN system is shown in the financial analysis summary in Figure 9.15. It appears to be an acceptable investment proposition to the firm.

| | |
|---|---|
| Total benefit per year | 57922 |
| Total cost per year | 32500 |
| Net benefit per year | 25422 |
| Payback | 2 years |
| ROI | 57.13% |

Figure 9.15    Financial analysis

After one year a post investment audit was performed. The cost of the investment was higher than anticipated on all counts. This is shown in Figure 9.16. However, the over-expenditure here was not regarded as material.

| Investment | Budget | Actual | Variance |
|---|---|---|---|
| Hardware | 30000 | 34550 | -4550 |
| Software | 9000 | 12500 | -3500 |
| Commissioning | 2500 | 3590 | -1090 |
| Training | 3000 | 4500 | -1500 |
| | 44500 | 55140 | -10640 |

| On-going Costs | Budget | Actual | Variance |
|---|---|---|---|
| Staff | 6000 | 6000 | 0 |
| Maintenance | 3000 | 3455 | -455 |
| Amortisation | 15000 | 17275 | -2275 |
| Communications costs | 6000 | 7500 | -1500 |
| Sundry | 2500 | 2000 | 500 |
| | 32500 | 36230 | -3730 |

Figure 9.16    Results of post investment audit

With regard to the on-going costs, these were also more than estimated. However, these cost over runs were again not considered material.

Figure 9.17 shows the amounts purchased by the individual subsidiaries. Some firms in the group experienced poor sales and thus their level of purchases were down, while others showed much better performance with purchases greater than forecast. The net result, however, was that the firms achieved a higher level of benefit than forecast.

|                        | Sub-A  | Sub-B  | Sub-C  | Sub-D  | Sub-E  | Sub-F   | Total   |
|------------------------|--------|--------|--------|--------|--------|---------|---------|
| Purchases by subsidiary | 999567 | 520986 | 450987 | 689342 | 765988 | 1456780 | 4883650 |
| Total purchases        | 4883650 |        |        |        |        |         |         |
| Additional discount    | 61046  |        |        |        |        |         |         |

**Figure 9.17    Purchases made through EDI system**

Figure 9.18 shows the summary financial assessment. It is clear from this that the overspends on the investment and the on-going cost have been partially compensated for by the increased discounts received.

| Total investment        | 55140    |
|-------------------------|----------|
| Total benefit for the year | 61046 |
| Total cost per year     | 36230    |
| Net benefit per year    | 24816    |
| Payback                 | 2 years  |
| ROI                     | 45.00%   |

**Figure 9.18    Overall financial assessment**

## 9.5  SUMMARY

The above four case histories are presented as examples of how firms actually perform their cost benefit analysis and how they assess whether their investments have produced the type and scale of benefit which they had originally estimated.

No critical evaluation has been made of these techniques by the authors. They have been presented as they have been used in real situations by real companies.

However, it must be remembered that research suggests that only about 10% of firms ever bother to perform this type of post investment audit.

# 10    Value for Money and Health Check Review Studies

## 10.1    EFFICIENCY AND EFFECTIVENESS STUDIES

A subject which is different, but relatively close to measuring IT benefits, is that of conducting value for money (VFM) and health check review (HCR) studies of the information systems department. These are very large subjects in their own right, and this chapter provides a brief overview of the area.

The aim of a value for money study is to establish whether the ISD is functioning efficiently, and whether the amount being spent on the department is proportionate to the service level being obtained. Questions such as "is the IS management making the most of the funds invested?", or "can the firm obtain the same service cheaper?" are asked. A value for money study may also ask if different ways of managing the ISD could be applied, so that a better level of service will be obtained for the same expenditure. Thus value for money studies often attempt to identify opportunities for improvements and areas for general cost saving. Furthermore, pending resource requirements are often addressed in a value for money study to see if there is any way of minimising, or simply reducing, this expenditure. In fact, a value for money study can address any of the operative issues faced by the ISD.

Some value for money studies extend beyond considerations of the efficiency of the ISD to also look at the effectiveness of the information systems function. Such studies are usually much more extensive than the relatively straightforward efficiency reviews. Effectiveness studies are sometimes referred to as health check reviews and focus on strategic issues as well as operational issues. Therefore, a HCR requires a much broader view of the firm and the role that the ISD plays.

## 10.2    A VALUE FOR MONEY STUDY

It is important to establish that a value for money study is not simply an audit. The term audit has a very negative connotation and can produce very unusual behaviour in those members of staff who feel threatened by an external inspection. A value for money study is aimed as much at highlighting areas of excellence, as identifying those areas requiring remedial action. The study includes a discussion of the many different ways in which an ISD may be improved, and the selection of the most practical and cost effect way of so doing with relation to the firm in question.

The deliverables of a value for money study inter alia include:

1. a balanced report presented as objectively as possible highlighting the strengths and weaknesses of the ISD.

2. a better idea of how to use the resources available to the ISD.

3. a clearer idea of what the ISD budget can actually buy.

4. a more motivated ISD management team who, as a result of participating in the study, have been highly involved in assessing their own work and that of their colleagues.

5. a top management team who are likely to better understand the challenges faced by their ISD.

6. a list of action points.

VFM studies may be conducted either internally, ie by the firm's own staff, or by external consultants.

There are a number of different approaches to value for money studies adopted by the large consultancies offering their own proprietary methodologies. Thus, Andersen Consultancy, Coopers & Lybrand Deloitte, Hoskins, Peat Marwick McLintock, to mention only a few of the larger firms, have their own methodologies for value for money studies. Firms who wish to conduct their own VFM studies should establish their own structured methodology before commencing.

If it is decided to use outside consultants to perform a VFM study, this must be approached in such a way that ISD personnel do not feel threatened. Failure to achieve this will lead to mis-information and inaccurate information being supplied. The most successful approach seems to be to use small teams involving both external consultants and selected internal personnel.

## 10.3   SETTING UP A VALUE FOR MONEY STUDY

Once the study team has been selected, the first step is a meeting to agree the objectives and the scope of the study in direct relation to the firm. Furthermore, the resources available for the study and the timescales must be clarified, and the deliverables defined. A team leader should also be appointed at this initial meeting. This should be someone from within the firm who will be responsible for co-ordinating the work of the study with the other team members.

In defining the objectives, four main questions feature:

1. Is the ISD providing value for money?
2. Are pending resource requirements for the ISD reasonable?
3. What opportunities exist for cost savings, improved efficiency and effectiveness?
4. What is the ISD doing especially well and how can this excellence be extended?

The precise scope of the study categories will vary extensively depending on the firm, but there are 12 identifiable areas which can be considered when setting up a study:

1. Hardware
2. Software
3. Staffing
4. Service levels
5. Security
6. Technical support
7. User support
8. Costs and charges
9. Application systems development
10. Networks
11. Integration with the rest of the firm
12. The information systems plan

The resources available for the study in terms of access to people, documentation, equipment, etc must be clarified. In addition, the overall timescale for the study must be clearly identified. A traditional approach to performing value for money studies is for the study team to examine documentation, interview personnel and generally to observe the function of the ISD. Progress meetings will be necessary to review the on-going progress of the study and to discuss the results to date. A time limit should be set for completing personnel interviews, reviewing documentation and other procedures, and progress meetings should also be scheduled from the outset. This enables a date to be put on the submission of the final report.

In the setting up stage of the study, the required presentation approach for the deliverables should be agreed. This should include a succinct management report of the findings and recommendations of the study. The first part of the VFM report should provide an assessment of the current situation, whereas the second part of the report will focus on an action plan indicating how the performance of the IS function may be improved. Where necessary, appendices may be attached showing results of the analysis used to support findings and recommendations. In addition, an action plan should be provided with definitive practical suggestions for improved cost effectiveness and department efficiency.

## 10.4   DETAILED PLANNING OF THE STUDY

The operational issues listed in the scope of the study incorporated most of the areas that an ISD might be involved with. However, this list will vary to some extent from firm to firm, and the study must be structured to meet the specific needs of the firm.

The following sub-sections indicate the type of information that the study team should aim to derive within each of the scope categories. In every case, having collected and analysed the information, an indication as to how well the ISD function is operating in that area should be reported, together with suggestions for improved costs effectiveness and efficiency. By the end of the study a pattern should develop which will show the broad areas where most improvement can be gained.

### 10.4.1   Hardware and software

It is important to determine exactly what hardware and software exists in the firm, and what is in use in the firm. This will, in most cases, involve personal computers on the desks of end-users, as well as the equipment under the direct control of the data processing department. The range of hardware configurations and versions of software in use should be established. In many cases this is a non-trivial task and the establishment of a hardware and software asset register is a key component in any VFM study. Other aspects of the hardware and software inventory include what software is installed on machines, but not actually used by the user? What are the future plans for hardware and software growth? What is already on order, and what capacity planning techniques are employed? How effective is the data processing function?

If possible, existing statistics should be reviewed, and an indication as to the relevance and application of current configurations with relation to workload should be established. Performance monitoring tools may already be in use, and if so, data from these should be analysed to suggest the value for money currently being obtained. Other monitoring and modelling procedures might be suggested by the study which could enhance cost effectiveness.

The areas of hardware and software maintenance should be addressed. How much of this is outsourced and how much is performed internally? The study should examine the approach currently employed by the firm and comment of the cost effectiveness of this approach.

### 10.4.2   Staffing

A headcount of ISD staff should be taken, as well as an organisation chart for the department. ISD staff who are placed in user departments must also be counted. Manpower planning procedures should be examined in relation to the current workload. It may also be useful to perform a study of the current working practices and conditions. This will involve reviewing rates of pay, leave entitlement, as well as training commitments. In so doing, 'good practice' may be identified and recommendations be provided as to how these may be implemented. The question of analyst, programmer and operator productivity must also be addressed, as well as the staff involved in data entry, data validation and information distribution. Key performance indicators should be identified for use in comparability studies in order that future objectives may be set and improvements may be monitored.

### 10.4.3   Service levels

This involves looking at the current agreements and commitments that the ISD has to clients in terms of turnaround times, response times, availability, etc. If a service or help desk exists, its efficiency in terms of staffing and response time should be examined. What tools for recording problems and solutions are used? It may be appropriate to suggest the creation of such a service if it has not already been established. As even quite small firms can benefit enormously from the introduction of sound service level agreements, this area is frequently given considerable attention.

### 10.4.4   Security

The study should examine all levels of computer related security, including physical access as well as controls over input, processing, and output procedures. How computer security fits in with the general security of the firm should be examined, and where the responsibility for security lies will be important. Physical access covers both control over access to the premises, as well as to machines, software and data. Special attention to the control of operating software should be given. What, if any, written procedures are there, and what happens in actual practice? How does the firm intend to minimise attacks from hackers and viruses? Potential problem areas should be highlighted. If the company has a disaster recovery plan, this should be reviewed and the methodology used compared to others. The cost effectiveness of this and alternative approaches can then be assessed.

### 10.4.5   Technical support

The present practices and procedures should be reviewed. This will include looking at how hardware and software upgrades are handled, what stand-ardisation is in place and how this can be improved. The commitment to training from the ISD should be examined as efficiency can be greatly enhanced if users are properly trained in the applications they are supposed to be using.

### 10.4.6   User support

How much support do users feel they get from ISD and how approachable do they feel ISD personnel are? Are requests dealt with promptly and sym-pathetically? Consider the establishment of departmental 'gurus' to filter trivial problems away from ISD.

### 10.4.7   Costs and charges

All the costs incurred in the IS area by the firm should be assessed and areas for potential savings highlighted. It is important that IS services should be charged for. However, this implies that all IS users must have a budget and a certain degree of discretion as to how to spend it. Charging formulae should be evaluated together with algorithms for efficiency and fairness.

### 10.4.8   Application systems development

Examine the standards and methodologies currently in use for systems de-velopment and ongoing maintenance. Are CASE tools or other development aids being used? Evaluate the efficiency and effectiveness of these procedures. Compare the perceptions of the systems as seen by terminal operators, user management and development staff. Derive a satisfaction quotient.

### 10.4.9   Networks

Examine the current design and configuration of online networks in terms of costs effectiveness and efficiency. Determine whether alternative approaches such as PC networks could be applied, whether networks have enough capacity and are performing to an efficient level. What is the loading and the downtime of the network? and can this be improved? How many users are currently connected and can this be increased. If the firm has not established a policy to network PCs, this is a potential area for dramatic cost improvements as software, data and peripherals can be shared and accessed more readily.

### 10.4.10   Integration with the rest of the firm

The study should clearly establish the relationship of the ISD to the rest of the firm. A review of the history of the department, its workload growth, reorganisations, management changes, etc is useful. Who is responsible for communicating with other departments within the firm as well as with clients and suppliers? What is the reporting hierarchy within the ISD and to the rest of the firm?

## 10.4.11   The information systems plan

If the firm has undertaken the development of a strategic information systems plan (SISP), this will provide important information for the VFM study. The plan should be examined to see how many of the recommendations therein are in practice, and how successful they are. Has the information systems plan been linked to the overall corporate plan of the firm? What monitoring of the plan has taken place and what results have been attained?

## 10.5   ANALYSING THE RESULTS

The performance of the ISD in each of the categories may be assessed on a scale of perhaps four points. Such a scale would have the categories: excellent, good, poor and very poor, where 4 is excellent, 3 is good, 2 is poor and 1 is very poor. The scores could be derived by averaging views obtained at interviews, or by collecting data using a questionnaire. Figure 10.1 shows the results of a study showing a relatively high VFM, and Figure 10.2 represents the results of a study showing a low VFM.

| Hardware | 3.2 | Costs | 3.9 |
|---|---|---|---|
| Software | 3.4 | Applications | 2.9 |
| Staff | 3.6 | Networks | 3.5 |
| Service | 2.8 | Security | 2.1 |
| Technical support | 2.9 | Integration | 2.8 |
| User support | 1.9 | IS Planning | 2.8 |

**Figure 10.1     Results of a high VFM study**

| Hardware | 2.4 | Applications | 2.8 |
|---|---|---|---|
| Software | 2.3 | Networks | 3.5 |
| Staff | 2.9 | Security | 2.1 |
| Service | 0.9 | Integration | 2.2 |
| Technical support | 2.2 | IS Planning | 1.8 |
| User support | 1.5 | | |
| Costs | 0.9 | | |

**Figure 10.2     Results of a low VFM study**

The results of the scores may be presented in a number of different ways. One method of presentation, used by Coopers & Lybrand Deloitte, is that of a wheel diagram. In Figure 10.3 this concept has been adopted to accommodate the twelve scope categories using the ratings shown in Figure 10.1. Figure

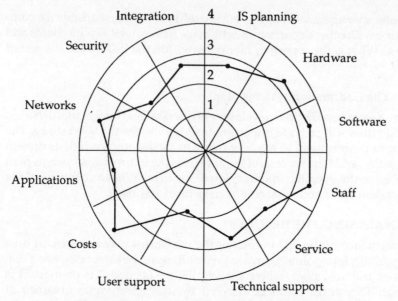

**Figure 10.3    Wheel diagram showing high VFM**

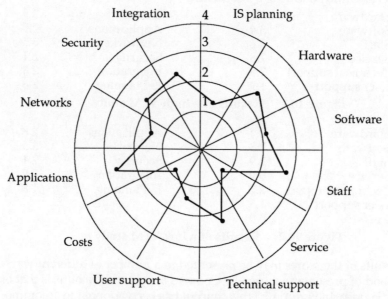

**Figure 10.4    Wheel diagram showing low VFM**

10.4 uses the data from Figure 10.2. The area of the polygon produced by joining the scores is a reflection of the VFM which the firm receives. If the area is large, the VFM is considerable, whereas if the area is small the VFM is low.

## 10.6  A LIST OF ACTION POINTS

A VFM study must indicate how the performance of the ISD may be improved and this should be expressed through a list of action points. These may address such issues as:

- Increasing/decreasing the staff complement.
- Replacing hardware/software.
- Initiating training programmes.
- Implementing additional security procedures.
- Initiating strategic information systems planning.
- Controlling end user computing.

The amount of detail which will be supplied with the action points will depend upon the terms of reference for the study. In some cases, the detail may be minimal, whereas in others the action points may be very specific.

## 10.7  A HEALTH CHECK REVIEW STUDY

Most of the topics discussed so far have been looked at from the point of view of assessing the level of efficiency in the ISD. Thus, the main focus has been on operational issues. In some cases, it can be useful to the firm to measure the value for money they are getting from an effectiveness viewpoint. In this case, a more strategic view of the IS function is required.

The National Computing Centre (NCC) are currently conducting a joint research programme, which they refer to as IMPACT, with a number of large UK establishments with the aim of discovering how effective IT is in their organisations and how this can be improved. They define effectiveness as the contribution made by the IS function to the organisation's objectives and the organisation's performance. Some aspects of the NCC IMPACT HCR study are described here to indicate how extensive a HCR study may be.

### 10.7.1  NCC IMPACT

The study is highly participative, comprising reviews, seminars, research projects, a Chief Executives' conference, as well as reports of the findings. Participants in the study decide for themselves the subjects to be covered in seminars and briefings, arising from the findings of the reviews. The first year of the study has recently been completed, during which the effectiveness of the IT function as seen by the ISD has been the centre of study. The second year aims to concentrate on how the rest of the organisation see the effectiveness of the IT function.

The main aim of the study is to define and measure what is meant by IT effectiveness. This was broken into three questions:

–   What are the most important elements in effectiveness?

–   How should each be defined?

–   On what scale can each be measured?

In order to approach these issues in some kind of structured way, the study prepared a pilot review of the IS function. Feedback from the pilot produced a second generation set of questions which formed the basis of a review procedure that could be applied and compared to each of the participating organisations.

The review was based on 12 elements in effectiveness, grouped under three main headings of IT Policy, IT Contribution and IT Delivery. The 12 elements were divided into the three main groups as follows:

*IT Policy*

–   Corporate IT strategy

–   IT planning and management

–   IT investment

–   IT budgeting

*IT Contribution*

–   Customer relations

–   Supply of IT services

–   Evaluation of existing systems

*IT Delivery*

–   Technology strategy

–   Development planning

–   Operations planning

–   Human resources strategy

–   Quality stratetgy

Each of the 12 elements had a definition and a list of issues to be discussed with each organisation during the review process.

From an independent assessment by a consultant, a qualitative scale of measurement was produced, consisting of five statements reflecting the level of sophistication, where A represented Advanced Practice and E represented Unsophisticated Practice. Ratings B through D represented points inbetween. The researchers emphasise that these results should not be taken purely at face value, seeing A as good and E as bad, but rather as a basis for discussion and refinement of the process.

An enhanced wheel or web diagram could then be produced giving a profile of each Partner's response to the 12 elements. Figure 10.5 is an example of such a diagram, but does not reflect a participant in the study.

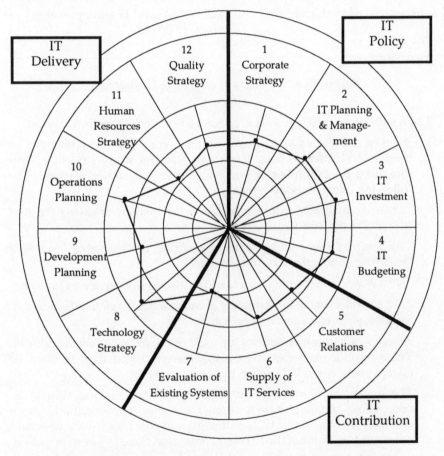

**Figure 10.5    Wheel diagram showing 12 review elements**

Although the individual results for each organisation are confidential, Figure 10.6 shows an example of the statements associated with the ratings.

| | |
|---|---|
| Most advanced performance found: | IT and Corporate strategies are closely integrated with effective feedback achievements. |
| Median performance: | Corporate and IT strategies are related but not integrated. |
| Least advanced performance: | Corporate and IT strategies are loosely linked. |

**Figure 10.6    Details of corporate IT strategy**

The results of the 1990 reviews produced a number of significant points:

1.  A set of definitions and measurements were produced which can be used to test effectiveness. Participants in the study saw how they measured on a number of key issues alongside other partners. The following quotations are typical:

    *"In our relationships with our customers, our practice is among the most advanced in the Joint Venture"*

    *"We thought we were doing a sound job on development planning, but most of the Partners are further advanced than us"*

    *"None of the Partners really has a handle on quality strategy; we are not alone"*

    *"The identification and presentation of best practice in information management has given us a standard to aim at"*

2.  A series of recommendations for each of the Partners was produced. These provide an objective base for internal discussions on how the effectiveness of the IS function can be improved.

3.  The reviews highlighted differences between Partners' individual pre-occupations and the current fashions. For example, fashionable IT issues currently include: using IT as a strategic weapon, user friendliness, and open systems. None of the Partners considered these as a preoccupation.

    A feature of the second year is to discover why these differences occur. One of the Partners sees the focus on IT development in terms of IS infrastructure and IS superstructure. Most organisations are still in the infrastructure phase, by which is meant automating clerical and routine operations, creating a communications network and establishing a base of routine transaction data. The IS department is forming a platform of understanding, confidence and comfort for users and, more importantly, for top management and line management. Superstructure refers to the adventurous, risk-taking, act-of-faith type of IS. Without substantial success on the infrastructure side, superstructure cannot be properly addressed.

4. The reviews showed that best practice is culture dependent. In a high-tech environment, where the top management are interested and involved in IS, performance expectations are different to those organisations where top management are more involved in other issues.

The key issues for continued study as seen by the Partners themselves were stated as:

- Effectiveness as top management see it
- Developing the definition and measurement of effectiveness
- Linking IS and Corporate strategies
- Sharpening and promulgating IS policies
- Human Resources
- Quality.

## 10.8   SUMMARY

Value for money analysis is a key issue. Studies should be conducted on a regular basis, perhaps every two or three years. Using, at least partially, external consultants is recommended in order to retain a level of objectivity. The results of a VFM study should be presented to top management in order that findings can be incorporated into the on-going development of the ISD. However, VFM analyses are operational in nature and if strategic issues are to be included, then a HCR is required. These studies are much more comprehensive.

# 11 Documentation of a Case for Investment in IT

## 11.1 AN IT INVESTMENT PROPOSAL

This chapter suggests some general guidance to assist in the preparation of a case requesting authority to spend a capital sum on IT. The same guidance could profitably be used by managers who have to review such cases. The second half of the chapter includes an example of a typical case.

Clearly, all firms have their own rules about how cases for financial authority must be prepared and presented, and at what level of expenditure such rules apply. However, most firms require a written commentary in addition to the financial details and it is the written half of the case with which this chapter is mainly concerned. The commentary is both explanation and plea and there are sufficient common points in most firms' requirements to be able to make some general comments.

The sole purpose of such a case is to persuade the relevant authority to spend the requested amount. That authority may reside in one person but, for amounts which require a full written case, is more probably vested in some form of capital approvals committee. In either case the intention is to gain agreement as quickly and painlessly, but honestly, as possible. Anything which detracts from this end should be removed from the case.

Although some of the comments below may seem arbitrary and petty, they are based on many years experience in a number of firms. Senior managers do not vary in their likes and dislikes as much as they would like to believe.

The basic form of the document is as follows:

1. Preamble
2. Main justification.
3. Possible negative effects.
4. The implications of not proceeding.
5. Summary.
6. All financial data. Costs of equipment, assumptions made, etc.
7. Cost benefit analysis, reduced to NPV, of all reasonable options, including the do nothing option.

213

8.    Effects on budgets, effects on cash flow.

Each of these sections is discussed below.

Most firms would probably not expect a full case as above for small projects, typically a simplified procedure with little documentation will apply for amounts below £25,000 or £50,000.

Many capital approval cases result from some company policy or legislative change. In such circumstances, there is relatively little freedom of choice for the capital approvals committee, and the main issue is to accommodate the change at minimum cost. However, most company rules still require a full approvals case as though a completely free hand was available. That case must of course refer to the policy change, with reference to the appropriate documentation, and explain how the change necessitates the current proposal.

## 11.2   THE SECTIONS IN MORE DETAIL

### 11.2.1   The preamble

The Preamble, or executive overview, should be less than a page of A4, preferably nearer half a page. The rest of the page should be blank; that is, the rest of the text should start on a fresh page. It is quite likely that this is the only part of the written case that some members of the approvals committee will read with any care. It is thus worth spending some time honing this section. It must include specific advantages of the project. Such advantages do not include general waffle to the effect that computers are considered a good idea by everyone else; the points must be specific to this proposal and should be reasonably detailed within the space confines. Attempted humour is probably misplaced in such a summary.

Thus, statements such as "the proposal will reduce operating costs in the mailing room by 15%" are necessary.

The company rules will probably require a form of words such as "the committee is invited to approve the expenditure of £56K, and note that non recurring current account expenditure of £15K will be incurred." The capital approvals secretariat will help with these formalities. If all else fails, get hold of a copy of a recently approved case and copy that.

### 11.2.2   The main justification

This section is intended to give a reasonably detailed description of the proposal. It would normally be made up of a number of shorter sections giving, for example, details of the background or current situation, descriptions of changed circumstances and discussion of the options considered. In total it should not be more than four pages of A4 and should include mention of all large amounts of money in the financial appendices. In complex cases there may be considerable amounts of supporting evidence; consultants' reports for example. Company preference will dictate whether these are attached as appendices or held available for inspection. Only the relevant conclusions need be quoted in this section of the case.

It should include a discussion of all reasonable options considered, including the do nothing option, and reasons why the recommended option is superior. This will usually be that, over the time period, the recommended option is the cheapest; but there may be lots of reasons for recommending other than the cheapest option. The golden rule here is to be honest about the real reasons, and not try to fiddle the figures in an attempt to favour the recommended option. All firms do, on occasion, spend money to gain intangible benefits, or in the hope of gaining an unquantifiable benefit. A statement that the recommended option, though not the cheapest, is preferable because the extra expense will bring some stated, but unquantifiable, benefit is reasonable; whereas a case based on fiddled figures will fall with little hope of rescue if the dishonesty is discovered.

The section must include a description of the problem to be rectified or the situation to be improved. Companies do not spend money without good reason and unless some improvement is intended this proposal is a waste of everyone's time. The measures which will be used to monitor and control the improvement must also be specified; including the current level of performance, and what target level the proposal seeks to achieve. Some firms will require a sensitivity analysis; how sensitive is the size of the return on capital to different levels of performance? Even if not required in the formal case, such a sensitivity analysis is recommended as a useful tool to be used by the project sponsor.

The measures used should preferably be one of the business ratios already used by the firm; they were presumably chosen because they reflect some important aspect of the firm's operations, and there will be a record of these figures going back some time and an understanding of cyclical changes or other trends.

If no suitable measure exists, which will be the case for most smaller projects, the proposal must devise one, explaining its relevance and how it is to be collected. Any costs of collection and analysis, if significant, are a cost of the proposal.

The necessity of stating, in clear numerical terms, the current and target performance cannot be too strongly emphasised. No sensible person will pay money without knowing in advance the benefit or goods he is to receive in return. No sensible firm should contemplate spending large sums of money without knowing in advance the details of the benefit sought, and knowing in advance how success is to be measured.

In similar vein, most proposals for larger projects should include some discussion of how the project manager will ensure that the target benefit will be achieved. This need not be in great detail, but some milestone dates and measures which will indicate whether or not progress is being maintained should be indicated.

Any significant issues that are likely to occur to the committee should be included. This is obviously a counsel of perfection, and it must be admitted that some members of capital approval committees will not be satisfied unless they can pick up some point no matter how abstruse. However, simple, obvious questions that remain unanswered will more or less guarantee a request to re-submit.

### 11.2.3   Possible negative effects

The main section described in 11.2.2 above should not contain a discussion of negative effects or dis-benefits. These should be kept together in one section, preferably as short as possible.

Every good idea has some potential risk or dis-benefit and no proposal will be taken seriously if it does not make mention of them. But for every point made in this section there should be an explanation of how those risks are to be minimised or how the dis-benefits are to be handled.

### 11.2.4   The implications of not proceeding

If the proposal has a benefit, and if it does not this document is worthless, then there must be a downside to not going ahead. It may be as simple as the fact that "operating costs in the post room will continue at an unnecessarily high level".

The purpose of this section is to counter the negative points made in section 11.2.3 and reinforce arguments advanced in section 11.2.2. It should be less than half a page of A4, preferably only a couple of short paragraphs.

### 11.2.5   The summary

The summary should be just that. Half a page at the most, and again it will probably be expected to include some agreed form of words. In the written case it is likely to repeat much of what was said in the executive overview and is often omitted for this reason. It should not be left out of a verbal presentation; never lose the opportunity to make a good point.

### 11.2.6   The financial appendices

These will probably be prepared by the finance group from information supplied by the proposer. In any event, these will vary so much that few general points can be made. The list quoted in Appendix 6 is a typical set.

The finance group will expect a list of all expenses that will flow from all of the options considered; on-going and non-recurring current account as well as capital. This is quite an onerous task but should have been completed before a formal proposal was initiated. Until the proposer has satisfied himself that the proposal is likely to be worthwhile he has no right to take up the time and energies of anyone else in considering it.

## 11.3   SOME GENERAL POINTS

- Contrary to what many people think, spelling and grammar are important in such documents. A simple spelling error will annoy and distract, spoiling the appearance of the document. The fact that it was the typist's mistake is no defence, the proposer is responsible for all the details in the document.

- For the same reason, details of the financial appendices should be checked; assistance should be sought with sections that are not clearly understood.

- The proposer may be called upon to present the paper in person. This is not an invitation to read out the text at dictation pace, nor to spend three quarters of an hour explaining every last detail. The presentation should last about four minutes – the average attention span of most managers when listening to a presentation on a subject that does not particularly interest them. The fact that the proposer finds the post room operations fascinating does not mean that everyone shares the obsession. The presentation should be structured in the same way as the first five sections above; 30 seconds for an introduction, two minutes for the main section and thirty seconds for each of the other sections. Practice beforehand, particularly the timing, in front of a mirror if necessary.

Clearly in such a short time it is impossible to cover the subject in any depth. It should be assumed that the audience has read the document (assuming that they have had it a few days) and emphasis should be placed on the problem to be resolved and the benefits of the suggestion as well as any major issues involved. The committee will then regulate the length of the presentation by the number of questions they ask.

Obviously, for major projects considerably more time will be required.

In that case, the presentation should start with a four minute overview which leads into more detailed discussion of the important points.

- When called upon to authorise expenditure, it is important to insist on details of what benefits the change is intended to bring about. Unless the measures are specified, the current level and the target level stated, the chances of achieving much return for the money are slim. Consideration should be given to determining how to ensure that the benefits are really achieved.

## 11.4   AN EXAMPLE OF CAPITAL EXPENDITURE REQUEST FOR IT

Appendix 6 illustrates an example of a typical, though fictitious, case requesting authority for the purchase of IT equipment. It includes a number of elements mentioned in this and other chapters; "must do" decisions resulting from policy or legislative changes, decisions justified on strictly financial bases, and intangible benefits.

It is based on GiantCo plc, which manufactures, sells, rents and maintains a wide range of metal- and wood-working tools and machines. Though the case as a whole is fictitious it is based on a number of real implementations. Little attempt has been made to give detailed or accurate technical specifications of the machinery; such details would distract from the main learning point. Similarly, reference is made to a number of appendices (all identified as Appendix N.n) which have not been included. The Child Safety Registration Act is a purely imaginary piece of legislation.

## 11.5   SUMMARY

The key features of an investment proposal are:

- to persuade the relevant authority that it is in the firm's interest to proceed. It should be designed to be as persuasive as possible for the target audience whilst remaining honest.

- to include a clear statement of the business reason for the investment, detailing the relevant measures, as well as the current and target performance.

- to provide criteria for measuring success, and responsibility for achieving targets.

Before submitting any proposal it is essential to check that it fully addresses each of the above points. If it does not, it is inadequate, and even if the proposal is approved it will probably lead to future difficulties.

# 12 Designing IT Surveys for Benefit Measurement

## 12.1 INTRODUCTION

In order to measure IT effectiveness most firms will need to administer a survey to its staff, suppliers and customers/end-users. To do this, considerable knowledge and skill relating to survey design, sample choice and so on is required. If handled correctly, a survey can provide detailed information about systems effectiveness, but conducted poorly, the survey may be useless and a complete waste of time and money.

It is not possible to describe a single, concise way in which to conduct a survey using questionnaires. There are many different approaches to a survey, and the appropriateness of the approach is entirely dependent on the particular circumstances being addressed. Furthermore, survey design is still regarded as more of an art than a science. Unfortunately, much of what has been written about survey design has been in the form of admonishments. The focus has been predominantly on what not to do rather than on those things that will help.

It is generally agreed that each study using questionnaires is unique. Therefore, every study requires that a questionnaire be specifically designed to fit the study's peculiar needs.

In designing a survey there are three main issues to consider. These are:

1. The survey method
2. The sampling scheme
3. Questionnaire design

Each of these components interacts with the others. In the following sections each will be discussed separately and the links that exist should become evident.

## 12.2 WHAT IS A SURVEY ?

A survey is a procedure for collecting information from individuals. The information sought can range from general background information such as age, income, size of the firm, the major areas of work of the firm, and the

219

location of the firm, to that relating to beliefs, feelings, attitudes, life-styles and intentions, etc. Methods for obtaining such information usually fall into two categories, namely self completion and interview administered. Self completion methods include mail surveys, computerised surveys and so called on-board or in-company surveys. Interview-administered surveys include personal interviews, telephone, and in-company/on-board surveys.

Each method possesses advantages and disadvantages. They do, however, all depend on the basic assumption that individuals subjected to questioning will be both willing and able to give truthful answers to the questions posed.

## 12.3   APPROACHES TO DATA COLLECTION

### 12.3.1   Mail surveys

This method involves mailing the questionnaire to predetermined respondents with a covering letter. This form of survey is only necessary if there are many information system users and they are spread widely around the country or world.

Arguments for this method are that it allows one to easily, at a relatively low cost, obtain a large sample with wide locational coverage. Furthermore, it allows respondents to complete the form at their own pace and also ensures that they are free from being influenced by the interviewer. Generally speaking, these samples are easy to select.

Arguments against this method include the need for a very simple questionnaire, possible biased responses, and the low response rate. Many suggestions for improving the response rate have been put forward. A good covering letter, follow up questionnaire or reminder can boost response and so can the offering of incentives. Also, the problem of bias can be addressed through interviewing a small sample of non-respondents, or by comparing early returns with the returns from the follow up questionnaire. The comparison is usually made on characteristics considered important to the study.

Typical response rates for this type of survey range from 1% to 60%.

### 12.3.2   In-company/on-board surveys

These surveys are carried out, for example, on board aircraft, in classrooms or in-company. In the information systems users' environment it may be possible to approach a group of IS users in the canteen, or perhaps a departmental head could be asked to bring his or her staff together for 25 minutes to fill out a questionnaire.

Arguments for this approach include that it provides a quick and cheap way of obtaining a large sample. This is because there is a captive audience. These surveys can be either interviewer or self administered.

Arguments against this approach are that it invariably only includes users and that there may only be limited time available.

Typical response rates for this method range from 35% to 75%.

### 12.3.3 Telephone surveys

This method is a low-cost form of personal interviewing which can be used to obtain information quickly. With a small number of users this is a fairly practical way of being able to collect data. Of course, if the users are spread around the country, Europe, or the world, telephone costs can be very substantial and, therefore, a major consideration against this approach.

Arguments for this method are that it is a good compromise in that it combines personal contact with cheapness and wide coverage; it provides information quicker than face-to-face interviewing and mail questionnaires; and it is easy to supervise the interviewing process, thereby reducing interview error.

Arguments against this method are that the telephone interview must be short; that it could be biased since it is limited to listed telephone owners; and that it could be expensive. A way in which this bias is overcome is through digit dialling. One such scheme is the so called Plus-One sampling where a single, randomly selected number is added to each of a randomly selected sample of telephone numbers chosen from the telephone directory.

Typical response rates for this method range from 35% to 75%.

### 12.3.4 Personal interviews

This method requires a face-to-face conversation between the interviewer and the respondent. This approach is widely used in marketing research.

In the information systems users' environment, personal interviews are frequently used, especially to canvass the opinions of the decision makers. It is an expensive means of collecting data in terms of time and money and therefore cannot be used with large groups where telephone or mail surveys are probably more appropriate.

The main argument for this approach is that in a long interview it is possible to probe complex issues that can be carried out in a relaxed atmosphere, developed by the interviewer. This should ensure a good quality response.

Arguments against this approach include the high amounts of time and cost involved. There are also the possibility of interviewer bias, and the difficulty to target users.

There are many factors that can influence the response rate but typical response rates for this method are between 50% to 80%.

### 12.3.5   Computer surveys

Where firms have electronic mail already established, a survey can be conducted across the network. This allows for instant data collection and summarisation. It is a relatively inexpensive method, easy to conduct and growing in popularity.

Arguments for this approach are that there is no need for printed questionnaires; interviewer bias is eliminated; checks can be built in so as to minimise response bias and optimise response consistency; and instantaneous analysis of the data is possible.

Arguments against this approach are that the design and programming of the questionnaire is likely to be a complex business involving considerable time and money up front; also respondents are restricted to E-mail users.

### 12.4   SAMPLING

All surveys require the selection of those individuals who are to provide the information. This set of individuals is called the sample. The sample comes from some much larger group of individuals or objects, called the target population. The target population referred to as the *population* in the sequel, is that group about which it is intended to make generalised statements based on the sample findings. The sample is ideally chosen so that no significant differences exist between the sample and the population in any important characteristics. In other words, the sample serves as a model for the population, and thus, from a statistical analysis of the sample data, it is possible to generalise to the whole population with a specified degree of confidence.

Sampling might be carried out in order to save expense (it would be impossibly expensive, as well as unnecessary, to carry out an opinion poll among the whole electorate). Using a sample also enables results to be obtained more rapidly.

Sampling has problems, however. It must be ensured that the sample is representative of the whole population, or the results will be biased and therefore will not be applicable to the whole population. For instance, an opinion poll carried out by knocking on doors in the afternoon is likely to result in a lot of people who work during the day being missed; if interviews are conducted in the canteen at lunchtime, staff who do not go to lunch will be missed; and the findings from interviewing accounting practices of 20 or fewer partners, with respect to software usage, cannot be extrapolated to larger accounting practices. Whether a sample is considered representative or not is a subjective assessment by those carrying out the survey or those using the results of the survey.

Sampling also has problems of variability. Even if great care is taken to avoid bias, the sample will never be exactly like the population. If another sample was chosen in exactly the same way, it would be different. This puts a limit on how accurate the sample can be, and therefore how accurately statements can be made about the population.

### 12.4.1 Choice of sampling frame

The sampling frame is a comprehensive list of individuals or objects from which the sample is to be drawn. For example, the membership list of a major association of data processing professionals or, perhaps, the membership list of the Institute of Chartered Accountants in England and Wales (ICAEW) could form the sampling frame. Other examples of sampling frames are the postal address file, the electoral register, the telephone directory, and companies listed on the London Stock Exchange.

In practice, the findings of a simple up-to-date list is highly unlikely. Combining more than one list can possibly help improve matters.

### 12.4.2 Types of sample

Sampling techniques fall into two broad categories, namely non-probability samples and probability samples.

For a *non-probability sample* there is no way of estimating the probability of an individual having been included in the sample. Such a sample can occur when individuals are included in the sample on a 'first arrive first questioned basis' and as a consequence, it is not possible to ensure that the sample is representative. Examples of non-probability samples include *convenience samples, judgment samples*, and *quota samples*.

In *probability sampling* each individual has a known, not necessarily equal, probability of being selected. Examples of probability sampling include *simple random sampling, systematic sampling, stratified sampling, cluster sampling*, and *multi-stage sampling*. Probability samples can be rigorously analysed by means of statistical techniques, whereas for non-probability samples this is not possible.

#### 12.4.2.1 *Non-probability sampling*

In non-probability sampling the subjective judgments of the researchers are used in selecting the sample. Clearly, this could result in the sample being biased. Non-probability samples are particularly useful in exploratory research. The more popular non-probability sampling methods are described below.

*Convenience samples* comprise those individuals that are most readily available to participate in the study. Such samples are extensively used in business school research, where the sample often comprises a group of MBA students or executives attending post experience courses at the time the research is being undertaken.

*Judgment samples*, also called purposive samples, are samples where individuals are selected with a specific purpose in mind. The composition of such a sample is not made with the aim to it being representative of the population. Such samples comprise individuals considered to have the knowledge and information to provide useful ideas and insights. This approach is extensively used in the exploratory research stage and is invaluable in ensuring a 'good' final questionnaire.

*Quota samples* are selected so that there is proportional representation of various sub-groups (or strata) of the target population. The selection of individuals to be included in the sample is done on a convenience basis. The interviewer is given information on the characteristics of those to be included in the sample, but the selection is left to the interviewer's judgment.

### 12.4.2.2 *Probability samples*

In obtaining a *probability sample*, use is made of some random procedure for the selection of the individuals or objects. This is done so as to remove the possibility of selection bias.

In *simple random sampling* each member of the population has an equal chance of being selected. This can be achieved by numbering individuals in the sampling frame and then selecting from these by some random procedure. An example of such a sample is a questionnaire mailed to say 600 information systems executives chosen at random from a mailing list of 3000 executives.

A *systematic sample* is selected from the sampling frame of size N in the following manner. Having decided what size sample n is to be selected from the sampling frame, calculate:

$$\left[\frac{N}{n}\right] \text{ where } [\;] \text{ denotes the largest integer } I \le \frac{N}{n}$$

Now select a random number i, say, in the interval $1 \le i \le I$. The sample size n then consists of the $i^{th}$, $(i+I)^{th}$; $(i+2I)^{th}$, and so on, up to the $(i+(n-1)I)^{th}$ item from the sampling frame.

Should there be some pattern present in the sampling frame, then such samples will be biased. For example, a systematic sample from the daily sales of a supermarket could result in picking out sales figures for Saturdays only.

In *stratified sampling* the population is subdivided into homogeneous groups, called strata, prior to sampling. Random samples are then drawn from each of the strata and the aggregate of these form the stratified sample. This can be done in one of two ways:

– The overall sample size n can comprise items such that the number of items from each stratum will be in proportion to the size of the stratum.

– The overall sample size can comprise items from each stratum where the number of items from each of the strata are determined according to the relative variability of the items within each of the strata.

The first approach is the one invariably used in practice.

In *cluster sampling*, the population is considered to be made up of groups, called clusters, where the clusters are naturally formed groups such as companies, or locational units.

A cluster sample from a large organisation could be achieved by treating the various departments of a company as the clusters. A random sample of departments could then be chosen and all individuals in the departments sampled. In other words a census of the selected departments (clusters) is performed.

An extension of cluster sampling is *multi-stage sampling*. The simplest multi-stage sample involves random selection of the clusters in the first stage, followed by a random selection of items from each of the selected clusters. This is called two-staged sampling. More complex designs involve more than two stages. For example, in selecting a sample of accounting software users in accounting practices in England and Wales, a random sample of geographic areas may be made from the ICAEW membership list. Then, from within the areas, a number of accounting practices may be randomly selected, and finally, in the third stage, a random sample of software users is selected from each of the previously selected practices.

### 12.4.3   Size of sample

Determination of the sample size is a complex problem. Factors which need to be taken into consideration include: type of sample, variability in the population, time, costs, accuracy of estimates required, and confidence with which generalisations to the population are made.

There exist formulae for computing sample size, which are based on sound scientific principles. These are briefly considered in section 12.4.3.1.

In practice, the sample sizes resulting from the application of the formulae are not slavishly adhered to and are frequently ignored. Often, the samples chosen are of a size that fit in with company policy or are regarded as credible through having been used by others conducting similar studies in the past. Such an approach is perfectly acceptable (Lehmann, 1989).

### 12.4.3.1    Statistical determination of sample size

This section describes two situations encountered in practice, namely, how to determine the sample size for estimating a population mean to a specified margin of error, or accuracy, with a specified level of confidence; and how to determine the sample size needed to estimate a population proportion (or percentage) to a specified margin of error, or accuracy, within a specified level of confidence.

These formulae only apply for probability samples taken from a very large population where the sample will be less than 10% of the population. Sample size calculations for more complex designs can be found in Lehmann (1989).

1.    Sample size to estimate the mean.

Suppose you wish to estimate the true average of a system's response time. In order to estimate this, a random sample of response times is taken and the average of these used to estimate the system's actual mean response time. The question now addressed is, what size of sample is needed to be 95% confident that the sample mean will be within E units of the true mean, where the unit of measurement of E can be in, say, seconds or minutes? E is therefore the accuracy required from the estimate. The sample size is given by:

$$ n = \frac{3.84\ \sigma^2}{E^2} $$

where $\sigma$ is the population standard deviation of response times. In practice $\sigma$ is inevitably unknown and will have to be estimated. This can be done by using response times for a pilot sample of size $n_p$, say, in the sample standard deviation formula:

$$ S = \sqrt{\frac{1}{n_p-1}\Sigma(x_i - \overline{x})^2} $$

where the $x_i$'s are the $n_p$ pilot response times, and $\overline{x}$ is the numerical average of the sample response times.

A simpler approach, often used, is to estimate $\sigma$ from the range of the pilot sample values. This is done according to the following formula:

$$ S_R = \frac{\max(x_i) - \min(x_i)}{4} = \frac{\text{Range}(x_i)}{4} $$

Some texts recommend dividing the range by 6. This is likely to result in an under-estimate of σ since pilots usually involve small samples. Of course a purely subjective estimate of σ is also possible.

Should it be required to estimate the mean to the same accuracy E as before, but now with a confidence level of 99% then the sample size is is given by:

$$n = \frac{6.66 \, \sigma^2}{E^2}$$

where σ can be estimated as described above.

2. Sample size to estimate a percentage.

Suppose you wish to estimate the actual percentage, p, say, of your customers who purchase software from a competing company. Suppose further that you require to know what sample size is needed to be 95% confident that the estimate of p resulting from the sample will be within E% of the actual percentage, p:

$$n = \frac{3.84 \, p(100-p)}{E^2}$$

The caveat in this case is that p is not known, as it is the parameter being estimated. In practice the value of p used in the above formula can be estimated in a number of ways. It can be estimated subjectively, or from a pilot sample or taken to be 50%. The latter results in the most conservative sample size estimate.

For a 99% confidence level:

$$n = \frac{6.66 \, p(100-p)}{E^2}$$

where p can be estimated as described above.

**Note:** where the sample is large, relative to the population, a finite population correction can be applied (Lehmann, 1989). Use of the previously described formulae will result in the use of larger sample sizes than needed.

## 12.5  QUESTIONNAIRE DESIGN

A questionnaire is not just a list of questions to be answered. It has to be designed with specific objectives in mind and is essentially a scientific instrument for measurement of the population characteristics of interest.

In designing the questionnaire consideration must be given to such issues as (Churchill, 1987):

- What does the firm want to achieve with the results of the questionnaire?
- What information is sought?
- What type of questionnaire will be used?
- How will the questionnaire be administered?
- The content of individual questions.
- The type of response required to each question.
- The number of questions to be used.
- The manner in which the questions are to be sequenced.
- After testing, by means of a pilot study, what revisions are needed?

Some of the above issues were dealt with in previous sections.

### 12.5.1   Prior to the main survey

The main survey makes use of a questionnaire comprised mainly of structured pre-coded questions. The construction of the main questionnaire is generally preceded by some qualitative or exploratory research involving the use of such informal techniques as unstructured interviews, brainstorming and focus groups. These activities include group discussions addressing many open ended questions. These activities combine not only to 'firm up' the study objectives, the method of data collection, and the definition of the target population, but also help identify appropriate questions to include in the survey and help ensure that the various concepts used in the survey are properly defined. A first draft of a questionnaire should then be tested by means of a pilot survey. Pilot surveys are used to test the structured pre-coded questions. It may include some open ended questions.

### 12.5.2   Things which help

A good starting point is to have clear terms of reference and objectives for the study, and to have made a thorough study of past surveys similar to the one being undertaken. In designing the questionnaire, consideration should be given to composing a good letter of introduction, the offering of incentives such as a draw for a magnum of Champagne, an attractive design, using no jargon, together with an easy to understand and relevant wording of the questions.

Also important is the sequencing of questions. This should be done so that the demographic and other potentially embarrassing questions are placed at the end of the questionnaire. Also, questions on the same topic should be kept together. The opening questions should be carefully designed so as to ensure the respondent's early co-operation, thereby increasing the chances of obtaining truthful and quality responses to all questions.

Pilot surveys are essential. Authors of questionnaires can never rely on knowing how clear a question is. This can only be established through pilot studies which should be completed by a range of possible respondents, including those least familiar with completing questionnaires. Every single question should be examined on the basis of how the answer will lead to a better understanding of what is being studied.

Questions that do not contribute to the specific objectives of the study should be removed. Furthermore, more sophisticated surveys may involve complicated terminology and concepts that could mean different things to different people. In such cases precise definitions of these concepts must be provided. An example of this can be found on page 3 of Figure 12.2.

Special attention should be given to the inclusion of demographic and usage questions so that adequate segmentation and cross tabulation can be performed. For example, of especial importance in IS studies is knowledge of who are the extensive users, minimal users and clerical users.

### 12.5.3   Things to avoid

The design should ensure that the questionnaire is not unduly long. Mail questionnaires requiring more than 15 to 20 minutes to complete are likely to have a dramatic impact on the response rate. Further, the design should ensure that there is no vagueness in the questions posed, that there are no loaded or leading questions, no double-barrelled or double negative questions, no on-sided and not too many open-ended questions. Good quality response to open-ended questions require the respondent to be articulate. Also, such questions are difficult to code for computer analysis. These two factors combine to produce problems in analysis and summarisation. The questions should not be too complex or involve concepts that are likely not to be clearly understood. Where jargon has to be used it is essential to supply a detailed glossary. Should the questionnaire involve branching type questions, then the branching instructions must be clear so as to ensure that the respondent does not become confused.

### 12.5.4   Techniques for questioning

The manner in which questions are structured, ordered, presented and, coded can affect the response rate, the quality of response, make accurate data capture easy, and facilitate statistical analysis. Some of ways in which this is done are set out below.

### 12.5.4.1 Sequencing of questions

It is generally agreed that the best way in which to order the questions is to place general questions first, specific questions next and attitudinal questions later. Hard questions should be placed fairly early interspersed with easy questions. Further, there is a need to ensure that the questions are structured in such a way that the respondent will find it easy to answer questions within a topic, and also not be burdened with questions that are irrelevant to him or her.

*Funnel Questions* are used to sequence within a particular topic. For example, consider the sequence of questions:

> Which of the following high level languages do you use?
> (Please tick appropriate box)
> Cobol ☐   Fortran ☐   APL ☐   C ☐   BASIC ☐

> Which of the following high level languages do you like most?
> (Please tick appropriate box)
> Cobol ☐   Fortran ☐   APL ☐   C ☐   BASIC ☐

> Which of the following high level languages did you not use
> in the past seven days?  (Please tick appropriate box)
> Cobol ☐   Fortran ☐   APL ☐   C ☐   BASIC ☐

In this type of question the respondent is guided from a general question to a specific question.

*Filter Questions* are used to exclude the respondent from being asked questions that are irrelevant to him or her. For example, consider the question:

> Do you ever use Cobol?

> IF YES: When did you last use Cobol?
> Within last 7 days  ☐   8-14 days  ☐   More than 14 days ago  ☐

> IF NO: Why is that?

The above filter question also illustrates the use of what can be referred to as a specific time period question.

*Specific Time Period* questions are used to avoid memory problems with respondents. Consider the question:

> How often do you use high level programming languages?  ☐

which is open-ended and has no prompt, against:

> When did you last use a high level programming language?
> (Please tick appropriate category)

Within last 7 days  ☐   8-14 days  ☐   More than 14 days ago  ☐   Never  ☐

### 12.5.4.2   Examples of pre-coded questions

Coding is the procedure for assigning numerical symbols to the categories or classes into which the responses are to be placed. This is usually decided when designing the questionnaire. For example:

> Which of the following best describes your position in the management structure? (Please circle the appropriate number)
>
> 1 Upper                     4 Lower middle
> 2 Upper middle              5 Lower
> 3 Middle

It is recommended that not more than six or seven categories be used. Also one must make sure that the categories fit, otherwise the respondent can become irritated.

### 12.5.4.3   Particular questions

The typology of data used in IS studies include demographics, attitudes, beliefs, interests, preferences, product, software and systems usage, determinants of usage, perceived benefits and desired benefits. Below are examples of questions for some of these categories (See also Figures 12.1 and 12.2 at the end of this chapter):

*Demographic variables* provide factual information about the individual or company and include information on:

> Industry in which the firm operates
> Number of IT staff employed in your firm
> Total investment in IT in the firm
> Degree of specialism of respondent
> (eg whether IS specialist or managerial user?)

*Socio-economic variables* relate to the economic status of the individual or company. Examples of variables which reflect this include:

> Income
> Turnover
> Market share
> Profits
> Education
> Spend on IT training as % of annual income
> Position in the company
> Function within the firm

*Attitudes* relate to a latent state of mind which in turn relates to feelings which can subsequently influence behaviour. Attitude measurement is usually achieved by use of a 5-point or 7-point scale. For example:

(7) Strongly agree
(6) Agree
(5) Slightly Agree
(4) Neither Agree or Disagree
(3) Slightly Disagree
(2) Disagree
(1) Strongly Disagree

Use of a scale with an odd number of points allows a neutral response. When using a 5-point scale leave out 'slightly'. Should it be desired to force the respondent to reveal his or her inclination, an even number of points is used. For a 6-point scale leave out the 'neutral' category. Sometimes a 4-point scale is used. This can be achieved by leaving out the three central categories.

Example: *Attitudes*

To what extent do you agree that the following should be used by/introduced into your practice?

Use the scale:

(5) Strongly agree
(4) Agree
(3) Uncertain
(2) Disagree
(1) Strongly Disagree

Q1. ☐  Computer assisted learning techniques
Q2. ☐  Public availability of current financial information on public companies.

*Beliefs* relate to an individual's subjective assessment, or opinion, of the likelihood of a statement holding.

Example: *Beliefs*

Answer the questions by indicating the strength of your opinion in terms of the use of your computer network if the following were available to you:

Use the scale

(1) Very likely to use it
(2) Somewhat likely to use it
(3) Neither likely or unlikely to use it
(4) Somewhat unlikely to use it
(5) Very unlikely to use it

Q1. ☐   Access to external databases through the system
Q2. ☐   A degree of technical competence of software and
hardware downtime

Answer the following questions on the scale:

(5) Very great benefit
(4) Great benefit
(3) Some benefit
(2) Little benefit
(1) No obvious benefit

What do you see as the main benefits of IT for your firm?

Q1. ☐   Providing better management information
Q2. ☐   Improving access to external sources of information.

Incidentally, the above scale can be regarded as unbalanced in that the emphasis is placed on the extent of belief and is loaded towards the respondent indicating a degree of benefit. In the previous example the scale is regarded as balanced in that there are an equal number of negative and positive categories.

*Usage of Product/Software/Systems* questions describe what is used, how it is used, the purpose of use, the benefit from use, the frequency of use and so on. Common variables include:

System used/planned to use
Usage rate of reports
Time between use
Satisfaction

Example: *Areas of use and amount of use*

Q1.   In which areas do you use SIS (Strategic Information
Systems)? (Please tick appropriate box)

☐ Sales and Marketing Systems
☐ Financial Planning and Mgmt Systems
☐ Inter-organisational systems
☐ Office automation
☐ Artificial intelligence based systems
☐ Other (Please specify) _____

Q2.   How many hours per week do you use a workstation?

___ Hours

Q3. Of these hours what percentage (whole numbers) do you use the following?

☐☐☐ % Word 5
☐☐☐ % Lotus 1-2-3
☐☐☐ % dBase III+
☐☐☐ % E/Mail
☐☐☐ % Time Management
☐☐☐ % Other(Please specify) _____

Example: *Benefit Identification*

Q1. Can you cite an instance in which ICON can be directly credited with giving the firm a competitive advantage? (Please tick appropriate box)
☐ Yes
☐ No
If yes please give a brief description _____

Example: *Satisfaction with software*

Q1. Look through the following list and state how satisfied you are with your firm's applications software in the following areas? Use the scale:

(1) Very dissatisfied
(2) Dissatisfied
(3) Not sure
(4) Satisfied
(5) Very satisfied

☐ Preparation of Accounts
☐ Tax Planning
☐ Stock Control
☐ Payroll
☐ Novell Network
☐ Other(Please specify): _____

*Determinants of use* questions are included with the view to explaining behaviour relating to the use of product/software/information systems. Variables used include:

Knowledge and understanding of the system
Ease of use
Influence of others
Relevance of report contents
Information systems needs
Information systems capabilities

Example: *IS needs*

Evaluate how *important* you feel that each attribute is
in ensuring that the overall computer based system will be
effective? Use the scale:

(1) Irrelevant
(2) Possibly useful
(3) Of some use
(4) Important
(5) Very critical

Q1. ☐ Availability and timeliness of report delivery
Q2. ☐ Communications between IS staff and managerial users.

Example: *IS capability*

Evaluate the degree of IS *performance* attained within
your organisation on the following scale:

(1) Very poor
(2) Poor
(3) Adequate
(4) Good
(5) Excellent

Q1. ☐ Availability and timeliness of report delivery

Q2. ☐ Communications between IS staff and managerial users.

## 12.6 MEASUREMENT SCALES

Section 12.5 reveals that the nature of data obtained from respondents are both qualitative and quantitative. Meaningful analysis requires that the responses be quantified.

There are four scales (or levels) of measurement that can be used. These are the nominal (or categorical), ordinal, interval and ratio measurement scales.

*Nominal* scales are used to identify the categories to which a respondent belongs. An example of such a scale can be found in Figure 12.1 question 2, where the response can be either yes or no. A nominal rating of '1' is assigned to a yes answer and a '0' to a no answer. A '1' therefore categorises the respondent as having had experience with a similar system to ICON. In this case the numbers assigned are arbitrary and are no more than labels for the categories. Counting is the only analysis possible on such data.

*Ordinal* scales are used when the respondent is asked for responses in the form of a rank ordering. An example of the use of such a scale is to be found in Figure 12.1 question 11. The ranks in this case provide information on the relative standing of the benefits when compared in terms of impact on ICON. For example, should efficiency be ranked '1', and effectiveness '2', then ICON is considered to have a greater impact on efficiency than on effectiveness. However, how much more impact it will have cannot be inferred from such numbers. Therefore the difference in the ranks does not provide information on the actual extent of the impact. Such scales do allow for more sophisticated analysis than was possible for the nominal scale. For this data it is meaningful to compute such non-parametric statistics as the median, quartiles and rank correlations.

*Interval* scales posses the property that the difference between the numbers on the scale can be interpreted meaningfully. Examples of a scale that is treated as interval is to be found in Figure 12.2, questions 1 through 20. For these questions the rating system is such that:

1 – denotes strongly agree

2 – denotes agree

3 – denotes disagree

4 – denotes strongly agree

In this case, the difference between the ratings of two individuals on the same item gives an indication of the extent to which the two individuals agree or disagree on the item. In other words, the difference between the numbers of such a scale can be interpreted as an absolute measure of how far apart individuals are with respect to the item. For example, in this case the difference between a rating of '1' and a rating of '2' is equal to the difference between ratings of '3' and '4'. Also the difference, say, between '1' and '2' is half the difference between '1' and '3'. For this scale the ratio of numbers on the scale is not meaningful. The reason for this is that the choice of the rating score of '1' to denote strongly agree was arbitrary, and could just as easily have been chosen as '0', say. However, intervals computed from numbers on these scales are comparable in terms of ratios.

Interval scale data can be analysed by virtually the full range of statistical procedures. For this scale the calculation of means, standard deviations and Pearson correlation coefficients provide meaningful statistics.

*Ratio* scales are scales such that the numbers on the scale possess not only the properties of the nominal, ordinal and interval scales, but in addition, ratios of numbers on this scale have meaning. An example of such a scale can be found in Figure 12.1 question 5.

This scale possesses the property that intervals between points on the scale are comparable. For example, the difference between an average workstation usage of 10 hours per week and 12 hours per week is the same as the difference between say 15 hours per week and 17 hours per week.

In addition, it is meaningful, for example, to compare an average usage of 15 hours per week with an average usage of 10 hours per week, by stating that the former usage of the workstation is 1.5 times that of the latter. For a ratio scale 'zero' has a physical meaning. In this case a response of zero is taken to mean that the individual does not use the workstation. Ratio data is the highest level of data and can be analysed by the full range of statistical techniques.

In practice, surveys generally make most use of data at the nominal, ordinal and interval level.

## 12.7 A GUIDE TO CONDUCTING A SURVEY

The following is a step-by-step guide to conducting a survey of the use of IT in the firm.

### 12.7.1 Terms of reference

Accurately define the purposes of the survey. These should be stated as the survey's terms of reference.

### 12.7.2 Data collection

Establish how the data will be collected, ie personal interview, mail, telephone, etc.

### 12.7.3 Determine the sample size and the sample frame

Estimate the response rate which will produce the appropriate sample size.

### 12.7.4 Focus groups

Form a focus group in order to identify the key issues to be addressed by the survey. Focus groups may be from six to ten informants.

### 12.7.5 Produce questions

From the key issues develop a list of appropriate questions.

### 12.7.6 Questionnaire design

From the questions draft a questionnaire. This task includes the selection of an appropriate scale.

### 12.7.7   Conduct a pilot study

Perform a pilot study using the questionnaire to determine initial responses. The pilot study may encompass between six and ten individuals.

### 12.7.8   Revise the questionnaire

Using the results of the pilot study, revise the questionnaire so that it focuses more closely on the key issues.

### 12.7.9   Distribute questionnaire

Distribute the finalised questionnaire to the chosen sample. Each respondent should be notified of the date by which return of the completed questionnaire is required.

### 12.7.10   Collect results

The completed questionnaires should be collected. It may be possible to discard partially complete questionnaires in favour of complete ones, depending on the response rate achieved.

### 12.7.11   Code results

The results of the questionnaires should be coded appropriately, in order to make analysis and interpretation easier.

### 12.7.12   Analyse and interpret

The coded results should be analysed to determine the overall results of the survey. Careful analysis will reveal both whether the survey was successful as well as whether the IT systems are meeting the requirements of the respondents.

## 12.8   SUMMARY

Survey design is very much an art and invariably results in economic considerations forcing the researchers to sacrifice what they ideally would require for what is practical in terms of the time and money available. It must be accepted that no survey will be found to be perfect. The key to a successful survey is the care taken in carrying out the time-consuming and costly up front work. This includes tasks such as clearly defining the purpose and objectives of the study, the running of focus groups, analysing transcripts of the focus group meetings, conducting fairly open ended interviews with appropriate persons, and the development and thorough pilot testing of the questionnaire. Also there is the need to ensure that the sample is representative and of credible size.

ICON User Survey
May 1989

## PART A – USER PROFILE

1.     Personal Details

| Group | Grade | How long in PMM | How long using PCs | How long using ICON |
|-------|-------|-----------------|--------------------|---------------------|
|       |       | years           | years              | months              |

2.     Have you used any other system similar to ICON?

       | Yes | No |

    If so where and what was it called?

3.     Do you find it easy to gain access to a workstation (tick one)

| Exclusive use | When required | Usually available | Not easy | Difficult |
|---------------|---------------|-------------------|----------|-----------|
|               |               |                   |          |           |

4.     Do you find it convenient to reach a Laserjet printer? (tick one)

| Locally attached | Same office | Available nearby | Not easy | Difficult |
|------------------|-------------|------------------|----------|-----------|
|                  |             |                  |          |           |

5.     How many hours per week on average do you use a workstation?

                        Hours

6.     Of these hours what percentage do you use the following:

    Note: Enter minimum 1% if you have ever used the service on ICON

| | % | | | % |
|---|---|---|---|---|
| a. WordPerfect | | i. E/Mail | | |
| b. Lotus 1-2-3 | | j. ICON Database | | |
| c. SuperCalc 4 | | k. Phone Directory | | |
| d. Harvard Graphics | | l. Time Management | | |
| e. PMW | | m. Other _____ | | |
| f. dBase III+ | | n. Other _____ | | |
| g. DataEase | | o. Other _____ | | |

7.     Please tell us which additional applications should be made available on ICON next

## Figure 12.1    First sample questionnaire – page 1

PART B – BENEFIT IDENTIFICATION

8.     Have your uses of ICON produced any benefits, direct or indirect, to you?
Please specify up to three, (but see also Part C below)

9.     What do we have to do in ICON to remove constraints to benefits?

10.     Can you cite an instance in which ICON can be directly credited with giving
the firm a competitive advantage?

| Yes | No |
|-----|-----|

If yes, please give a brief description

11.     Please rank these areas of benefit into the order in which you think that ICON
will have the most impact to Peat Marwick:

(5=high, 1=low)

| | | |
|---|---|---|
| a. Efficiency | (doing more things) (doing things faster) | |
| b. Effectiveness | (doing the right thing) | |
| c. Innovation | (new ways of work) | |
| d. Utilisation | (Hours billed to client) | |
| e. Job Satisfaction | (work environment) | |

**Figure 12.1     First sample questionnaire – page 2**

ICON User Survey
May 1989

12.  Now please tick one answer in each heading (as defined above) for the
     impact of ICON on you own work:

| It has enhanced my: | Strongly agree | Agree | Disagree | Strongly disagree | Don't know |
|---|---|---|---|---|---|
| a. Efficiency | | | | | |
| b. Effectiveness | | | | | |
| c. Innovation | | | | | |
| d. Utilisation | | | | | |
| e. Job Satisfaction | | | | | |

Please write any comments on the above

13.  I have received adequate training to use the ICON system effectively:
     (tick one)

| Strongly agree | Agree | Disagree | Strongly disagree | Don't know |
|---|---|---|---|---|
| | | | | |

Please give a brief explanation of your answer:

14.  I have received adequate support from the ICON Help Desk:
     (tick one)

| Strongly agree | Agree | Disagree | Strongly disagree | Don't know |
|---|---|---|---|---|
| | | | | |

Please give a brief explanation of your answer:

**Figure 12.1     First sample questionnaire – page 3**

## PART C – DIRECT EFFECT ON PROPOSALS AND REPORTS

If you are involved in preparing or typing proposals or reports please
answer the following:

15.    My use of ICON has contributed to the speed with which I can prepare
       a proposal/report:
       (tick one)

| Strongly agree | Agree | Disagree | Strongly disagree | Don't know |
|---|---|---|---|---|
|  |  |  |  |  |

Please give a brief explanation of your answer:

16.    My use of ICON has contributed to my ability to produce better
       quality reports/proposals:
       (tick one)

| Strongly agree | Agree | Disagree | Strongly disagree | Don't know |
|---|---|---|---|---|
|  |  |  |  |  |

Please give a brief explanation of your answer:

## PART D – GENERAL

17.    From my experience to date I feel that ICON will make a strong impact
       on the way that Peat Marwick does business:
       (tick one)

| Strongly agree | Agree | Disagree | Strongly disagree | Don't know |
|---|---|---|---|---|
|  |  |  |  |  |

Please give a brief explanation of your answer:

If you have any further comments or suggestions to improve the ICON system please use the space
overleaf.

Thank you for your help

Dan Remenyi
Research Associate
Henley – The Management College
Greenlands
Oxon. RG9 3AU

Figure 12.1     First sample questionnaire – page 4

## Management Research into Strategic Information Systems

This questionnaire is being used to collect data which will be part of a dissertation for a doctor of philosophy (PhD) degree presented at Henley – The Management College by Dan Remenyi. The content of individual questionnaires will not be divulged nor will the identity of those completing them.

Some of the language used in the questionnaire is quite specific to the subjects of corporate planning and information systems and therefore a list of definitions is provided on page 3 of this document.

## Introduction to the Questionnaire

This questionnaire has been designed to test the validity of certain theories concerning management practice in the formulation, planning and implementation of Strategic Information Systems (SIS). The theory being investigated is that:-

*SIS occur as a result of pressure or opportunities directly related to industry drivers. This pressure or opportunity is influenced by the firm's strategy and by its CSFs and these issues determine the formulation of the SIS. The decision to attempt to take advantage of SIS is made with little attention to detail concerning cost/justification and supplier selection but with more attention to communicating with the staff, training appropriate people and setting up support facilities.*

This questionnaire is aimed at executives who have been involved in the formulation and/or implementation of a SIS. It is hoped that several from the same firm, but who are working in different functional areas, will complete separate copies of this questionnaire.

The questionnaire is looking for two sets of views from executives concerning how their firms have *actually* coped with the practical management of SIS and how the executives believe their firms, and/or firms in general, *should* go about the formulation, planning and implementation of these systems. Thus it is of paramount importance for respondents to clearly distinguish between what actually happened in their organisations during the formulation, planning and implementation of their SIS and what they now believe should have occurred. The questions are in the form of statements and the respondents are asked to state whether they Strongly Agree, Agree, Disagree or Strongly Disagree with each statement. After each question in the questionnaire there are two answer diagrams, one for replies concerning how the firm *ACTUALLY* coped and one for how the respondent believes they *SHOULD* have formulated and implemented their SIS.

There are 20 questions in the main body of the questionnaire as well as nine questions on the background of the person completing the form which will together require about 20 minutes to complete.

Thank you for participating in this research.

Dan Remenyi BSocSc MBA
Research Associate
Henley – The Management College
Greenlands, Henley-on-Thames
RG9 3AU

(0734) 724148

November 1989

1

**Figure 12.2      Second sample questionnaire – page 1**

## DETAILS OF RESPONDENTS

Name of Respondent

Name of Firm

Type of SIS* with which involved

Industry in which working

Function within firm

Number of years working with IS

Number of years working in management

Number of IT staff employed in your firm

| Up to 100 | 101 – 500 | 501 and above |
|-----------|-----------|---------------|
| ☐ | ☐ | ☐ |

The total investment in IT in your firm

| Up to £500 000 | £500 001 – £10 000 000 | £10 000 001 and above |
|----------------|------------------------|------------------------|
| ☐ | ☐ | ☐ |

*Examples of SIS include

| | |
|-----|-----|
| SMS | Sales and marketing systems |
| FPMS | Financial planning and management systems |
| IOS | Inter-organisational systems |
| OA | Office automation |
| AI | Artificial intelligence based systems |
| MRP | Materials requirements planning |
| FMS | Flexible manufacturing systems |

If another type of SIS has been formulated and/or implemented, please give a brief description

(A SIS may have aspects of more than one of the systems. If this is the case please indicate which of the above categories could be described as the dominant one).

2

**Figure 12.2    Second sample questionnaire – page 2**

## Definitions

Because some of the terminology in the questionnaire can mean different things to different people the following are definitions of some of these terms.

*Strategic Information Systems (SIS)* are information systems which directly assist the firm in achieving its corporate strategy. These applications are sometimes referred to as competitive edge systems.

*Systems formulation* refers to the process of identifying and specifying the requirements and the subsequent expected or forecast benefits to be derived from a system.

*A business or strategic vision* refers to a view of how the firm can successfully function in the marketplace in the medium to long term. It usually encompasses how the firm will find, get and keep its clients.

*An industry driver* is a condition which directly influences or affects the performance of all the firms in the industry. Examples of industry drivers include major changes in competition, deregulation and new technological developments.

*Top management* refers to members of the board of directors and those who report directly to them.

*Systems implementation* refers to those activities required after the system has been installed which are necessary in order to make the system fully functional.

*Management Information Systems (MIS)* refers to those information systems which perform routine data processing and which supply regular reports to the firm including the firm's management.

*A centrally planned approach* refers to an IS strategy whereby top management plays a key role in the planning of IS activities including the search for SIS.

*Information Systems Department (ISD)* is the department in the firm responsible for managing the information systems function.

*A systems champion* is an important executive who is fully committed to the success of the SIS and who takes an active role in ensuring that it succeeds.

*Critical Success Factors (CSF)* are those aspects of the business which must be right in order for the enterprise to succeed in achieving its objectives.

*A software platform* is an already existing IS which may be extended so that it acquires a strategic dimension. An example would be an order entry system to which clients are given access through an external network so that they can monitor the progress of their orders.

## How to Tick the Boxes

The following may assist respondents in deciding which boxes to tick, especially in the ACTUAL row. The statements are expressed in the present continuous tense because the research seeks to establish both what happened to your firm and what *you currently believe* should be the approach to the challenge of formulating and implementing SIS.

Using question 1 as an example, the following shows the difference between the boxes.

1.      A business or strategic vision which combines the issues of competitive advantage with information systems is critical to the success of SIS.

If, when your firm implemented its SIS, a business or strategic vision was a very important consideration, then tick the STRONGLY AGREE box. If a business or strategic vision was an issue the tick the AGREE box. If a business or strategic vision was not considered then tick the DISAGREE box. If a business or strategic vision was considered, an it was believed to be irrelevant, then tick STRONGLY DISAGREE.

**Figure 12.2      Second sample questionnaire – page 3**

Please score the following remarks in terms of whether you Strongly Agree, Agree, Disagree, or Strongly Disagree. Please remember to score each question twice – once for what *actually* happened and once for what you feel *should* have happened.

1.  Industry drivers play an important role in determining where the firm should look for SIS opportunities.

| ACTUAL | Strongly Agree | Agree | Disagree | Strongly Disagree |
|---|---|---|---|---|
| SHOULD | Strongly Agree | Agree | Disagree | Strongly Disagree |

2.  An understanding of the industry drivers is a key starting point for formulating SIS.

| ACTUAL | Strongly Agree | Agree | Disagree | Strongly Disagree |
|---|---|---|---|---|
| SHOULD | Strongly Agree | Agree | Disagree | Strongly Disagree |

3.  Changes in industry drivers frequently suggest where to look for SIS opportunities.

| ACTUAL | Strongly Agree | Agree | Disagree | Strongly Disagree |
|---|---|---|---|---|
| SHOULD | Strongly Agree | Agree | Disagree | Strongly Disagree |

4.  SIS exploit the informational aspects of changing business conditions and relationships, rather than create new opportunities in their own right.

| ACTUAL | Strongly Agree | Agree | Disagree | Strongly Disagree |
|---|---|---|---|---|
| SHOULD | Strongly Agree | Agree | Disagree | Strongly Disagree |

5.  Most SIS are formulated through the process of matching industry drivers with corporate strategies.

| ACTUAL | Strongly Agree | Agree | Disagree | Strongly Disagree |
|---|---|---|---|---|
| SHOULD | Strongly Agree | Agree | Disagree | Strongly Disagree |

6.  SIS are formulated by direct reference to the firm's CSF.

| ACTUAL | Strongly Agree | Agree | Disagree | Strongly Disagree |
|---|---|---|---|---|
| SHOULD | Strongly Agree | Agree | Disagree | Strongly Disagree |

7.  To ensure success with SIS it is necessary to adopt a central planning perspective for the management of IS.

| ACTUAL | Strongly Agree | Agree | Disagree | Strongly Disagree |
|---|---|---|---|---|
| SHOULD | Strongly Agree | Agree | Disagree | Strongly Disagree |

8.  SIS evaluation is generally treated beyond the rules of the firm's normal capital investment appraisal procedures.

| ACTUAL | Strongly Agree | Agree | Disagree | Strongly Disagree |
|---|---|---|---|---|
| SHOULD | Strongly Agree | Agree | Disagree | Strongly Disagree |

4

Figure 12.2    Second sample questionnaire – page 4

9. Less attention is paid to finding the most cost effective vendor where SIS are concerned.

| ACTUAL | Strongly Agree | Agree | Disagree | Strongly Disagree |
|---|---|---|---|---|
| SHOULD | Strongly Agree | Agree | Disagree | Strongly Disagree |

10. SIS are systems which management believe must be implemented and therefore the short term measurable benefits are not as important as for MIS.

| ACTUAL | Strongly Agree | Agree | Disagree | Strongly Disagree |
|---|---|---|---|---|
| SHOULD | Strongly Agree | Agree | Disagree | Strongly Disagree |

11. In the medium to long term SIS will produce better than average financial results.

| ACTUAL | Strongly Agree | Agree | Disagree | Strongly Disagree |
|---|---|---|---|---|
| SHOULD | Strongly Agree | Agree | Disagree | Strongly Disagree |

12. More attention is paid to staff briefing when implementing SIS than with other IS.

| ACTUAL | Strongly Agree | Agree | Disagree | Strongly Disagree |
|---|---|---|---|---|
| SHOULD | Strongly Agree | Agree | Disagree | Strongly Disagree |

13. Training is a more important issue in the successful implementation of SIS than other IS.

| ACTUAL | Strongly Agree | Agree | Disagree | Strongly Disagree |
|---|---|---|---|---|
| SHOULD | Strongly Agree | Agree | Disagree | Strongly Disagree |

14. A continuing support centre plays an important role in the success of SIS.

| ACTUAL | Strongly Agree | Agree | Disagree | Strongly Disagree |
|---|---|---|---|---|
| SHOULD | Strongly Agree | Agree | Disagree | Strongly Disagree |

15. It is important to perform regular post implementation audits on SIS.

| ACTUAL | Strongly Agree | Agree | Disagree | Strongly Disagree |
|---|---|---|---|---|
| SHOULD | Strongly Agree | Agree | Disagree | Strongly Disagree |

16. A strategic vision is not necessarily initiated by a top manager.

| ACTUAL | Strongly Agree | Agree | Disagree | Strongly Disagree |
|---|---|---|---|---|
| SHOULD | Strongly Agree | Agree | Disagree | Strongly Disagree |

17. SIS are frequently developed from software platforms which are already well established IS.

| ACTUAL | Strongly Agree | Agree | Disagree | Strongly Disagree |
|---|---|---|---|---|
| SHOULD | Strongly Agree | Agree | Disagree | Strongly Disagree |

5

Figure 12.2     Second sample questionnaire – page 5

18    There are no real opportunities to use IS strategically and the current interest in this
      subject is misplaced.

| ACTUAL | Strongly Agree | Agree | Disagree | Strongly Disagree |
|--------|----------------|-------|----------|-------------------|
| SHOULD | Strongly Agree | Agree | Disagree | Strongly Disagree |

19.   Formulation and implementation issues are considered together as SIS will benefit
      from a seamless approach from start to finish.

| ACTUAL | Strongly Agree | Agree | Disagree | Strongly Disagree |
|--------|----------------|-------|----------|-------------------|
| SHOULD | Strongly Agree | Agree | Disagree | Strongly Disagree |

20.   SIS will generally produce only non-quantifiable benefits.

| ACTUAL | Strongly Agree | Agree | Disagree | Strongly Disagree |
|--------|----------------|-------|----------|-------------------|
| SHOULD | Strongly Agree | Agree | Disagree | Strongly Disagree |

6

Figure 12.2      Second sample questionnaire – page 6

# 13 How to Develop an IT Benefits Management Department

## 13.1 ESTABLISH THE NEED FOR THE FUNCTION

The development of an IT benefit management department begins with the need for improved information management being accepted at the highest level in the firm. This simply means that the board of directors have to accept that information management is no longer an issue which may be left up to the ISD alone. It also means that IT must be recognised as not just being the domain of the so-called techies but rather a central issue to the prosperity of the business as a whole. The establishment of these needs should lead to a call for someone to manage this area. It is important that both IS management and general management want this role to be created. If either side resists the suggestion further persuasion is required. Without these attitudes being established there is no point in proceeding, and in any case, the funds required will almost certainly not be forthcoming.

## 13.2 THE POST OF IT BENEFITS MANAGER

The first step in the action plan must be to establish a new function or a new post in the firm. The position will probably be called something like IT Benefits Manager. This post must be created with quite wide responsibilities for both IT proposals and post implementation audit and benefit management. It is essential to start the benefit management function or process at the IT proposal stage because it is at this juncture that the potential benefits which will ultimately have to be managed are initially conceptualised. Except in the smallest firms a couple of people may be needed to staff this area.

The IT benefits manager must be capable of soliciting co-operation from both the IS staff and from operations personnel who are actually using the system.

### 13.2.1 Primary aptitudes

The staff required have to have an excellent understanding of how the business functions at both an overview and a detail level. The individuals chosen must understand IT and how it is likely to impact on the business.

249

Therefore, an individual with just an IT background will not be adequate for this job. This is a necessary but not a sufficient condition.

The post of IT benefits manager requires a highly analytical mind with a high propensity to measure corporate performance. Thus, the individuals who might take this position must have considerable aptitude with numbers and be familiar with a range of different measuring instruments. These measuring instruments range from Strategic Analysis and Evaluation templates to Capital Investment Appraisal spreadsheets to Opinion Surveys.

### 13.2.2    The location of the post of IT benefits manager

Within the hierarchy of the firm the post of IT benefits manager must be a fairly senior one. It is essential that this person report to a very senior member of staff, preferably at board level, but at least to the chief information officer. Three possible organisation charts are shown in Figures 13.1, 13.2 and 13.3.

Figure 13.1 shows the position of IT benefits manager having a very high degree of visibility, reporting directly to the MD. This will give the incumbent in this position a lot of prestige and possible power, but will also put considerable pressure on him/her to perform.

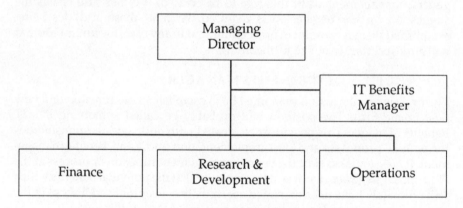

**Figure 13.1      Location of the post of IT benefits manager
reporting to the MD**

In Figure 13.2 the position of the IT benefits manager has much less visibility and probably much less power. As a result the job could be made less easy to perform. Another scenario for the positioning of the IT benefits manager is to place him/her in the Corporate Services Division. Some firms have elevated corporate services to the board and in such firms the structure would appear as in Figure 13.3.

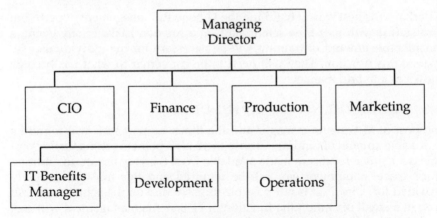

**Figure 13.2    Location of the post of IT benefits manager reporting to the CIO**

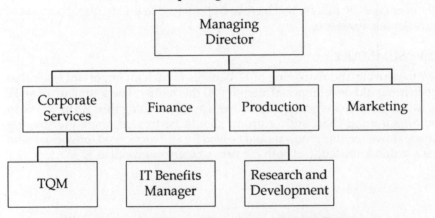

**Figure 13.3    Location of the post of IT benefits manager reporting to the corporate services division**

Staff for the IT benefits management department must be at an appropriately senior level in the firm, as without adequate status, they will not be taken seriously by either the other IS professionals or by the heads of department with which they will have to work. There are difficulties and possible conflicts with this requirement for a senior man or woman because of the dilemmas and paradoxes relating to experienced staff and exploring staff. It is quite possible that a person of the required seniority level may not want to undertake such an analytical type of job which requires exploring what is going on in a variety of circumstances and situations. On the other hand, a junior and more inquisitive person may not have the experience or seniority.

Perhaps the best way of handling the IT benefits management department is to staff it with part-time senior staff on a rotation basis. In any event, a considerable amount of training will be necessary for the individuals who operate this function. They will need to be converted to what has become known as a hybrid manager.

### 13.3   OBTAIN THE NECESSARY FUNDING

The post of IT benefits manager and the other support staff will require a reasonable amount of funding. Clearly there is no point in setting up this post unless adequate funds are made available from the very outset. In addition office space, equipment etc, will be required and this must be properly provided for. Clearly it is not possible to generalise on the actual costs, but even in a small operation the function of IT benefits management will cost tens of thousands of pounds.

The post of IT benefits manager will not necessarily be a popular one and whoever takes on this job will have to be prepared to find frequent pockets of considerable resistance.

### 13.4   SUMMARY

The measuring and managing of IT benefits is such an important issue that the firm should devote special attention to this matter. The setting up of an IT measuring and managing group is one way of handling this. As to where in the organisation chart such a group should be located, there are varying views. However, this group should be lead by an experienced individual who has a sound knowledge of both the firm's business as well as IT matters.

# 14    Guidelines to More Effective Use of IT

## 14.1   THE MORE EFFECTIVE USE OF IT

The effective use of IT firstly requires a partnership between top management, users and information systems staff. Top management involvement is simply required to ensure adequate funding for the IT function. Users must be committed if IT is to succeed as they are the only people who can make the systems actually deliver the benefits. And only information systems staff have the expertise required to ensure that the systems really work. Research conducted by the Kobler Unit into the role which IT has in firms showed that only 57% of organisations regarded the ISD as an equal partner. This is shown in Figure 14.1.

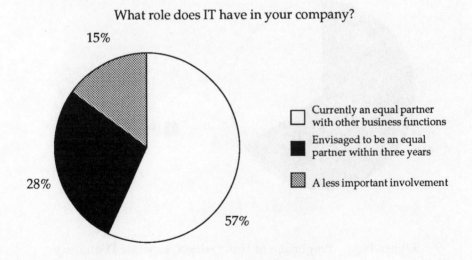

Figure 14.1    The role of IT in the firm

The second key to the effective use of IT requires the firm to regard IT investment in exactly the same way as it does any other so-called core business investment. Of course, this is rapidly occurring in those firms where IT is being used to directly support the business through mission critical systems. This trend needs to be extended to all IT investments. However, like any other investment the firm should establish a financial threshold which the investment must exceed before it is necessary to initiate capital investment appraisal and implementation audit procedures.

It is essential that responsibility for IT investment, on-going costs and benefits be firmly vested in line or user management. However, the partnership referred to above will ensure that user management obtains continuous and adequate support from the ISD. Where appropriate the ISD should be proactive suggesting to user management how costs may be minimised and how benefits may be optimised. To achieve this it is most helpful to have a corporate IT strategy in place, however, as demonstrated by the Kobler Unit, most firms do not have such a strategy. This is shown in Figure 14.2.

Does your company have a corporate IT strategy in place?

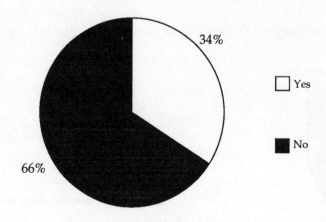

Figure 14.2    Proportion of firms with a corporate IT strategy

For firms which do not yet have an explicit corporate IT strategy it is essential that they conduct a Strategic Information Systems Plan (fully described in Remenyi, 1991).

In addition, systems should be categorised at specification into the broad groups of automate, informate and transformate. These generic systems' thrusts should underpin managements approach to the measurement and management of IT benefits.

It is very difficult to effectively employ IT in the firm unless there is a systematic approach to both IT investment justification and post implementation audit. An *ex-ante* investment justification control is not sufficient unless it is followed up by detailed *ex-post* analysis. The difficulties associated with the *ex-ante* justifications are mostly associated with establishing the estimated value of benefits and various suggestions as to how to cope with these problems were given in Chapter 6. The difficulties with the *ex-post* analysis are mostly related to the firms accounting systems and this may present more difficulties than with the original benefit estimations. A considerable amount of attention may have to be given to the firm's accounting procedures if the benefit of IT are to be highlighted.

## 14.2   MEASUREMENT OF IT BENEFITS

The first point to establish is that there is no one single metric. The search for a single metric is similar to the search for the holy grail or the philosophers' stone. A single metric for the IS function would be as meaningful as a single metric to describe the whole business or one measure to combine the age, weight and height of a human being. Therefore, a different IT assessment metric (ITAM) is required for each of the three main system thrusts or dimensions, ie automate, informate and transformate. These three dimensions have been expressed in an interesting and novel way by John Scott-Simpson (1991) as $E^3$. The expression $E^3$ stands for efficiency, effectiveness and exploitation. According to Scott-Simpson the benefits which may be derived from an effectiveness or informate system may be ten times greater than those available from an efficiency or automate system. In turn, the potential benefits in an exploitation or transformate system are ten times greater than an effectiveness system, and 100 times greater than an efficiency system.

### 14.2.1   An ITAM for automate systems

Automate systems generally lend themselves to cost displacement and/or cost avoidance analysis. There is also frequently an element of information which requires decision analysis. Intangible benefits should be primarily treated as serendipitous and measured by surveys.

### 14.2.2   An ITAM for informate systems

Informate systems require decision analysis. There may be some element of automate and this can be isolated using the cost displacement and/or cost avoidance techniques. Informate systems frequently contain a considerable element of intangible benefits such as what-if analysis. Use a scoring method to measure this.

### 14.2.3    An ITAM for transformate systems

Transformate systems require full capital investment appraisal techniques which will focus on measuring the viability of new business investments. Little or no emphasis should be placed on intangibles. However, the horizon for the investment will tend to be larger than both automate and informate projects.

### 14.2.4    Holistic measures

When the firm requires an holistic assessment of the IS function it may conduct a VFM or a HCR study. Also a user survey may be conducted. User satisfaction with the IS department is generally agreed to be a surrogate for the efficiency with which the ISD functions. Certainly it is difficult to envisage how the IS function could be effective if the user population is dissatisfied with its performance, although it is possible for satisfied users not to be as effective as they could be. Firms are recommended to conduct VFM or HCR or user satisfaction surveys regularly.

Furthermore, it is important to note that some benefits may not be very obvious in the short term. Nolan Norton (Waller 1991) claim that it may require two or three years for systems to develop sufficiently so that the benefits are obvious and therefore may be measured. The Nolan Norton view is demonstrated in Figure 14.3 below.

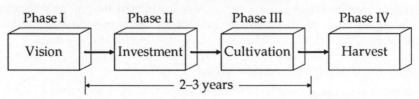

Realising the benefits from IT investments must
be looked at over the long term

**Figure 14.3    Long-term realisation of IT benefits**

### 14.3    MANAGEMENT OF IT BENEFITS

Although this is the responsibility of several groups, IT benefit management must be masterminded and driven by the ISD or by a new section set up specifically for that purpose.

1.   Management of IT benefits requires the detailed management of systems on an individual basis. This is the responsibility of users or line management supported by the partnership concept. Therefore, the first step is to create awareness and acceptance of the partnership concept which will lead to each of the parties to the system recognising their responsibility to achieve the projected benefits.

2.   Nominate an IT benefits measurement and management officer. As described in Chapter 13, this requires a fairly senior appointment which in most firms probably should not report to the information systems director.

3.   Set up the necessary infrastructure around the measurement and management officer. On a physical basis this refers to offices, equipment as well as clerical and secretarial support. However, infrastructure does not stop at these issues. It also refers to creating a climate in the firm which will accept the new approach to measuring and managing IT benefits. This may require some training. This process may also require discussion with the accountants to modify the reporting system or even involve the introduction of new accounting procedures. New forms for presenting costs justification and implementation reviews will have to be developed. However, the primary task is to ensure that measurement of value is accepted at all levels in the firm.

4.   A successful measuring and management of IT benefits function requires historical statistics because business measurements are most meaningful when they are observed in relation to other comparable measures. Therefore, create a database of measurement statistics using all three measurement approaches.

5.   It is important to assist those parts of the firm which are not succeeding to generate adequate IT benefits. This will be achieved primarily by training. Successful role models within the firm are important in this respect. Therefore, give maximum visibility to successful systems in order to encourage the transfer of learning.

6.   Make sure that experience gained is fed back into the management of the systems. This is particularly true for mistakes from which value may be derived if they may be subsequently avoided.

## 14.4   SUMMARY

To measure and manage IT benefits professionally is a complex, multifaceted and therefore difficult task. It is a subject which has traditionally not been given the amount of attention which it deserves but which, with the growing concern to improve corporate efficiency and effectiveness, will attract a growing amount of attention.

It is believed that this book represents a step towards establishing improved practices in this field. As stated in the foreword it is not claimed that this book is in any way a definitive work but rather a guide which will hopefully help the reader towards a better understanding of the many diverse issues involved in coming to terms with this subject.

# Appendix 1
# Glossary

**AI**
**Artificial Intelligence**

An approach to developing systems so that they will function in a way not dissimilar to the human brain. The most frequently encountered application for artificial intelligence is expert systems which allow very efficient rule processing to be performed.

**Benefit**

A term used to indicate an advantage, profit or gain attained by an individual or oganisation.

**Bottom-up Planning**

Bottom-up IS planning is an approach which addresses the current IS requirements and focuses on priority settings and resource allocation to achieve these requirements.

**Business Vision**

The business vision is what the management want to achieve with the enterprise in the future. A business vision usually refers to the medium to long term. It is often expressed in terms of a series of objectives.

**CAD**
**(Computer Aided Design)**

A computer system or software package providing facilities for simplifying the design of items. Systems may be specialised towards engineering, architectural or electronic applications.

**CAM**
**(Computer Aided Manufacture)**

Wide ranging term to describe computer systems that improve the firm's ability to improve its manufacturing efficiency.

**CASE**
**(Computer Aided Systems Engineering)**

Term used to refer to software products that improve the efficiency of systems planners, systems analysts and systems designers. Some CASE tools will also include code generators which can produce final programs in Cobol.

259

**Corporate Strategy**  The method through which the firm finds, gets and keeps its clients. In a broad sense it refers to how the firm relates to and interacts with its environment, including its stakeholders.

**Cost Benefit Analysis**  The process of comparing the various costs associated with an investment with the benefits and profits that it returns.

**Cost Leadership**  A generic strategy by which the firm presents itself to the marketplace as a low-priced, no-frills supplier.

**CSF**
**(Critical Success Factors)**  Those aspects of the business which must be right for the enterprise to succeed in achieving its objectives. It is also sometimes said that even though all other aspects of the business are going well, if the critical success factors are not, then the business will not succeed.

**Differentiation**  A generic strategy by which the firm presents itself to the market as a high quality supplier, and therefore asks for a premium price for its goods or services.

**DP**
**(Data Processing)**  Early term given to the use of computers in business for the purposes of record keeping and providing regular reports to assist in the functioning of the firm. The term was originally referred to as Electronic Data Processing (EDP), but the E was dropped by most members of the industry.

**DSS**
**(Decision Support Systems)**  Information system that supports semi or unstructured decisions that are made in the area of strategic planning, management control or operations control.

**EDI**
**(Electronic Data**
**Interchange)**  Technology which facilitates computer application to computer application communications. EDI is designed to allow structured messages to be transmitted across a network. It relies on adherence to data communications standards. These standards have to include details of how EDI partners are prepared to re-

ceive standard business documents such as purchase orders, sales invoices, etc. This means that careful attention must be given to the definition of such documents.

**EIS**
**(Executive Information Systems)**

Systems used by top executives to assist in the planning and control process of the firm. It involves the use of an information warehouse or repository which is accessed through a series of easy to use tools. EIS also normally implies the use of communications to address external databases.

**EPOS**
**(Electronic Point Of Sale)**

Technology of recording retail sales directly onto a computer. This can be achieved through a variety of devices ranging from computerised tills where operators enter the data, to various forms of scanning machines. EPOS produces instant updates to inventory records as well as valuable sales information. It can also have a very much lower error rate than traditional systems.

**ETO**
**(Electronic Trading Opportunity)**

Use of computers to buy or sell in the marketplace. This is a wide-ranging term which includes systems such as airline reservations through which organisations can sell their services, as well as applications used for purchasing from a vendor or vendors.

**EUC**
**(End User Computing)**

Term referring to the supply of computer power to management in order to increase its efficiency and effectiveness.

**Factory System**

A computer system which assists the firm in achieving its required level of efficiency and effectiveness. These systems are also sometimes referred to as critical information systems (CIS).

**Generic Strategy**

One of the basic ways in which a firm can find, get and keep its clients. There are two generic strategies, which are *cost leadership* and *differentiation*. A generic strategy may be broad based or focus on a niche in the market.

Hard Cost

Costs associated with an investment that are agreed by everyone to be directly attributable to the investment, and which can be easily captured by accounting procedures.

Hidden Cost

A non-obvious cost associated with an investment that may in fact appear to be due to another source.

Industry Driver

Condition which directly influences or affects the performance of all the firms in the industry. Examples include major changes in competition, deregulation and new technology developments.

Industry Value Chain

A concept developed by Michael Porter which shows how the value chains of individual firms within an industry are related. It is an excellent basis from which to find SIS opportunities.

Information Weapon

A term used by a number of authors to describe the firm's efforts to gain a competitive advantage through the use of IT.

IRR
(Internal Rate of Return)

The return generated internally by an investment throughout its life, also referred to as the Yield of the Investment.

IS
(Information Systems)

General term to describe the use of hardware and software to deliver information to businesses.

ISD
(Information Systems
Department)

Department in the firm responsible for managing the information systems function.

Information Technology

Wide-ranging term to describe the use of computers and telecommunications.

Intangible Benefit

Benefits produced by an investment which are not immediately obvious and/or measurable.

IT Benefit

The benefit produced by an investment in information technology. It is likely that such an investment will produce both tangible and intangible IT benefits.

| | |
|---|---|
| **JIT**<br>**(Just In Time)** | Approach to manufacturing which requires raw material to be delivered to a firm exactly when required. The objective of a Just In Time system is to minimise raw material inventory and work in progress. |
| **LAN**<br>**(Local Area Network)** | The joining together of a number of personal computers or other devices in a network which operates within a limited geographical area. |
| **MIS**<br>**(Management Information Systems)** | There is no general agreement in the industry as to a precise meaning of the term MIS. Initially, it was used to describe systems which would play an active role in assisting managers make decisions. However, with the arrival of Decision Support Systems and Executive Information Systems, the term MIS has been used to describe information systems which perform routine data processing and which supply regular reports. |
| **MSS**<br>**(Management Support Systems)** | Information system which provides reports which assist management in its decision making function. |
| **Network** | A series of important points connected together. In IT terms a network may be defined as a number of computing devices connected together electronically. |
| **Niche** | A clearly defined market segment at which the firm aims its corporate strategy. |
| **OA**<br>**(Office Automation)** | Provision of computer power to white collar workers in order to improve their efficiency and effectiveness. The key to an office automation system is its connectivity whereby data is shared between a group of people working in the same office or the same firm. |
| **Opportunity Cost** | The opportunity cost of an investment is the amount which the organisation could have earned if the sum invested in IT was used in another way. |

**Payback**

The amount of time, usually expressed in years and months, required for an original investment to be repaid by the cash-in flows.

**PMW**
**(Project Management Workbench)**

Software product used to plan and control projects. It produces various forms of Gantt chart etc.

**ROI**
**(Return on Investment)**

Accounting or financial management term to describe how well the firm has used its resources. It is usually calculated by dividing net profit after tax by total net assets.

**SIS**
**(Strategic Information Systems)**

Information systems which directly assist the firm in achieving its corporate strategy. These applications are sometimes referred to as competitive edge systems.

**Soft Cost**

Costs associated with an investment that are not readily agreed by everyone to be directly attributable to the investment, and which are not easily captured by accounting procedures.

**Software Platform**

An already existing IS which may be extended so that it acquires a strategic dimension. An example would be a sales order entry system to which clients are given access through an external network so they can monitor the progress of their orders.

**SOG**
**(Strategic Option Generator)**

A system application developed by Charles Wiseman which may be used to identify SIS.

**Strategic Vision**

How the top management of an enterprise believes it can achieve its objectives in the medium- to long-term.

**Strategy**

The formal use of this word refers to the way a firm finds, gets and keeps its clients. Common usage has reduced the meaning of strategy to be synonymous with plan. See also Corporate Strategy and Generic Strategy.

**Support Systems**

Basic record keeping systems which the firm requires to function. These systems are also

|  | sometimes referred to as vital information systems (VIS). |
|---|---|
| **Tangible Benefit** | Benefits produced by an investment which are immediately obvious and measurable. |
| **Technology Vision** | How the organisation considers the application of technology within the business. This term is usually used to refer to a relatively mechanistic application of technology within the firm. |
| **Top-down Planning** | Top-down IS planning attempts to develop IS which support business objectives and strategies. |
| **Top Management** | A term used to refer to the chief executive and other senior members of the board of directors. |
| **TPS (Transaction Processing Systems)** | Computer systems which process large volumes of data. These systems are normally on-line or real time. |
| **Turnaround System** | Experimental information systems developed by the firm. This is the R & D aspect of the information systems department. It is hoped that turnaround systems will eventually become SISs. |
| **Value Activities** | The term used by Michael Porter to describe the individual aspects or functions of an enterprise. |
| **Value Chain** | A value chain is a method described by Michael Porter for the detailed analysis of an enterprise. |
| **VAN (Value Added Network)** | Regulatory term in the United Kingdom to describe a facility whereby a firm may sell its network to third parties, thus allowing them the facility of large scale data communications without its initial setup costs. |
| **Vision** | Sometimes referred to as Strategic Vision or Business Vision, this term refers to a view as to how the firm can successfully function in the marketplace in the medium- to long-term. It usually encompasses how the firm will find, get and keep its clients. |

# Appendix 2
# Acronyms

| | |
|---|---|
| **CAD** | Computer Aided Design |
| **CAM** | Computer Aided Manufacturing |
| **CASE** | Computer Aided Systems Engineering |
| **CBA** | Cost Benefit Analysis |
| **CIS** | Critical Information System |
| **CSF** | Critical Success Factor |
| **DCF** | Discounted Cash Flow |
| **EDI** | Electronic Data Interchange |
| **EIS** | Executive Information System |
| **EPOS** | Electronic Point Of Sale |
| **EUC** | End User Computing |
| **HCR** | Health Check Review |
| **ICAEW** | Institute of Chartered Accountants of England and Wales |
| **IRR** | Internal Rate of Return |
| **ISD** | Information Systems Department |
| **IS** | Information System |
| **ITB** | Information Technology Budget |
| **IT** | Information Technology |
| **I/O** | Input/Output |
| **JIT** | Just In Time |

| KMO | Kaiser-Meyer-Olkin |
| KPI | Key Performance Indicators |
| MBA | Master of Business Administration |
| MD | Managing Director |
| MIS | Management Information System |
| MIT90s | Management In The 90s |
| MIT | Massachusetts Institute of Technology |
| NPV | Net Present Value |
| OA | Office Automation |
| OECD | Organisation for Economic Co-operation and Development |
| PC | Personal Computer |
| PIA | Post Implementation Audit |
| PIN | Personal Identification Number |
| PI | Profitability Index |
| PLC | Public Listed Company |
| PSIS | Potential Strategic Information System |
| ROI | Return On Investment |
| R&D | Research and Development |
| SISP | Strategic Information Systems Plan |
| SIS | Strategic Information System |
| SOG | Strategic Options Generator |
| SPSS/PC | Statistical Package for the Social Sciences/Personal Computer Based |
| TQM | Total Quality Management |
| UIS | User Information Satisfaction |
| US | User Satisfaction |

| | |
|---|---|
| **VAN** | Value Added Network |
| **VDU** | Visual Display Unit |
| **VFM** | Value For Money |
| **VIS** | Vital Information System |

# Appendix 3
# Bibliography and Reading List

Ahituv N, A Systematic Approach Toward Assessing the Value of an Information System, *MIS Quarterly*, Volume 4 Number 4, December 1980

Ahituv N, Techniques of Selecting Computers for Small Business, *Proceedings of the 24th Annual Conference of the International Council for Small Business*, June 1979 (a)

Ahituv N, *A Cost Benefit Analysis of Data Entry and Validation Systems*, Faculty of Management, University of Calgary, March 1979 (b)

Amdahl Research Report, *Clues to Success: Information Technology, Strategies for Tomorrow*, Amdahl, April 1988

Arrow K J, McGuire C B, Radner R, *The Value of Demand for Information in Decision and Organisation*, North Holland Publishing Company, 1972

A.T. Kearney, *Corporate Organisation and Overhead Effectiveness Survey*, A.T. Kearney, 1987

Bailey J E, Development of a Tool for Measuring and Analysing Computer User Satisfaction, *Management Science*, Volume 29 Number 5, May 1983

Baroudi J, An Empirical Study of the Impact of User Involvement on System Usage and Information Satisfaction, *Communications of the ACM*, Volume 29 Number 5, March 1986

Benbasat I, Vessey I, Programmer and Analyst Time/Cost Estimation, *MIS Quarterly*, Volume 4 Number 2, June 1980

Bjorn-Anderson A, 1986, cited by Willcocks L, *Unpublished Chairman's Introduction to a Conference on Managing IT Investment*, conducted by Business Intelligence, London 20 May 1991.

Bostrom R P, Heinen J S, MIS Problems and Failures: A Socio-Technical Perspective. Part I: The Causes, *MIS Quarterly*, Volume 1 Number 3, September 1977 (a)

Bostrom R P, Heinen J S, MIS Problems and Failures: A Socio-Technical Perspective. Part II: The Application of Socio-Technical Theory, *MIS Quarterly*, Volume 1 Number 4, December 1977 (b)

Brown S W, Swartz T A, A Gap Analysis of Professional Service Quality, *Journal of Marketing*, April 1989

Butler Cox Foundation, Value from Information Technology: The Business Perspective, *Proceedings of the Management Conference, Wishaw*, June 1990

Cameron I, *Unpublished Management Application Project Report on Measuring IT Benefits at Henley – The Management College*, June 1991

Cash J I et al, *Corporate Information Systems Management: Text & Cases, Second Edition*, Irwin Homewood, 1988

Chandler J S, A Multiple Criteria Approach for Evaluating Information Systems, *MIS Quarterly*, Volume 9 Number 1, March 1985

Churchill G A, *Market Research*, 4th Edition, Dryden Press, 1987

Clark F, Cooper J, *The Chartered Accountant in the Information Technology Age*, Coopers & Lybrand, 1985

Danziger J N, Computers and the Frustrated Chief Executive, *MIS Quarterly*, Volume 1 Number 2, June 1977

Dennis A R et al, An Evaluation of Electronic Meeting Systems to Support Strategic Management, *Proceedings of the 11th ICIS*, December 1990

Dexter A S, Evaluating a Time Sharing Information System: A Step Towards Optimisation, *Proceedings of AIDS, Western Regional Meeting*, March 1974

Dhananjay K et al, On The Economics of the Software Replacement Problem, *Proceedings of the 11th ICIS*, December 1990

Doll W J, Ahmed M U, Diagnosing and Treating the Credibility Syndrome, *MIS Quarterly*, Volume 7 Number 3, September 1983

Drury D H, An Empirical Assessment of the Stages of DP Growth, *MIS Quarterly*, Volume 7 Number 2, June 1983

Ein-Dor P, Segev E, Organisational Context and the Success of Information Systems, *Management Science*, Volume 24 Number 10, June 1978

Epstein D H, King W R, An Experimental Study of the Value of Information, *Omega*, Volume 10 Number 3, September 1972

Feltham G A, The Value of Information, *The Accounting Review*, Volume 43 Number 4, October 1968

Feltham G A, *Information Evaluation*, American Accounting Association, 1972

Gallagher C A, Perceptions of the Value of Management Information Systems, *Academy of Management Journal*, Volume 17 Number 1, March 1974

Ginsburg M J, Early Diagnosis of MIS Implementation Failure: Promising Results and Unanswered Questions, *Management Science*, Volume 27 Number 4, April 1981

Glennon J T, MIS Systems: The Role of Authority and Responsibility, *MIS Quarterly*, Volume 2 Number 2, June 1978

Gould J P, Risk Stochastic Preference and the Value of Information, *Journal of Economic Theory*, Volume 8 Number 1, May 1974

Guthrie A, Attitudes of the User Managers Towards MIS, *Management Infomatics*, Volume 3 Number 5, October 1974

Hamilton S, Chervany N L, Evaluating Information System Effectiveness - Part II: Comparing Evaluation Approaches, *MIS Quarterly*, Volume 5 Number 4, December 1981 (a)

Hamilton S, Chervany N L, Evaluating Information System Effectiveness - Part I: Comparing Evaluation Approaches, *MIS Quarterly*, Volume 5 Number 3, September 1981 (b)

Henry G T, *Practical Sampling*, Sage Publications, April 1990

Hochstrasser B, Griffiths C, *Regaining Control of IT Investments*, Kobler Unit, 1990

Huff S L, Munro M C, Information Technology Assessment and Adaption: A Field Study, *MIS Quarterly*, Volume 9 Number 4, December 1985

Ives B et al, The Measurement of User Information Satisfaction, *Communications of the ACM*, Volume 26 Number 10, October 1983

Keen P G W, Value Analysis: Justifying Decision Support Systems, *MIS Quarterly*, Volume 5 Number 1, March 1981

Kerlinger F N, *Foundations of Behavioural Research*, Holt Rinehart & Winston, 1969

King J L, Schrems E L, Cost Benefit Analysis in Information Systems Development and Operation, *ACM Computing Surveys*, Volume 10 Number 1, March 1978 (a)

King W R, Epstein B J, Assessing the Value of Information, *Management Datamatics*, Volume 5 Number 4, 1976

King W R, How Effective is Your Information Systems Planning, *Long Range Planning*, Volume 21 Number 5, October 1988

King W R, Rodriguez J I, Evaluating Management Information Systems, *MIS Quarterly*, Volume 2 Number 3, September 1978 (b)

Kleijnen J P C, *Computers and Profits: Quantifying Financial Benefits of Information*, Addison Wesley, 1980

Kyu Kim K, User Information Satisfaction: Towards Conceptual Clarity, *Proceedings of the 11th ICIS*, December 1990

Lehmann D R, *Marketing Research Analysis*, 3rd Edition, Richard D. Irwin, 1989

Lucus H C, Performance and the Use of a Management Information System, *Management Science*, Volume 3 Number 4, April 1975

Mace D R et al, The Econometrics of Data Validation, *Management Datamatics*, Volume 5, 1976

Madrick S E, *The C. 'egic Use of Information Technology*, Oxford University Press, 1987

Marschak J, Economics of Information Systems, *Journal of the American Statistical Association*, Volume 66 Number 333, March 1971

Matlin G L, How to Survive a Management Assessment, *MIS Quarterly*, Volume 1 Number 1, March 1977

Matlin G L, Wh ' is the Value of investment in Information Systems?, *MIS Quarterly*, Volume 3 Number 3, September 1979

McFarlan F Warren, Information Technology Changes the Way You Compete, *Harvard Business Review*, May–June 1984

Miller J, Doyle B A, Measuring the Effectiveness of Computer-Based Information Systems in the Financial Services Sector, *MIS Quarterly*, March 1987

Miller J, *The Effectiveness of Computer-Based Information Systems: Definition and Measurement*, Unpublished PhD Thesis, University of Cape Town, 1989

Miller W B, Building an Effective Information Systems Function, *MIS Quarterly*, Volume 4 Number 2, June 1980

Mock T J, Concepts of Information Value and Accounting, *The Accounting Review*, Volume 46 Number 4, October 1971

Money A H, Tromp D, Wegner T, The Quantification of Decision Support Benefits Within the Context of Value Analysis, *MIS Quarterly*, June 1988

Morse C, *Unpublished Paper Presented at a Seminar on Measuring and Managing IT Benefits*, Conducted by Mondanock International, March 1991

Neumann S, Segev E, A Case Study of User Evaluation of Information Characteristics for System Improvement, *Information and Management*, Number 4, 1980-81

OECD, *A Report on the Management of Marketing Information*, Oasis, 1988

Onions C T, ed, *The Shorter Oxford English Dictionary*, Guild Press, 1983

Owen D E, Information Systems Organisations: Keeping Pace with the Pressures, *Sloan Management Review*, Volume 27 Number 3, Spring 1986

Parasuraman A, Zeithaml V, Berry L, A Conceptual Model of Service Quality and its Implications for Research, *Journal of Marketing*, Fall 1985

Parasuraman A, Zeithaml V, Berry L, SERVQUAL: A Multi-Item Scale for Measuring Consumer Perceptions of Quality, *Journal of Marketing*, Volume 64 Number 1, Spring 1988

Parker M M et al, *Information Strategy and Economics*, Prentice-Hall, 1989

Peters G, Evaluating your Computer Investment Strategy, *Journal of Information Technology*, Volume 3 Number 3, September 1988

Porter Michael E, *Competitive Advantage – Creating and Sustaining Superior Performance*, The Free Press, 1985

Porter Michael E, *Competitive Strategy – Techniques for Analysing Industries and Competitors*, The Free Press, 1980

Raymond L, Organisational Characteristics and MIS Success in the Context of Small Business, *MIS Quarterly*, Volume 9 Number 1, March 1985

Raymond L, Validating and Applying User Satisfaction as a Measure of MIS Success in Small Organisations, *Information and Management*, Volume 12, 1987

Remenyi D, *Introducing Strategic Information Systems Planning*, NCC Blackwell, 1991

Remenyi D, *Strategic Information Systems – Development, Implementation, Case Studies*, NCC Blackwell, 1990 (a)

Remenyi D, *Strategic Information Systems: Current Practice and Guidelines*, Unpublished PhD Thesis, Henley – The Management College, 1990 (b)

Rivard S, Huff S L, User Developed Applications: Evaluation of Success from the DP Department Perspective, *MIS Quarterly*, Volume 8 Number 1, March 1984

Robey D, User Attitudes and MIS Use, *Academy of Management Journal*, Volume 22 Number 3, September 1979

Romtech Report, *Computing Opinion Survey*, Romtech, 1989

Saunders L, MIS/DSS Success Measure, *Systems Objectives Solutions*, Volume 4, 1984

Schmitt J W, Kozer K A, Management's Role In Information System Development Failures: A Case Study, *MIS Quarterly*, Volume 3 Number 2, June 1978

Scott-Simpson J, *Unpublished Paper Presented at a Personal Computer Conference*, April 1991

Senn J A, A Management View of Systems Analysis: Failures and Shortcomings, *MIS Quarterly*, Volume 2, Number 3, September 1978

Sharp W E, *The Economics of Computers*, Columbia University Press, 1969

Silk D J, *Course Workbook Prepared for Managing Strategic Information for MBA Students*, Henley – The Management College, 1990 (a)

Silk D J, Managing IS Benefits for the 1990s, *Journal of Information Technology*, Volume 5, 1990 (b)

Srinivasan A, Alternative Measures of System Effectiveness: Associations and Implications, *MIS Quarterly*, Volume 9 Number 3, September 1985

Strassman P A, *Information Payoff: The Transformation of Work in the Electronic Age*, Free Press, 1985

Strassman P A, *The Business Value of Computers*, The Information Economics Press, 1990

Streeter D N, Cost Benefit Evaluation of Scientific Computing Services, *IBM Systems Journal*, Volume 11 Number 3

Waller R R, *Unpublished Paper Presented at a Seminar on Measuring and Managing IT Benefits*, Conducted by Mondanock International, March 1991

Willcocks L, *Unpublished Chairman's Introduction to a Conference on Managing IT Investment*, conducted by Business Intelligence, May 1991

Wiseman C, *Strategy and Computers - Information Systems as Competitive Weapons*, Dow-Jones Irwin, 1985

Zmud R W, Individual Difference and MIS Success: A Review of the Empirical Literature, *Management Science*, Volume 25 Number 10, October 1979

Zuboff S, *In the Age of the Smart Machine: The Future of Work and Power*, New York Basic Books, 1988

# Appendix 4
# Financial Measures used in
# Cost Benefit Analysis

## PAYBACK

The payback may be defined as the amount of time, usually expressed in years and months, required for the original investment amount to be repaid by the cash-in flows. This measure is sometimes used with nominal cash-in flows and sometimes used with discounted cash-in flows. Nominal cash flows are the amounts unadjusted for the time value of money. The most popular form of payback used today is referred to as the exhaust method. The exhaust method of payback calculation involves the deduction of each year's cash-in flow from the original investment until the original amount is reduced to zero. This method should be contrasted with the average payback method which only gives a rough approximation of the period of time required to recover the investment amount when the cash-in flows are relatively constant.

### Exhaust Method

**Payback in time (Years, months, etc) = Investment − Cumulative benefit**

The calculation of the payback by the exhaust method is a reiterative process which requires the cumulative benefit to be subtracted from the investment until the result is zero. The time at which the result is zero represents the period which is required for the investment amount to be returned.

### Average Method

$$\text{Payback in time} \quad = \quad \frac{\text{Investment}}{\text{Average annual benefit}}$$

This average method is only useful if the annual benefits do not materially vary from the average. If there is any substantial variability in the annual benefits this method will produce meaningless results. Many firms use the payback as the primary criteria for deciding whether an investment is suitable or not.

It is generally considered that the cash flows used to calculate the payback

277

should have first been discounted. This is referred to as a discounted payback. If this is done it will produce a time value based payback measure which will reflect the cost of capital. A discounted payback will always show a longer period than one based on nominal values.

## NET PRESENT VALUE (NPV)

The net present value may be defined as the difference between the sum of the values of the cash-in flows, discounted at an appropriate cost of capital, and the present value of the original investment. Provided the NPV is greater than or equal to zero the investment will earn the firm's required rate of return. The size of the NPV may be considered as either a measure of the surplus which the investment makes over its required return, or as a margin of error in the size of the investment amount.

$$\text{Present value of benefit} = \frac{\text{Benefit}}{(1+i)^n}$$

Where
　i = rate of interest
　n = number of years

$$\text{NPV} = \Sigma \text{ Present value of benefit} - \text{Present value of investment}$$

The interpretation of the NPV should be based on the following rules:

**If NPV>=0 then invest**
**If NPV <0 then do not invest**

The size of the NPV represents the margin of error which may be made in the estimate of the investment amount before the investment will be rejected.

## PROFITABILITY INDEX (PI)

The profitability index is defined as the sum of the present values of the cash-in flows divided by the present value of the investment. This shows a rate of return expressed as the number of discounted pounds and pence which the investment will earn for every pound originally invested.

$$\text{PI} = \frac{\Sigma \text{ Present value of benefits}}{\text{Present value of investment}}$$

## INTERNAL RATE OF RETURN (IRR)

The internal rate of return is the rate of interest which will cause the NPV to be zero. It is the internally generated return which the investment will earn throughout its life. It is also frequently referred to as the yield of the investment.

**IRR = i such that NPV=0**

## RATE OF RETURN OR RETURN ON INVESTMENT (ROI)

The rate of return or return on investment, which is sometimes referred to as the simple return on investment, is calculated by considering the annual benefit divided by the investment amount. Sometimes an average rate of return for the whole period of investment is calculated by averaging the annual benefits while on other occasions the rate of return is calculated on a year by year basis using individual benefit amounts.

$$ROI = \frac{\text{Annual benefit}}{\text{Investment amount}}$$

# Appendix 5
# Issues Addressed in
# Effectiveness Surveys

## FUNCTIONING OF EXISTING TRANSACTION/REPORTING SYSTEMS

The following represents the issues on which the 38 questions in the Miller-Doyle effectiveness measurement instrument are based.

- Completeness of output information
- Accuracy of output information
- More monitor systems
- Relevance of report contents
- Currency of output information
- Volume of output information
- Report availability and timeliness
- More exception systems

## LINKAGES TO STRATEGIC PROCESSES IN THE FIRM

- Top management involvement
- Strategic IS planning
- Business-related systems priorities
- Using database technology
- Overall cost-effectiveness of IS
- Use of steering committee

## AMOUNT AND QUALITY OF USER INVOLVEMENT

- Users' feeling of participation
- Users' control over IS services

- IS-user management communications
- Users' understanding of systems
- User confidence in systems

## RESPONSIVENESS TO NEW SYSTEMS NEEDS

- Prompt processing of change requests
- Short lead time, new systems development
- Responsiveness to changing user needs
- IS support for users preparation of new systems proposals
- Flexibility of data and reports

## END USER COMPUTING

- More analysis systems
- More enquiry systems
- Effective training programmers or users
- Ease of user access to terminals

## IS STAFF QUALITY

- User-oriented systems analysts
- Competence of systems analysts
- Technical competence of IS staff
- Larger IS effort to create new systems
- Positive attitude to IS to users

## RELIABILITY OF SERVICE

- Low % hardware and systems downtime
- Efficient running of current systems
- Data security and privacy

# Appendix 6
# A Typical Case Requesting Authority for the Purchase of IT Equipment

CAPITAL APPROVALS COMMITTEE PAPER 14/91

17th June 1991

UPGRADE OF COMPUTER EQUIPMENT AT

THURSTON COMPUTER CENTRE

## OVERVIEW

A provision of the Child Safety Registration Act requires all companies selling or maintaining a specified range of metal working machines located near any school to inform the Local Education Authority, and to make monthly returns.

The information required for GiantCo to comply with the Act is held in a number of computer systems running on the Thurston centre. Suitable software is available commercially but cannot be mounted at Thurston with the current operating system. The software and the necessary operating system upgrade costs £243K, plus £51K pa licence fees, and will require hardware modifications. The modification recommended costs £75K, plus £9K pa maintenance.

Currently each Customer Service Centre (CSC) has access only to details of those customers within its local area. A by-product of the changes referred to above is that the restrictions which have prevented giving each CSC access to data about all customers would be removed, and it would become possible to allow customers to deal with their choice of CSC. Many customers with multiple sites are known to want this facility. The additional capital costs necessary to fully develop this extension of customer service are £139K, plus operating costs of £49K pa.

There are non-recurring current account costs of £78K for installation, commissioning and training.

The Capital Approvals Committee is invited to approve the expenditure of £457K, and note that non-recurring current account expenditure of £70K, and recurring current account costs of £117K pa will be incurred.

**Upgrade of Computer Facilities at Thurston**

1.  Background and legislative changes

1.1   The Thurston computer centre is currently equipped with a HAL 4080-200 computer which provides an on-line service for 37 Customer Service Centres (CSC) in England and Wales. The systems supported are the Order Handling System (OHS), National Billing System (NBS), Customer Enquiry System (CES) and the Repair Service System (RSS). There are a total of 1256 terminals in the CSCs and at the National CSC at Lichfield. Appendix N gives a schematic of the current network.

1.2   All systems run under the HAL BAD-DOS operating system which limits the size of any open file to 32K fields. This is sufficient to cater for approximately 2,000 average customer sites. There are approximately 83,000 customers with machines on some 98,000 sites throughout England and Wales. For this reason the systems are structured to divide the customer base into sections, called Logical Customer Groups (LCG). Most CSCs have access to a single LCG, though some of the larger are responsible for two, three or four LCGs. In these cases the CSC is run as a number of independent units.

1.3   Customers can only deal with the CSC (or that part of it) which has access to their LCG. There are a total of 57 LCGs at the moment. A number of larger customers, with multiple sites, have asked for the facility to pass all orders, or invoicing queries, through a single CSC. This is not possible with current systems.

1.4   Appendix N is a report from the marketing department on the subject. Included in the report are the results of a survey of customer satisfaction with the service they get from their CSC. 86% of customers with a single site are satisfied or very satisfied; however only 23% of customers with more than one site are in the same categories. Focus group research has shown that the principal reason for this disparity is the inability to pass all queries to a single CSC. About 40% of customers have more than one site.

1.5   Appendix N is a summary of the Child Safety Registration Act (1991), which becomes effective in September 1991, and the implications for Giant-Co's customer service systems. GiantCo will be required to check the records of all the metal working machinery maintained for customers, and any sold since April 1990, to ascertain whether they are either on school premises or within two kilometres of a school ("Designated Sites"). For machines which fall into this category GiantCo must inform the relevant Local Education Authority (LEA) by March 1992 of their responsibility; Appendix N details the information required. Thereafter, monthly returns to every LEA are necessary, giving information of all new sales which go to Designated Sites, and certain information about maintenance visits to such sites. Nil returns are required. The Act specifies that LEAs must accept notification by electronic file transfer or written on a magnetic medium, to standards laid down in the Act.

1.6  A small sample survey conducted in three CSCs suggests that about 80% of the machines maintained by GiantCo are on Designated Sites.

1.7  The Act lays down stringent timetables for the monthly reporting; returns will have to be with the LEAs by the 15th working day of the following month. It also specifies that the preferred method of Designating Sites is by a digital mapping system developed by the Ordnance Survey in conjunction with post codes.

1.8  GiantCo's current systems include provision to enter the post code for all maintenance sites. However only about 75% of site records held in RSS include the post code; NBS holds invoice addresses, about 95% of these include the post code. For outright sales since March 1990 the only permanent record is of the invoice address on NBS. There are no digital mapping facilities in the company.

## 2.  Options

2.1  The Child Safety Registration Act has now gained Royal Assent; it will come into force in September 1991. The only options considered in this case are those which involve compliance with the terms of the Act; all of which will incur some expense.

2.2  A manual system of complying with the provisions of the Act has not been fully costed. It would require completion of a return for about 80,000 sites, plus an analysis of all new sales to ascertain whether they were to Designated Sites, in the first three weeks of each month. Estimates from the Organisation and Methods group, in consultation with CSC managers, suggest that this would require approximately 50 staff; who would have little to do for the rest of the month. Such a manual system would be very prone to errors.

2.3  A software company called Moorhill Technical Services (MTS) has developed a package which meets all the requirements of the Act and which will strip data automatically from our existing systems. This costs £75K, plus an annual licence fee of £10K. However, it will not run under our current version of BAD-DOS.

2.4  Appendix N is a report from the GiantCo central software development centre at Milton Keynes. This estimates that the in-house development of a package to meet our requirements, and run under our current version of BAD-DOS, will cost about £125K and take two years. Annual maintenance costs are estimated at £5K. The report also estimates that there would be no significant resale opportunity for such a package in two years time, principally because the MTS package will by then be predominant. No other division of GiantCo is known to need a similar package.

2.5   No bureau is known to be offering a suitable service.

2.6   Thus the only viable option is to proceed with the MTS package; para 2.3 above.


3.   Implications of recommended option

3.1   The MTS package is designed to run under BAD-DOS/X, an extension of the operating system currently in use. The upgrade cost for this version of BAD-DOS is £168K, plus an additional annual licence fee of £41K.

3.2   However BAD-DOS/X requires 360MBytes additional filestore, arranged as three identical 120MByte partitions. The current disk drive controllers, HAL 3845, cannot support triple partitions. The HAL 3863 is the cheapest controller to have this facility, but is incompatible with the present disk drives. In any event, allocating 360MBytes of disk space to the operating system would exhaust the spare disk capacity, which had been intended for the NBS upgrade planned for October 1991.

3.3   A single HAL 3863 controller, with a HAL 3868 disk drive, can be added to the present configuration with no other changes. The 3868 is the smallest drive that is compatible with the 3863, with a capacity of 640MBytes; 280MBytes more than required. That spare capacity could be configured as additional filestore.

3.4   Appendix N includes a quotation from HAL for a 3863 controller and 3868 disk drive. Two prices are quoted, depending on which maintenance contract is chosen. The standard price is £85K, assuming the usual annual maintenance contract; we can expect the annual renewals to be at prices that have increased roughly in line with inflation. HAL offer an alternative deal with a reduced purchase price, £75K, in exchange for a five year maintenance contract; the price of which will rise faster than inflation. In both cases, there are no maintenance charges in the first year.

3.4   Appendix 1 includes a discounted cash flow calculation reducing both options to net present value at the current GiantCo discount rate. This shows that the cheaper option is to pay the higher price now, which accords with GiantCo policy of not being tied to specific maintainers.

3.5   The additional disk drives and controller described above will occupy 2.8 square metres leaving 34 square metres of floor space for future expansion.

3.6   They will consume 3.8 KW. The present protected power supply has 12 KW spare capacity, and the air conditioning plant is capable of coping with an additional 24 KW without upgrade. The extra energy costs are included in the recurring current account estimates.

## 4.   Further enhancements

4.1   BAD-DOS/X will support the HAL RAndom File Search And Retrieval System (RAFSARS). This package cannot be mounted with the current version of BAD-DOS. The costs are in appendix 1.

4.2   The use of RAFSARS will allow any CSC to search all files in all LCGs for a specified customer name or account number. Once the correct details have been identified changes can be written, via a temporary file, to the customer's records irrespective of its correct LCG.

4.3   To take full advantage of this enhancement all CSCs would need digital connections to Thurston. Currently 5 of the 37 have only an analogue connection. The costs of upgrading these five private circuits are included in appendix 1.

## 5.   Timescales and responsibilities

5.1   The upgrade from BAD-DOS to BAD-DOS/X will take 36 hours. The job can thus be completed in a weekend, giving adequate testing and contingency allowance. The disk drive and controller are available ex-stock from HAL and can be installed during the working week.

5.2   MTS estimate the configuration and set up of their package requires about two man weeks of work. This would be undertaken by existing computer centre staff. Some six man months work is necessary by Service Division for data entry and data cleanse. They intend to employ ten short term contractors for one month to do this work and relieve CSC staff whilst they are trained. The costs are included in appendix 1. Very little of this work can proceed before the MTS package is mounted.

5.3   The computer manager will ensure that the MTS package is installed and running within one month of capital approval. The service manager will ensure that the MTS package is usable within three months of capital approval.

5.4   Thus the first monthly report will be available during the fourth month after capital approval. This needs to be early enough to allow about three months to ensure that the monthly report is correct, and to check the distribution arrangements, before the Act's 'go live' date of March 1992. This is a service division responsibility.

5.5 RAFSARS can be installed and tested in one working week. The current lead time for 64 Kb circuits is five weeks.

5.6 The computer manager will ensure that all computer and network upgrades to permit full inter-working of CSCs will be complete within three months of capital approval. The service manager will ensure that all training and subsidiary changes at the CSCs will be complete by the same date.

5.7 The service manager expects that the level of satisfaction, measured in the same way as in the marketing report, among customers with multiple sites, will rise to 65% by March 1992 and to 80% by September 1992. Productivity in the CSCs will be held at least at current levels.

5.8 Appendix N includes two service level agreements and a full timetable for the project. These have been agreed by the computer manager and the service manager.

6. Possible resistance to the recommended option

6.1 CSC staff are very proud of the service they offer to their 'own' customers. Indeed, some rivalry has been encouraged in the past as a means of improving the overall level of service. There is the possibility that a few staff will see the extension of access as a dilution of their special relationship with their local customers.

6.2 In order to overcome this risk, the service manager has planned a series of events to talk all CSC staff through the reasons for the change, and to build a team spirit between as well as within CSCs. The details are included in the timetable in appendix N.

6.3 There will be extensive training of CSC staff before the extended service is offered. It is seen as important that the extension is not marred by unprofessional handling of customers by a few CSC staff.

7. Implications of not adopting the recommendation

7.1 The Child Safety Registration Act now has Royal Assent and the company thus has no real choice about complying with its provisions. The option recommended is the only practical means of achieving those ends.

7.2 The implications of not going ahead with the proposal to extend CSC access are continuing very high levels of dissatisfaction among our larger customers. It is likely that this will result in a number transferring their business elsewhere.

**Appendix One**

1  Capital Costs                                                    £K

1.1  Hardware

| | |
|---|---|
| HAL 3863 disk controller | 35 |
| HAL 3868 disk drive | 40 |
| 5 x Kilostream controllers | 9 |
| Total | 84 |

1.2  Software

| | |
|---|---|
| BAD-DOS/X | 168 |
| MTS Package | 75 |
| RAFSARS | 130 |
| Total | 373 |

2  Recurring Current Account

2.1  Hardware Maintenance

| | |
|---|---|
| HAL 3863 | 4 |
| HAL 3868 | 5 |

2.2  Software Licence Fees

| | |
|---|---|
| BAD-DOS/X | 41 |
| MTS Package | 10 |
| RAFSARS | 40 |

2.3  Other     (additional to current charges)

| | |
|---|---|
| Kilostream circuits | 9 |
| Electricity | 8 |
| Total | 117 |

3  Non recurring Current Account

| | |
|---|---|
| Hardware installation | 12 |
| Network Upgrades | 8 |
| Training | 20 |
| Agency staff | 30 |

# Index